# INNOVATION IN INTERNATIONAL LAW

# LAW IN AN EMERGING GLOBAL VILLAGE

# LAW IN AN EMERGING GLOBAL VILLAGE:

## A Post-Westphalian Perspective

Richard Falk

Transnational Publishers, Inc.
Ardsley, New York

Richard Falk is Professor of Law at Princeton University.

**Library of Congress Cataloging-in-Publication Data.**

Falk, Richard A.
Law in an emerging global village : a post-Westphalian perspective / Richard Falk.
p. cm.
Includes bibliographical references.
ISBN 1-57105-066-3
1. International law. I. Title
KZ3110.F35 1998
341—dc21
98-35606
CIP



Manufactured in the United States of America

FOR HILAL

A cherished presence

# TABLE OF CONTENTS

*Part II: Substantive Concerns*

*Part III: Toward Humane Governance*

# ACKNOWLEDGEMENT

As with any book written over a period of years, this one is partly collaborative and partly an ongoing dialogue with friends and colleagues. It should come as no surprise that we often learn more from adversaries than from those with whom one feels deep affinities in matters of perception and value. But it should be even less surprising that the sharing of commitments makes the drudgery of scholarship seem more valuable and certainly more satisfying. In this spirit, without naming names, I would like to thank both opponents and collaborators for their encouragement, which was probably not the intention of the former group.

I would, however, like to make a few more explicit acknowledgments. First of all, I continue to feel a deep affinity with The New Haven School of International Law and especially to its recently deceased founder, Myres S. McDougal. After several decades Professor McDougal remains my abiding mentor as well as my fiercest adversary, admittedly a delicate balance, yet extremely satisfying nonetheless.

I want also to mention Saul H. Mendlovitz, friend and collaborator since our days together at Harvard Law School in the late 1950s, who conceived and directed the World Order Models Project for thirty years. This adventure in transnational collaboration was a wonderful learning experience for those of us fortunate enough to take part, although it never fulfilled Saul's dream of attaining a warless, equitable, and sustainable world order. Tragically, we may actually be moving further and further in the opposite direction, shaping a violent, unjust, and ecologically doomed world order.

Another important formative intellectual relationship for me has been with Burns Weston, Anthony D'Amato, and Hillary Charlesworth in our successive struggles to produce the three editions of INTERNATIONAL LAW AND WORLD ORDER. The undertaking was inspired by Burns' strong sense of bringing values to bear at every phase of inquiry into the workings of international law that guided and structured this effort, and made it worthwhile despite the inevitable tensions that arise when scholars combine their sometimes diverse talents and conflicting professional priorities.

Closer to home, I want to thank the Princeton University's Center of International Studies, and its energetic recent directors, Henry Bienen, John Waterbury, and Michael Doyle, for doing so much to provide a stimulating and efficient working community devoted to the various dimensions of international political life. And as has been true for more than twenty-five years, I have been blessed by my gifted and gracious secretary, June Garson, who does so much more than anyone could reasonably ask or expect.

I also want to say that it has been a satisfying experience to work with Heike Fenton and her associates at Transnational Publishers over the years, and I am grateful to them for being so efficient and friendly in relation to this manuscript.

Finally, and more intimately, my recent years owe virtually everything that is positive to my wife, Hilal Elver, to whom this book is dedicated, and to our challenging, yet wonderful children, Dimitri, Noah, and Zeynep.

It is also my pleasure to thank the following publications for permission to use portions of previously published materials:

"The Grotian Moment: Unfulfilled Promise, Harmless Fantasy, Missed Opportunity?" *International Insights*, Vol. 13, Special Issue (Fall 1997), 3-34.

"The World Order between Inter-State Law and the Law of Humanity: The Role of Civil Society Institutions." In Daniele Archibugi and David Held, eds. *Cosmopolitan Democracy*. Cambridge, England: Polity Press, 1995, 163-179.

"The United Nations, the Rule of Law and Humanitarian Intervention." Reproduced from Mary Kaldor and Basker Vashee, eds., on behalf of the United Nations University, World Institute for Development Economics Research (UNU/WIDER). *Restructuring the Global Military Sector, Volume I: New Wars*. London and Washington: Pinter, 1997, 108-133, by permission of Pinter, an imprint of Cassell, Wellington House, 125 Strand, London WC2R 0BB, England.

"The Complexities of Humanitarian Intervention: A New World Order Challenge." *Michigan Journal of International Law*, Vol. 17, No. 2 (Winter 1996), 491-513.

"Environmental Protection in an Era of Globalization." *Yearbook of International Environmental Law*, Vol. 6 1995 (1996), 3-25, by permission of Oxford University Press.

"A Peaceful Future for the Oceans?" In Elisabeth Mann Borgese, ed. *Peace in the Oceans: Ocean Government and the Agenda for Peace,* The Proceedings of Pacem in Maribus XXIII, Cost Rica, 3-7 December 1995, IOC Technical Series No. 47. Paris, France: UNESCO, 1997 (English), 45-51.

"Nuclear Weapons, International Law and the World Court: A Historic Encounter." *The American Journal of International Law,* Vol. 91, No. 1 (January 1997), 64-75. Reproduced with permission by the American Society of International Law.

"The Nuclear Weapons Advisory Opinion and the New Jurisprudence of Global Civil Society." *Transnational Law and Contemporary Problems,* Vol. 7, No. 2 (Fall 1997), 333-352.

"The Coming Global Civilization: Neo-Liberal or Humanist? In Antony Anghie and Garry Sturgess, eds. *Legal Visions of the 21st Century: Essays in Honour of Judge Christopher Weeramantry.* The Hague, The Netherlands: Kluwer Law International, 1998 (forthcoming).

"The Quest for Humane Governance in an Era of Globalization." In Don Kalb, Marco van der Land, Richard Staring, Bart van Steenbergen, Nico Wilterdink, eds. *Globalization, Inequality, and Difference: Consequences of Transnational Flows.* (forthcoming 1998).

Richard Falk

# FOREWORD

The books in the series devoted to Innovation in International Law have had the overall objective of highlighting emergent concerns (future generations, equity, and terrorism) and identifying fundamental change that calls for conceptual clarification. This fourth volume of the series falls into this latter category, focusing on a framework for international law that can no longer be usefully associated *exclusively* with the interaction of sovereign territorial states. It also deploys a global village metaphor to capture the higher degrees of integration that pertains to many of the most important aspects of the relations among the peoples of the world. The specific argument of the book is set forth in its introduction, and need not be restated here.

It may be clarifying to point out three qualifications that pertain to the global village thesis. First of all, no claim is being made to the effect that the state is disappearing as the paramount actor on a global level, but only that other actors are assuming sufficient importance that the framework for law needs to be rearticulated to capture this reality. Secondly, the degree of globality varies with the issue area, being far greater in relation to the flows of money, ideas, information, and goods than it is with respect to security or immigration. In the end, it is the rise of global market forces and capital markets in tandem with the widespread application of information technology that makes it at all plausible to view world order as "post-Westphalian." And thirdly, the emphasis on the global is not meant to challenge the view that the most revolutionary innovations in world order are occurring on the regional level in this period, especially within the setting of the European Union.

Because this is a time of adjustment and change it seems particularly important to nurture the innovative spirit, both to identify large-scale change in the substance and circumstance that shape the role of law in human affairs and to propose more helpful ways of addressing world order challenges that are looming on the horizons. In this regard, gaining distance from the Westphalian outlook may be a crucial step in bringing to bear the full potential of law as a healing and stabilizing force. Such distance may enable the political imagination to operate more freely in responding to such distinctive challenges of the current period as weaponry of mass destruction, large-scale terrorism, transnational crime, climate change, intellectual property rights, and post-colonial claims of self-determination. In particular, conceptual distance may encourage a more critical approach to the use of force to solve the problems of security. It is my hope that future volumes in the Innovation series will be devoted to some of these issues, and others of a kindred character, and will help us to gain greater confidence and experience in nonviolent methods of accommodation and conflict resolution.

Of course, it is hardly necessary to add, not all forms of innovation are to be welcomed, and this includes some of the erosions in state capacity. The impact of neo-liberal ideas on the role of government has weakened the capacity of the state to regulate business and financial operations. Such ideas have also eroded the provision of public goods by the state, including in relation to education, health, and poverty reduction. The decline of the state is even more evident with respect to global public goods such as support for the United Nations or contributions for the protection of the global commons. The innovative character of economic globalization is playing itself out in complex ways with mixed results for human wellbeing. Until the Asian crisis began in mid-1997 there was generalized euphoria about the human benefits of globalization. But with the financial meltdowns and economic turmoil in an increasing number of countries, now including Russia and Japan, there is a rising tide of concern about globalization and the consequent decline of state power.

But no signs are pointing in the same direction as far as the role of the state is concerned. In a central respect, with regard to the oceans, the main innovative energy has been to endow the state with great authority than ever over a wider band of coastal waters. This momentous expansion of authority arising from the innovative idea of the Exclusive Economic Zone reflected the realities of state practice, but also the realization that the alternative to coastal management was chaos and decay at an accelerating rate. The Law of the Seas Treaty was a massive move within the Westphalian structure to encourage what might be called "responsible sovereignty" as a sequel to the earlier ideology of "unconditional sovereignty" that had been bound up with the rise of the modern state from the 15th century onward. That is, the spirit of innovation can be as manifest within the state system as it is beyond it. The state may yet revive its central role in relation to upholding the security and wellbeing of persons, but not without fundamental changes in outlook and method.

As we are poised on the threshold of a new century, and indeed a new millennium, the pretext for boldness of the imagination is all too apparent. It is difficult to assess this historical moment due to wild gyrations of political mood and strongly contradictory tendencies. The crowding of the planet, and its attendant environmental and resource woes, continues to be a cause of deep concern verging on pessimism, as is the slowness to establish modes of governance that correspond in capability to the potency of various forms of transnational activity. At the same time, miracle technologies involving free access to information and instant connectivity throughout the planet offer vistas of possibility that we are only beginning to glimpse. There is a welcome lull in strategic conflict among the leading states that might, with enlightened leadership at the level of the state and civil society, shift the attention of policymakers operating in all arenas to matters of longer range concern of regional and global scope. As we approach the year 2000 it is difficult to say whether this is the best of times, or the worst.

It is my hope that the Innovation series can point in some positive directions with respect to law, and thereby contribute to a process of creative adjustment that could make those of us in the present happily envy the destiny of future generations. The legal profession seems characteristically slow to seize such opportunities, and seem more comfortable with the most minute assessment of what is past. It is our wish that the Innovation series counters this backward gaze of lawyers and jurists, and entices scholars to devote some of their energy to the threats and promises associated with the emergent future. Only then could we pronounce this venture to be a success. To reach this goal we invite anyone with ideas and proposals responsive to this challenge to step forward and make contact.

Richard Falk
Princeton, NJ
September 10, 1998

# INTRODUCTION

As this millennium comes to a close, there is a growing consensus that the fundamental structure of international law that has prevailed for several centuries, or roughly since 1648 at the time of the Peace of Westphalia, is no longer adequate as a framework of inquiry. And yet the realist mainstream, built around the statist paradigm of sovereign, territorial units, retains much of its hold on the political imagination of the legal profession that addresses global issues.

Several years ago, a fairly diverse group of distinguished scholars were asked to consider whether the Westphalian framework was being superseded, in particular, by world community intervention under the auspices of the United Nations.[1] Although there were some suggestions that territorial sovereignty was being eroded in various ways, the editorial consensus was to the effect that there had been as yet no shift in authority from the level of the state to the United Nations. The United Nations was not consistently in a position to override territorial opposition to its activities.

Such a conclusion seems a healthy antidote to the heady atmosphere about collective security under the auspices of the United Nations that took shape after the collapse of the Berlin Wall (1989) and, especially, in light of the strong response to Iraqi aggression against Kuwait (1990–1991). This apparent availability of the U.N. Security Council for collective measures led George Bush to proclaim exultantly that "a new world order" of the sort that Woodrow Wilson had dreamed of establishing after World War I could finally come into existence. This enthusiasm proved to be short-lived and, in retrospect, appeared more opportunistic than principled, intending to mobilize support for the use of force against Iraq on this particular occasion, but not involving any kind of sustained commitment to rely more heavily on the United Nations in the future. There was also no willingness on the part of leading governments to support the sort of

1. *See* BEYOND WESTPHALIA? STATE SOVEREIGNTY AND INTERNATIONAL INTERVENTION (Gene M. Lyons & Michael Mastanduno eds., 1995).

structural buildup of U.N. capabilities that would be needed to carry out an expanded sense of its role in relation to international peace and security.

By late in 1993, it became obvious that the path was not clear for humanitarian intervention by the United Nations as soon as serious difficulties emerged with the peacekeeping mission undertaken in Somalia. Such a realization became clearer, still, in relation to the reluctance by members of the Security Council to support a strong response to the genocidal killings occurring on a large scale in Rwanda since 1994.[2] What this experience confirmed was the inability of the organized international community to mount any effective response to complex humanitarian emergencies on the basis of altruistic motivations. Effectiveness of response, even in the face of genocidal behavior, continued to depend on a favorable combination of strategic calculations and civic pressures exerted on the key geopolitical actors. During the Cold War, such pressures could occasionally advance the humanitarian agenda even in the face of contrary strategic interests. This was the case with respect to the grudging support given to sanctions against the apartheid regime in South Africa during the 1980s by conservative governments in the United Kingdom and the United States.

But the issue is miscast as a test of whether the Westphalian system of world order retains its purchase on reality. The strongest foundation for a post-Westphalian approach to the role of law is not connected with the peace and security agenda. In this policy setting, the role of states has not been seriously diminished, although interstate war appears to be of declining importance. Major states remain unwilling to accept constraints on their discretion to use force. This conclusion is confirmed by recent comprehensive studies of international practice during the last half-century.[3] To the extent that world order is evaluated in relation to war and peace the traditional framework of international law suffices, and needs to be retained, and any reforms will continue to be negotiated within its parameters.

There is another problem with using the Lyons/Mastanduno yardstick of a transfer of powers to the United Nations as a test of whether the state system had been transformed. The United Nations is itself a creature of the state system. Only states are members, and only

2. On Bosnia, *see* DAVID RIEFF, SLAUGHTERHOUSE: BOSNIA AND THE FAILURE OF THE WEST (1995).

3. *See* A. MARK WEISBRUD, USE OF FORCE: THE PRACTICE OF STATES SINCE WORLD WAR II (1997); ANTHONY C. AREND AND ROBERT J. BECK, INTERNATIONAL LAW AND THE USE OF FORCE: BEYOND THE UN CHARTER PARADIGM (1993).

states have full access to most activities conducted by the organization. By comparison, the European Union is much more receptive to structural transformations and can be taken as moving toward a postmodern form of regional governance. Even the recently constituted Asian Regional Forum has made formal space available for Track II diplomacy, that is, initiatives arising from Asian civil society.

I find myself in much closer jurisprudential accord with the work of Anthony D'Amato.[4] His critique of "the Sovereignty Paradigm" in the context of explaining the legal character of human rights obligations is closely parallel to the critical discussion of "the Westphalian framework" set forth here. Similarly, D'Amato's proposed "replacement paradigm," consisting of "a neutral paradigm" that identifies both interstate *and* interpersonal law as simultaneously operative, is a valuable way of depicting the transitional character of the current era. It deliberately rejects the idea that the state and interstate relations have been superseded either by the rise of the individual as an important subject of law (complementary to the state) or by the impact of global civil society on the structure of world order. The state remains a critical actor in relation to the generation and implementation of legal norms, as well as for the mobilization of resources to enable various types of international institutions to function effectively.

This book adopts a similar view of the changing setting of world order that generates a more affirmative response to the question "beyond Westphalia?" than results from a study of the allocation of authority between the U.N. and its member states, and the extent to which the United Nations defers to the rights of sovereign states. In essence, the various tendencies associated with economic globalization are rapidly and fundamentally eroding the autonomy of sovereign states, and giving increasingly important roles to actors that represent global market forces, including corporations, banks, and international financial institutions.[5] To a substantial extent, governments and mainstream political parties have been persuaded to adhere to the discipline of global capital as the precondition of governance at the level of the state. This acceptance has tended to

4. *See especially* ANTHONY D'AMATO, INTERNATIONAL LAW THEORY: COLLECTED PAPERS, VOL. III (1998).

5. D'Amato also gives global TV a critical role in creating a shared human field of awareness that encompasses the planet as a whole.

depoliticize governments in state/society relations, fostering considerable passivity by states in global arenas, and turning policy initiatives over to such bodies as the International Monetary Fund and the World Bank.

This disabling of the state as guardian of the global public good and as autonomous actor helps account for the weakness of the United Nations in the late 1990s, despite the end of the Cold War, the complexity of international life, and the ongoing strife and poverty that engulfs tens of millions in misery and acute danger. This marketization of global political and economic life is reinforced by an ethos of consumerism that is disseminated by a global media closely tied to gigantic transnational media empires and further reinforced by the libertarian political culture of the internet that places its confidence in the viability of self-organizing systems.[6] The direct effect of these tendencies is to discourage deliberate efforts to improve human well-being beyond what can be achieved by the pursuit of self-interest through applications of technology to increase productivity and of the idea of comparative advantage to improve the efficiency of trade and exchange. These developments are having a cumulative effect on the capacity and function of government, making the state more and more perform as an instrument for the advancement of globalization. The private sector magnates who gather each year in Davos at the World Economic Forum to design global policy on the basis of economistic reasoning set the geopolitical agenda to a greater extent these days than do the political leaders who meet at the Annual Economic Summit, forming the Group of Seven, and essentially existing to ratify and implement the outcomes at Davos. The overall effect of these developments has been to strengthen a set of forces that can be cumulatively associated with globalization-from-above.[7]

There is a second, generally countervailing, set of tendencies that are also bypassing the state in their efforts to achieve political goals. Citizens have come to realize that transnational networks based on normative commitments and access to information may be a more effective and satisfying mode of democratic political participation than electoral politics and the dynamics of representative democracy at the level of the state. Such a shift in civic energies has been particularly notable in relation to concerns about the environment and human rights, but also with respect to peace and security, and

6. D'Amato sees the consumer in a more positive vein as an indication that the person is displacing the primacy of the state.

7. *See* Richard Falk, *The Making of Global Citizenship, in* GLOBAL VISIONS: BEYOND THE NEW WORLD ORDER 39–50 (Jeremy Brecher, John Brown Childs & Jill Cutler eds., 1993).

increasingly with respect to macroeconomic policy. The Treaty to Ban Anti-Personnel Landmines, signed by over 120 countries at the end of 1997, has been aptly called "a people's treaty," and a principal organizer (Jodi Williams) along with a coalition of NGOs (Campaign to Ban Landmines) was awarded the Nobel Peace Prize in recognition of the impressive contributions of these grassroots efforts to the goal of prohibition.

Similarly, the World Court Project, a coalition of more than 700 NGOs representing all parts of the world, organized a campaign in the 1990s that eventually induced the Assembly of the World Health Organization and the U.N. General Assembly to pass formal resolutions seeking clarification in the form of an Advisory Opinion from the World Court as to the legal status of nuclear weapons. What is most notable is that these requests challenged the policies of the leading geopolitical actors in the world, that is, the five nuclear weapons states. And the Court, despite its statist character and rigorously positivist jurisprudence, issued a highly significant majority decision that was generally supportive of the transnational call for the elimination of nuclear weaponry.[8]

It is these cumulative efforts of a normative character that are identified here as globalization-from-below in chapter 2, challenging to varying degrees the climate of opinion that shapes the role of the state in this emergent global context where territoriality and tangibility seem to mean far less than they did for the first three hundred years or so after Westphalia. The nonspatial character of money and infomatics is steadily undermining the ordering role of territorial sovereignty and its usefulness as an account of how authority is distributed among states. This erosion of territoriality (as well as conventional ideas about acting-in-time), in turn, is challenging statist ideas of citizenship and national identity. In one respect, a question that is central to this move toward the reconceptualization of world order is "how to be a good citizen in an era of globalization?" To some extent, the obvious response is a shift to "thick" or "complex" citizenship in which the nature of loyalty and affinity is distributed among several overlapping political frameworks and zones of identity. To some further extent, the citizen of the global village is by necessity, in this period of transition, a citizen pilgrim on a journey

8. The decision is admittedly "equivocal" or "ambiguous" in key substantive respects, and yet it suggests the leverage being exerted on the development of international law by transnational social forces. *See* chapters 3 and 4, *infra*, for exposition.

to a better future. Such a citizen replaces the geographical framing of citizenship by reference to space with the aspirational framing of world order values and time. Such ideas are just beginning to take hold of the political and legal imagination, but it is all part of the move to an early stage of a post-Westphalian world.

This book explores various aspects of this emergent reality from the perspective of the changing role of law. The overriding issue is posed provocatively in the form of a question: how should the nature and function of law be reconceived in relation to the global village? The question follows from a pervading preoccupation with how to understand and evolve law as a dimension of this early phase of a post-Westphalian world order. The effort to generalize by referring to "law for a global village" is a very provisional terminology that points to the central reality that we, concerned with international law, have to adjust our frames of reference to the yet unfamiliar features of a post-Westphalian world. The circumstance of the state in this setting is problematic; it has become the most important among several categories of international actors rather than the exclusive source and focal point for the formation and enactment of legal obligations.

There is an important ambiguity that arises from the terminology of "a post-Westphalian world." It is not meant to cast doubt on the persisting preeminence of the state as global actor, but to acknowledge that the state must now share the stage with a variety of actors representing both global civil society and regional institutional frameworks. How to deploy the concept of "law" in relation to this transformed global reality is a question that underlies this entire book.

The conceptualization of "law" under these circumstances is itself an awkward aspect of the academic challenge. The substitution of "global law," "global public order," or "the law of humanity" for "international law" seems to go too far, implying that the normative role of the state is no longer descriptive of the place of law in global society. Perhaps the best solution, although far from satisfactory, is to retain "international law" as the basic term. It is unexpectedly useful that international law was always a misnomer to a certain degree, or at least confusing, if scrutinized. After all, the units of the Westphalia system were states, not nations (except in the formalistic sense that states conferred "nationality" and sought to conflate national identity with loyalty to the state). International law, in a real sense, has never been international law!

And so, it is more of a semantic adjustment than a distortion to extend the ambit of international law now to cover the entire range of actors on the global stage. International law as a focus also lends itself, as well, to a conception of law that combines norms, community expectations, and processes of decision and implementation. In any event, the various chapters that follow develop facets of this central idea that law in a strict statist sense must now share our jurisprudential concern with a variety of other subjects of law that represent different sectors of civil society, as well as express the political will of distinct civilizational traditions.[9]

The book is arranged in three parts to divide its principal approaches. Part one considers the prevailing historical circumstances from the standpoint of whether the time is right for an innovative synthesis of the past, present, and future of international law, "a Grotian moment." Its second chapter sets forth some of the evidence that supports a normative hypothesis that states are losing the normative high ground to "humanity" as articulated by transnational social forces, the creative basis for positing the rudimentary reality of "global civil society."

Part two, in a series of substantive chapters, explores this overarching interpretation in relation to more specific issue-areas: humanitarian intervention, environment, public order of the oceans, and the legal status of nuclear weaponry. Each of these concerns addresses a major problem of world order by reference to the adequacy of traditional conceptions of the international legal order as shaped by the logic of state sovereignty. And each observes both the tenacity (or resilience) of the state and statecraft, and its deficiency, from the perspective of world order values.

Part three returns to the more general level of analysis in a pair of concluding chapters. Chapter 9 is both a tribute to the juridical vision of Judge Christopher G. Weeramantry and an expression of an alternative view of the future that is centered on the encounter between global market forces and transnational social forces. This outlook is then developed in the final chapter by reference to a coherent vision of a transformed world order specified by reference to "humane governance."[10] Whether humane governance is a viable political project

9. At this time, it is also crucial to be sensitive to the problematic impact of "false universalism" that is associated with the historical reality that the normative order embodied in international law was predominantly evolved during its period of geopolitical ascendancy. For analysis in the human rights setting, *see* Richard Falk, *False Universalism and the Geopolitics of Exclusion*, 18 THIRD WORLD Q. 7–23 (1997).

10. For an elaboration, *see* RICHARD FALK, ON HUMANE GOVERNANCE: TOWARD A NEW GLOBAL POLITICS (1995).

or mere utopianism, only time will tell. But let us not forget the rapidity with which such utopian undertakings as self-determination for the countries of East Europe or racial equality for South Africa became transformative experiences!

# Part I

# THE EMERGING FRAME

# CHAPTER I

# THE GROTIAN MOMENT: UNFULFILLED PROMISE, HARMLESS PHANTASY, MISSED OPPORTUNITY?

> It was a time when the unthinkable became thinkable and the impossible really happened.
>
> Arundhati Roy[1]

## A. THE IDEA OF A GROTIAN MOMENT

Often the sense of decisive historical moments of the location of a boundary between one epoch and another obscures the slow, gradual tectonic shifts in values, beliefs, ideas, and behavior that are hidden from the general view, and if noticed at all, then only by the trained, observant eye of a gifted scholar. Nevertheless, to facilitate our understanding of change and continuity in human experience, the selection of key moments or dates seems almost indispensable in our search for clues about what the future will bring.

Such an understanding seems particularly crucial with respect to the future of world order these days for a variety of reasons: the apparent waning of influence of the territorial, sovereign state, which has been the defining unit of international political life for centuries; the shifting hierarchical structure of international relations following the collapse of the Soviet Union; the rising influence of global economic forces and the associated reality of integrated regional and global markets; the growth of informatics, artificial intelligence, and virtual diplomacy; the widespread sense that a "new world order" is emergent, but not so clearly delineated as to be yet nameable; and the ending of a momentous century and millennium with the prospect of new beginnings.

1. Arundhati Roy, The God of Small Things 31 (1997).

Characterizing the present unsettled reality of international society as "a Grotian Moment" is a way of underscoring the view that this is a time of *potential* transition from one type of world order to another, that the prospects for change are of qualitative significance that calls for a possible reformulation of world order, and that the authoritative interpretation of these circumstances has yet to be made from a juridical perspective in a manner comparable to what Hugo Grotius contributed to our grasp of international law and society in the early modern period.

My own understanding of the Grotian Moment was initially connected with a rather simplistic appreciation of Grotius' own distinctive contribution as historically situated early in the seventeenth-century Europe of feudalism and Christendom: he was rooted in the medieval world and yet he was receptive, perhaps not altogether wittingly, to an emergent world order of his day composed of sovereign territorial states that required a normative framework to guide their interactions given the loss of legitimacy and capability that had been earlier associated with Christian supranationalism.[2] Indeed, so receptive to the new was Grotius seen to be by the gatekeepers of the old order that his great treatise on international law was viewed by the religious establishment in the Vatican as essentially heretical; it was treated as a prohibited text, and duly placed on the papal index. It was not until some decades later, by way of the Peace of Westphalia in 1648 that ended the Thirty Years' War, that the modern system of states was formally established as the dominant world order framework, and it was not for another century or so that it seemed possible to appreciate that indeed Westphalia had provided a defining threshold—of course, overgeneralized and simplified, but yet a convenient shorthand by which to situate the transition from the medieval to the modern.[3] This transition has been generally treated as one of global scope, but it was in reality an exclusively European phenomenon at the outset that underpinned a Eurocentric phase of world order that has still not been entirely displaced, although it has

2. My initial portrayal of this Grotian identity was expressed in Richard Falk, *Introduction, in* CHARLES S. EDWARDS, HUGO GROTIUS: THE MIRACLE OF HOLLAND xiii–xxi (1981).

3. The continuing convenience of the Westphalian notation is evident, for instance, in a book evaluating U.N. peacekeeping activities in the 1990s to assess whether the United Nations was in the process of displacing the state and states as the main organizing force in international political life, the basic test still being formulated by reference to Westphalian benchmarks. *See* BEYOND WESTPHALIA? STATE SOVEREIGNTY AND INTERNATIONAL INTERVENTION (Gene M. Lyons & Michael Mastanduno eds., 1995).

been much weakened by the collapse of the colonial empires in the last half of the twentieth century, and by the growing appreciation and significance of Asia/Pacific countries, and especially China, for the global economic and strategic balance.[4] It remains true that states, and only states, assert sovereignty claims in relation to authority over bounded territorial units in a manner that is formally recognized within contemporary annals of diplomacy.

## B. THREE ACCOUNTS OF THE GROTIAN MOMENT

Let us ask ourselves whether it is reasonable to consider whether we are currently at a Grotian Moment in this sense, that is, at a time of deep transition from the statist framework of Westphalia to some differently constituted, emergent, and normatively enhanced world order. If so, we await a Grotius to convey that special juridical aura of inbetweenness, as we seemingly have not crossed the type of bright line that Westphalia provided, at least in retrospect. Of course, a few recent candidates have stepped into the sunshine to proclaim the new era and claim their maximum allotted fifteen minutes of fame—the interval allowed by Andy Warhol, that post-modernist arbiter of mass culture—to explain just what is changing and what is to come.[5] The prominence accorded these attempts at depicting what is new in the world confirms the impression that the old forms of world order are under dreadful pressure, and that society is seeking to find a sweeping account that restores a measure of coherence and meaningfulness to the world. But the short-lived attention that has been devoted to these efforts suggests strongly their inability to withstand critical judgments and their lack of capacity to explain real-world behavior.

Looking to the future is generally more problematic than interpreting the past, which, while subject to continuous reinterpretation, still possesses settled categories of understanding that are widely relied upon to identify defining moments of discontinuity. In contrast, to insist that one's own time and place is at the core of the change is almost always problematic, tarnished by a suspect autocentrism that gives undue weight to the significance of changes that coincide with

4. Samir Amin, Eurocentrism (1989).

5. *See* Charles Jencks, The Architecture of the Jumping Universe (1989) for a stimulating discussion of influential trends and the idea of an emergent aggregate in settings of pervasive complexity.

one's mortality and preferences, as well as with one's particular vantagepoint in time, space, and societal position, leading to an overall pattern of exaggeration and wish-fulfillment (or fear-fulfillment) that can be appropriately derided as a form of "presentism." Yet posing the question of whether we are at a Grotian Moment in the evolution of world order is a call for just such an assessment, and more than this, it presupposes the possibility of providing innovative normative horizons that help restructure our understanding of the role of law and morality as a regulative mechanism for the whole of humanity. Such an expectation is expressed in a globalist manner despite the realization that Grotius was himself insensitive to the exploitative implications of his juridical imaginings for non-European peoples, especially indigenous peoples.[6]

The end of the Cold War, the symbolic breaching of the Berlin Wall, and the implosion of the Soviet Union give to this exercise of generalizing about the recent past and near future a superficial historical validation, strongly sustained by a popular craving for interpretative guidance ("What does it all mean?"). Certainly, the preceding period generated a consensus in the North, at least, that world order was being shaped by the nuclear stand-off between two superpowers and their subordinate allies, creating a condition of ideological and geopolitical bipolarity that dominated our understanding of political reality. Ending this set of circumstances helps illuminate several interrelated, previously backgrounded, realities: trends of the recent past that had been subsumed beneath Cold War categories of perception (e.g., economic integration, regionalization, civilizational identification, decline of the state, the rise of informatics) and social forces that were released from structures of constraint that had been one feature of a specific sort of stability, bipolar geopolitical discipline, and conflictual behavior associated with Cold War practices (e.g., ethnic passions and micro-nationalism, religious politics, post-colonial applications of the right of self-determination and secessionism, and new forms of ideological purification that were no longer nearly as constrained in their political expressions as they were in a bipolar world).

6. Hedley Bull defers to the normative sensibility of the historical setting within which Grotius worked, but more recent commentators tend to adopt a more critical demeanor; the issues raised are important, but tangential to the inquiry in this chapter. For Bull's assessment, see Hedley Bull, *The Importance of Grotius in the Study of International Relations, in* Hugo Grotius and International Relations 65 (Hedley Bull, Benedict Kingsbury and Adam Roberts eds., 1990).

In light of these considerations, it is instructive to consider three attempts to depict the bridge between past and future that were directly or indirectly stimulated by the end of the Cold War era, taking note of the fact that all three were done by American males who were close to mainstream consciousness, that no one of the three made any effort to provide a new *juridical* synthesis, and that each perceptively highlights a particular feature of what might be called "the new world order" while ignoring other features. Although it lacked the pretension of an overarching explanation, the terminology of new world order initially made prominent by George Bush in the build-up to the Gulf War in 1990–1991 represented another line of response to a perceived condition of geopolitical rupture, and will be briefly considered below as a separate and influential, if flawed, effort to step into the void of geopolitical incoherence.

The first attempt to capture the essence of the historical experience following the events of 1989 was made by Francis Fukuyama in a widely discussed article entitled "The End of History?"[7] Fukuyama interpreted the ideological surrender of the Soviet Union mainly in a triumphalist spirit, suggesting that Western ideas about constitutionalism and a strong private sector had not only prevailed in a specific struggle but, far more spectacularly, had exhausted the possibilities for any future rise of meaningful resistance to these ideas in the form of alternative approaches at the level of the state about either the governing process or the economy. Fukuyama grounded his interpretation of this historical mutation by reliance upon an elaborate neo-Hegelian framework that supported the view that the discrediting of socialism marked the last phase in the evolution of human society, and that as a result ideological conflict would disappear, allowing an era of moderation to shape the future of world order in which the homogenizing tendencies associated with market forces and technological innovation would continue to spread the liberal model of governance to all corners of the planet, and where there would be nothing to fight over, or even argue about, at the level of ideas.

In effect, the American way of life would be universalized, and history as the progression of dominant ideas in a process of continuous contestation would come to an end, as this sort of liberalism will be treated as having won out decisively. Although widely criticized

7. Francis Fukuyama, *The End of History?*, 16(3) NAT'L INTEREST 3 (1989); also *A Reply to My Critics*, 18 NAT'L INTEREST 21 (1990); the extended book version of Fukuyama's world picture was published under the title THE END OF HISTORY AND THE LAST MAN (1992).

from the moment of publication, Fukuyama's ideas sparked the imagination, at least briefly.As has been the fate of other grand explanations of the end of the Cold War, this one had a short life; the book version attracted only a tiny fraction of the attention accorded to the initial article, despite spelling out the argument in far more detail and depth. What was wrong with Fukuyama's effort? In brief, it overstated the significance of the Soviet collapse and the discrediting of Marxism. Its reading of history didn't correspond sufficiently with other aspects of the emergent international reality, including widespread religious resurgence, a renewed emphasis on distinct cultural traditions, transnational activism, the overpowering of the state by transnational market forces, and the eruption of an array of new patterns of social and political disorder (inviting the contrarian label of the emergent reality as the "new world disorder").

Next came Samuel Huntington's bold thesis depicted in an article, "The Clash of Civilizations?," that was featured in the Summer 1993 issue of *Foreign Affairs*,[8] and was subsequently expanded to a substantial book entitled *The Clash of Civilizations and the Remaking of World Order*.[9] Intriguingly, as with Fukuyama, the tentativeness implied by the question mark that followed the title of the article version was dropped from the book title, and yet the reformulated and much extended argument has attracted only a fraction of the attention that was provoked by the article, and while discussion of the Huntington clash hypothesis persists, it is based on treating the initial publication as the definitive statement. What caught the imagination, literally around the world, was Huntington's contention that the next phase of history would be dominated by inter-civilizational war, and would most likely, in his words, pit "the West versus the rest."[10] The timing of the article overlapped with a rise in Western anxieties about Islam linked, misleadingly, to outbreaks of international terrorism and especially inflamed when Islamic extremists exploded a large bomb in New York City at the World Trade Center. These developments seemed to express an influential view that Islam's challenge to Western security was on a scale at least comparable to that associated with the Communist challenge that had produced the Cold War. Arguably, Huntington's thesis was substantially misconstrued by dwelling upon its sensationalist call for Western vigilance in the face of an Islamic threat, whereas the real force

8. Samuel Huntington, *The Clash of Civilizations?*, 72 Foreign Aff. 22 (1993).

9. Samuel Huntington, The Clash of Civilizations and the Remaking of World Order (1996).

10. *See* Huntington, *supra* note 8, at 39–49.

of his presentation was more conceptual, and less linked to a particular spin on conflict patterns. What Huntington argues is that "civilizations" rather than "states" will resume their roles as the defining units of world order. In this regard, the Grotian quest would have to include and emphasize a world order based on inter-civilizational relations and norms, as well as on the realities of intra-civilizational values and traditions. While highly suggestive, such a reframing of political life immediately poses questions, not convincingly addressed by Huntington, as to whether civilizations can be given meaningful spatial boundaries under existing circumstances, given the migrations of peoples and the mixing of civilizational identities in many places.

Interestingly, in the book Huntington reverts to a more traditional geopolitically grounded image of future conflict and projects a possible scenario of inter-civilizational war arising out of Western concerns about global balance centering on the containment of China, and activated by a struggle between China and Vietnam over control of hydrocarbon resources in the South China Sea in which, with an obvious historical irony, the United States enters the conflict in support of Vietnam's claims.[11] Huntington seems to soften, or to bracket, the view that states will be superseded by civilizational units in the near historical future, although he continues to stress the extent to which security and conflict will in the future be increasingly configured by civilizational identities and that the prospects for the West retaining its global role will depend on its leaders and citizenry becoming self-conscious about protecting its distinctive core values and beliefs against civilizational rivals. Such an undertaking commends to Huntington the desirability of actively protecting cultural identity, including the adoption by the West of a restrictive approach toward immigration from non-Western societies.

Even more so than Fukuyama's, Huntington's views ignited a firestorm of protest. His analysis was taken seriously throughout the world and treated as tantamount to an official manifestation of strategic thinking in the United States that was released at a given time to unveil a new ideological crusade-in-the-making behind closed doors in Washington.[12] In terms of conflict and violence, as well as the

11. *See* Huntington, *supra* note 9, at 312–18.

12. This impression of authoritativeness was undoubtedly strengthened by the publication of the Huntington piece as the lead article in an issue of *Foreign Affairs*, a journal notorious over the years for providing the government with space to release trial balloons on new directions of foreign policy.

delicate issues of civilizational differences, Huntington's interpretations touched a raw nerve, while Fukuyama was bland in comparison, presenting the Western victory in the Cold War in a grandiose, almost utopian, form that could be seen as nothing more than the latest of many efforts to package and set forth the American way of life as the inevitable wave of the future. Fukuyama's assessments of the end of history were so obviously overstated and idiosyncratic that they seemed unlikely to worry others for very long, while Huntington's outlook set off alarm bells that are still ringing; the clash thesis was interpreted outside the West as threatening and divisive, as an expression of the real opinions of the leadership of the greatest power-center in the world, and as supportive of chauvinistic reactions to economic globalization. Somewhat overlooked in the Huntington worldview was his strong insistence that the West stay out of conflicts involving non-Western antagonists and, in that regard, his prescriptions were non-interventionist and defensive in a manner that could have been regarded as reassuring to the rest of the world even if issued as part of the defense of the West and its superiority to the non-West.[13]

Huntington's views have by now receded into the background, but not necessarily forever. In the event that inter-civilizational tensions rise or civilizational regionalism takes hold, Huntington's clash thesis will undoubtedly be revisited. In the meantime, such a conceptualization of security and conflict seems to underestimate, and even ignore, globalizing tendencies associated with the market and the internet that tend to diminish civilizational differences and blur geographical divisions. Huntington downplays, as well, the difficulty and danger at this stage of attempts to reverse the mixing of civilizations through inter-civilizational mobility; it seems too late to consider separating civilizations by drawing geographical fault-lines, and the options of expulsion and cleansing seem too distasteful to consider seriously. The West, in particular, is already multi-civilizational, and any effort to ideologize and homogenize its historical identity based on spatial boundaries and cultural/ethnic characteristics would be oppressive toward millions of non-Westerners, and likely to foster the already existing attractions of chauvinistic and multicultural politics now making a comeback at the level of the state. (For example, in France, the rightist leader Jean-Marie Le Pen already in 1997 said

13. Huntington, *supra* note 9, at 316–17.

that "France will disappear" unless it moves rapidly to implement an anti-immigration program.) Such a view passes no judgment on functional regionalism of the European or Asia/Pacific variety that draws loosely on shared civilizational identities, and seems unlikely to become the basis for inter-civilizational rivalry, but at most an ordering of competing trading blocs and associated also with some distinct cultural claims.

Finally, there is the stark vision of Robert Kaplan, initially set forth in an article appearing in *The Atlantic Monthly* under the title "The Coming Anarchy"[14] and then later in a book called *The Ends of the Earth: A Journey to the Frontiers of Anarchy.*[15] Again, as with Fukuyama and Huntington, the main impact came from the shock effect of the article. By the time the more extended argument was embodied in book form, the mood had shifted and there was little interest in assessing an extended version of the position. Kaplan regards the recent disorders of Africa and the Middle East as world order signatures for the future. The outlook of this perceptive journalist attracted attention, in this instance, almost exclusively in the West, and particularly in the United States, because it provided a vivid account of deeply destructive and disturbing occurrences that were surfacing in the Great Lakes region of Africa, in Somalia, and in Bosnia, a pattern especially associated with the so-called "failed states" or "political meltdowns" of the early 1990s. Kaplan's negative view was the polar opposite of the principled optimism of Fukuyama, and indifferent to the civilizational contours that Huntington foresaw as shaping forces for the next major phase of world history. Unlike Fukuyama and Huntington, Kaplan is interpreting trends that are not coupled with either a triumphalist or a confrontational United States and, as such, do not arouse interest elsewhere in the world on the part of those seeking to decipher the implications of U.S. geopolitical predominance so as to protect themselves against such perceived threats. Kaplan's projections of an enveloping and expanding anarchy of a destructive character had their main resonance in the United States and reinforced the view that interventionism in the 1990s, even for humanitarian goals and under the auspices of the United Nations, was misguided, futile, costly, and dangerous. In a sense, the world order depicted was a partial complement to that given expression by Huntington, with the breakdown of states into disorganized fragments

14. Robert Kaplan, *The Coming Anarchy*, THE ATLANTIC MONTHLY, Feb. 1994.
15. ROBERT KAPLAN, THE ENDS OF THE EARTH: A JOURNEY TO THE FRONTIERS OF ANARCHY (1996).

presented as an alternative scenario to the process of states being humbled by the reassertion of "civilizations" as the main repositories of human loyalty and identity.

## C. TWO ADDITIONAL DEPICTIONS OF THE GROTIAN MOMENT

Let us consider two additional accounts of this Grotian Moment that have not yet been conceptualized in any serious way, but nevertheless respond to developments in this period on the assumption that world order could be and was being transformed. The first was associated with George Bush's much-heralded effort to mobilize support for a strong response to Iraq's 1990 invasion of Kuwait by contending that the global setting now provided the foundation for a "new world order" based on the effective use of collective security potentialities of the United Nations. In Bush's view, the conditions were finally favorable for the permanent members of the Security Council to cooperate in response to aggression precisely in the manner contemplated by the U.N. Charter, but heretofore stymied by the geopolitical stalemate between East and West. It was Bush's claim that if Iraq's aggression could be successfully reversed in this manner, then a whole set of possibilities to establish the Rule of Law in international relations would materialize and make Woodrow Wilson's vision of global security approach closer to practical reality, thereby overcoming the war-proneness of a states system based on self-help. The call to establish a new world order formed part of a successful campaign by Bush to mobilize political support for waging war against Iraq under U.N. auspices, with operational and financial responsibility spread among the members of an American-led coalition. The military undertaking attained its principal goal of restoring Kuwaiti sovereign rights, as did the financial undertaking of assessing rich states in a manner that relieved the United States from shouldering the burden of paying for an expensive war. Despite these successes, serious problems with the claim of a new world order became immediately apparent when the fighting stopped.

Countries of the South were deeply suspicious of the U.S. sponsorship of such a design for the future, especially given the degree of unilateral control that was exercised over the conduct and goals of the war and the negotiation of a cease-fire. The new world order was seen as a smokescreen for a U.S. hegemonic project to use the United

Nations to lend an aura of legitimacy to its geopolitical undertakings. In that regard, the Gulf War was interpreted elsewhere in the world as being mainly about access to the Gulf oil reserves and upholding Israeli security rather than representing a normative occasion on which to form a united front against Iraqi aggression and restore Kuwaiti sovereign rights. Such a skeptical interpretation of American intentions was reinforced by the reluctance of the United States to mount any comparable effort within the United Nations framework to meet what was widely viewed at the time as Serbian aggression (along with gross crimes against humanity) in Bosnia, by the exposure of Iraqi civilian society to punitive sanctions that were having a devastating impact, and by the manipulation of the Kurdish population. After encouraging the Kurds to overthrow Saddam Hussein, immediately after the cease-fire the U.S. allowed Baghdad to reassert its control over the Kurdish regions through reliance once more on oppressive tactics (which were in the end partially constrained by Security Council action, but only after strong public pressures were generated by CNN coverage that portrayed the desperate nature of the human ordeal as the Kurds were driven into the barren mountains of Northern Iraq during the onset of winter).

What is more, the Bush Administration itself became quickly uncomfortable with the implications of the new world order as a generalized directive to keep the peace by reliance on American-dominated U.N. procedures. It was one thing to mount a major effort where the strategic interests of the U.S. government were at stake, but it was quite another to make peacekeeping commitments to correct the range of disorders that were afflicting a variety of poor societies, especially those in sub-Saharan Africa. During the Cold War the political destiny of virtually any country was of some strategic interest as a barometer of who was winning and losing on the global stage, but with no such geopolitical encounter, it was of far less concern who ran a particular society and with what ideological outlook. This indifference also reflected a climate of ideological subservience in which the postulates of neo-liberalism were being endorsed by almost every government in the world, and thus there were not even economic incentives to control political outcomes, although to reinforce this consensus on governance and economic policy the United States used its leverage to induce governments that came to power in emergency circumstances (as in Haiti when Jean Baptiste Aristide was restored or Zaire after Mobutu Sese Seko), to adopt a liberal policy agenda by linking it to reconstruction aid. Furthermore, the citizenry of the United States, despite its government being the advocate (and arguably the main beneficiary) of the new world order along the lines proposed by Bush, and even while exulting in the military prowess exhibited during the Gulf War, was not inclined to take on the responsibilities associated with a provocative role in the United Nations. This reluctance became dramatically evident in reaction to a firefight in Somalia that cost 18 American lives in the fall of 1993. As one American diplomat expressed privately, in light of these developments, "the new world order" was put back on the shelf.

But there is one other way of conceptualizing the emergent discontinuity in international life. It is to anticipate a cumulative trend toward globalization giving rise inevitably to a corresponding trend toward global governance, although not necessarily in a statist form. Such an evolution would follow from the need to manage complexity, to take account of the fragility of an unregulated world, and to compensate for the inability of the state to cope with either economic interdependence or cyberspace. The establishment of the World Trade Organization, as the institutionalized expression of the negotiated GATT framework for world trade, suggested that states were quite willing to transfer sovereign prerogatives to achieve a more reliable form of global economic governance. Such moves are provisional, and there are indications that portions of governing elites at the state level are trying to retrieve some of the authority that had been earlier so easily negotiated away. The U.S. government, initially unconditionally enthusiastic about the GATT process and the WTO, subsequently cast doubt on the degree of its commitment. It refused to abandon its efforts to disrupt Cuba's trading and investment relationships by imposing secondary boycotts although such tactics seemed definitely inconsistent with the U.S. global legal obligations under GATT. The U.S. government adopted a rejectionist posture by refusing to resolve the controversy over the boycotts with its European allies by recourse to the WTO dispute-settlement mechanism.

A neo-liberal world order based on the functional imperatives of the market is not likely to be a Grotian Moment in a normative sense. That is, economic globalization might in time produce a transition to a post-Westphalian world order, but not one that is likely to enhance human well-being, and seems instead to intensify polarizing tendencies associated with unequal returns on capital and to justify benign neglect of those victimized by the drive toward the most efficient uses of capital in the global marketplace. The normative effects of globalization, it must be acknowledged, remain uncertain and contradictory. The polarizing and marginalizing impacts seem definite, although their severity and extent are in doubt, and might well shift over time. As well, there are some definite beneficial social effects of globalization, including positive overall impacts on the standard of living in previously impoverished countries that have recently managed high, sustained growth rates. As a result, hundreds of millions of people have been rescued from poverty even in the face of continuing rapid population expansion. Those who emphasize these positive trends associated with economic globalization are probably in the best position to respond normatively to a set of circumstances that may add up to a Grotian Moment.[16]

## D. IS THERE A GROTIAN MOMENT BUT NO GROTIUS?

But taken as a whole, these considerations discussed in relation to the various explanations of a major shift in world order, both of an empirical and normative character, suggest a posture of caution toward the contention that we are indeed experiencing a Grotian Moment. The realization that there has been a wide range of transformative images set forth, without any of them commanding sustained acceptance, in the last several years seems to vindicate this attitude of doubt. Such doubt is intensified by the awareness that only in the United States is the current historical period being portrayed as one that is generating change of a defining magnitude. And if this were not enough to discourage optimism about an emergent world order responsive to human needs and desires, the climate of ideas fostered by the neo-liberal consensus is quite hostile to the provision of public goods by governmental authority, making it difficult to maintain even the present scale of social commitments under United Nations auspices despite a remarkable period of sustained economic growth and trade expansion. That is, there may be a Grotian Moment, but until the response is one that is persuasively articulated by reference to human betterment, there is no Grotius.

The failure of these attempts to define the Grotian Moment, despite perceiving correctly that something decisive was underway in

16. And, perhaps, such a viewpoint is expressed by such writers as Kenichi Ohmai who are enthusiastic about economic globalization. *See, e.g.*, KENICHI OHMAI, THE BORDERLESS WORLD: POWER AND STRATEGY IN THE INTERLINKED ECONOMY (1994).

relation to world order, should not be surprising. Each attempt perceived a fragment of an emergent world order, but none has seen enough of the whole to provide an image that is convincing, except as a very temporary fiction that controversially interprets what is baffling or menacing to the rest of us. That is, these attempts were not able to sustain explanatory credibility, and did not seriously even try to achieve normative credibility. As already suggested, each of these conceptions of the Grotian Moment originally appeared in a magazine or journal article that achieved instant and notorious prominence, and each was followed by a book that failed to attract comparable attention. That is, the more careful and comprehensive arguments were virtually ignored, while their superficial rendering was widely discussed and commented upon; similarly, as noted, the Bush avowal of a new world order was abandoned as soon as its opportunistic use in the Gulf War was fulfilled. Only the transforming potential of economic and cybernetic globalization seems to remain relevant as an effort to establish the reality of a Grotian Moment, which is quite different from acknowledging that a Grotius has been able to articulate the normative bridge between past and future.

Apparently, such a short lifespan for world order explanations is the dismal fate of cultural and geopolitical fad; perhaps a postmodern glimmering of the shape of things to come is all that we can expect. The absence of a generally endorsed account of the Grotian Moment is itself a smoke signal of sorts, indicative of a failure to supersede the Westphalian realities of the state system despite numerous superficial claims to the contrary. Where no explanation of a phenomenon is able to command adherence, it would seem likely that existing circumstances remain too inchoate to assume a definitive shape. In this sense, possibly it is best to conclude that the Grotian Moment has not yet arrived, and thus, it becomes impossible for a Grotius to provide a normative imprint for the age. Such an assessment is complicated by the cultural mood that seems to repudiate any generalized explanation of societal patterns as one more "meta-narrative" that is inherently flawed by the very character of the undertaking, being self-serving on behalf of ruling ideas and elites, silent about those who are being victimized, and uncritically evasive about the viewpoint from which a conceptualization of world order derives.

A closely related difficulty arises from the proximity of the Cold War, and the temptation to view its end as fundamental rather than as one more marker in statist geopolitics. It is notable that Fukuyama, Kaplan, and Huntington are Americans, and that it is the United

States, as unipolar claimant and self-anointed global leader, that sought a coherent account of world order in this period, and was regarded elsewhere on the planet as virtually the sole source of planning for a new world order that was perceived as little more than a cosmetically disguised design for abiding global hegemony. Such a view gained credibility in the immediate aftermath of the Gulf War, although it has been badly eroded in subsequent years by the refusal of the United States to follow through in U.N. peacekeeping contexts, most evidently in relation to the outcomes in Somalia, Bosnia, Rwanda, and Zaire. The whole perceptual process may be distorted to the extent that governments of major states have become, to an extent yet to be determined, themselves instrumentalized by global capital forces and their representatives.

On this basis, it seems appropriate to ask whether the Grotian Moment needs to be recast as a question: is the present global setting usefully understood as a transitional interval in world order, or are the essential ingredients of the state system still descriptive of the structure and exercise of authority at the global level? Contributors to a recent book, *Beyond Westphalia?,* answered their own question mainly in the negative, focusing on whether U.N. and world community claims were consistently enough overcoming territorial sovereignty in relation to matters of humanitarian concern, environmental protection, and the nonproliferation of nuclear weapons to support the view that a post-statal world order was coming into being. The scholarly consensus set forth in the book confirmed and affirmed the persistence of statism as the basis of world order, but it did so mainly by focusing on a single critical dimension of world order, namely, the extent to which sovereign claims retained their territorial authority in the face of global claims, especially those associated with claims by the United Nations to engage in humanitarian intervention.[17]

There is another good reason for reluctance to proclaim a Grotian Moment. Perhaps we should take precautions against what might be called "the illusion of historical climax"—the tendency to regard one's own period as a decisive historical turning point, a strong expression of mortal curiosity about how history will turn out. Quite possibly, the approach of a new millennium accentuates this illusion that we are living at a decisive turning point in human history. After all, before the year 1000 the air was filled with both dire prophesy

17. *Compare* Lyons and Mastanduno, *supra* note 3, at 1–18, 250–265 *with* Rosenau, *Sovereignty in a Turbulent World, in* Lyons and Mastanduno, *supra* note 3, at 191–227.

and transcendental hopefulness: the end of the world, the second coming or the reign on earth of the Holy Spirit after the two preparatory stages of Mosaic law and the ministry of Jesus Christ, thereby interpreting history by reference to the Christian doctrine of the Holy Trinity.

Let me consider this theme of endings and new beginnings differently by way of reference to Frank Kermode's important book, *The Sense of an Ending*.[18] As Kermode suggests, "the survival of [the] paradigms is as much our business as their erosion."[19] Kermode sharply observes that:

> It is commonplace to talk about our historical situation as uniquely terrible and in a way privileged, a cardinal point in time. But can it really be so? It seems doubtful that our crisis, our relation to the future and to the past, is one of the important differences between us and our predecessors.[20]

And finally, as Kermode points out, "the whole concurrence of *fin de siecle* phenomena" encourages us to "project our existential anxieties onto history; there is a real correlation between ends of centuries and the peculiarity of our imagination, that it always chooses to be at the end of an era."[21]

For most peoples of the world, we are coming to the end of a millennium—not merely the end of a century—and so the tendency to exaggerate danger and possibility should be magnified by a factor of ten, or more. Indeed, there has been a flood of "endist" books: "the end of nature," "the end of the Cold War," "the end of marriage," the end of absolutely everything, even the end of endings. And maybe this suppressed yearning for historical climax partially explains the instant, if awkwardly ephemeral, notoriety of the Grotian candidacies of Fukuyama, Huntington, and Kaplan, and their equally abrupt dismissal as useful presentations.

As earlier suggested, the postmodern cultural circumstance has also played its part in disavowing overarching explanations and evaluations of historical process: nothing can be worse, according to this critical outlook, than the acceptance of a meta-narrative. Hence, any attempt to define the Grotian Moment necessarily runs the gauntlet

18. Frank Kermode, The Sense of an Ending: Studies in the Theory of Fiction (1968).
19. *Id.* at 43.
20. *Id.* at 95.
21. *Id.* at 97.

of this posture—unless one succumbs to the temptation to say (cleverly) that the loss of meaning and purpose is itself the defining feature of an emergent world order, the new reality being in its essence a cauldron of shifting perceptions and contradictions.

## E. VISIONARY FATIGUE AT THE THRESHOLD OF A NEW MILLENNIUM

But, in fact, I want to consider and support the *opposite side* of Kermode's effort to puncture the balloon of hyped historical expectations. What I find startling is not the mood of millennial boldness, stimulating a splurge of the imagination that should be viewed with suspicion, but rather the grayness of our current expectations about the future even as we approach the year 2000. What I find to be the spirit of this moment is not the excessiveness of conjectures about the future, but rather what I would call the meagerness of the millennial moment.[22] It was this suppressive attitude that was on display during the fiftieth anniversary celebrations of the United Nations. President Bill Clinton's speech at the United Nations was particularly emblematic of this discouraging outlook, especially as the United States is the leading member of the organization and has generally, in this century, been the country to put forward at critical moments a visionary prospect for the reform of international society. The only plausible way to grasp Clinton's anti-inspirational message is as a dampening counsel to set sights lower—by learning to do more with less, given tangible reality by a massive dose of downsizing medication. It is true that this downsizing approach toward the future of the United Nations was domestically driven by conservative pressures in America, but such a domestic mood, especially if unchallenged, reveals a wider skepticism about world order ambitions.

## F. JURIDICAL CANDIDATES FOR THE SECOND COMING OF GROTIUS

The same kind of disappointment relates to the comparatively slight sigh of relief about the collapse of oppressive Communism and the termination of the Cold War. After World War I and World War II,

22. Richard Falk, *The Paucity of the Millennial Moment: The Case of Nuclearism*, *in* THE YEAR 2000: ESSAYS ON THE END 169–79 (Charles B. Strozier and Michael Flynn eds., 1997).

there were public pressures to sustain a peaceful world and political leaders, especially the Americans Woodrow Wilson, Franklin Roosevelt, and even Harry Truman, put forward proposals on future war prevention. The League of Nations and the United Nations, however restricted in their actual capabilities, represented the realization of dreams on the part of those who wanted to see the end of war as a social institution and who believed that moving toward such a goal depended on shifting peacekeeping roles from major states to international institutions over time. Substantial demobilization took place at the national level and disarmament was placed high on the international agenda, as were efforts to impose criminal accountability on leaders of the losing side in the war. World War II ended with the founding of the United Nations and the trials of major war criminals at Tokyo and Nuremberg. These developments were soon followed by the Acheson/Baruch/Lilienthal plan for complete nuclear disarmament and, shortly thereafter, by such normative breakthroughs as the Universal Declaration of Human Rights, the endorsement of the Nuremberg Principles, and the adoption of the Genocide Convention. Could this series of earlier normative initiatives qualify the historical setting as a Grotian Moment lacking only a Grotius to imprint on public consciousness a widely accepted understanding that a discontinuity in world order had occurred? Or were these normative developments deceptive in their rhetoric and purported scope, and incapable of providing the foundations for a genuine world community? Given these circumstances, the Grotian Moment arguably existed in the years after 1945, but it was not theorized as such, thus its potential significance was not generally appreciated.

One notable exception to this generalization were the efforts associated with the world federalist movement that believed that World War II and its atomic finale demonstrated the necessity, and hence created the opportunity, for world government, that is, the transformation of a statist world order into a world order with the requisite capabilities to maintain peace and security for all the peoples of the world. This perspective was given its most serious academic expression in *World Peace through World Law* by Grenville Clark and Louis B. Sohn,[23] a carefully elaborated design for the centralization of authority in international life that took the form of a drastic revision of the United Nations Charter so that the organization would be transformed into a type of limited world government with formal

23. Grenville Clark and Louis B. Sohn, World Peace Through World Law (1960).

responsibility for and effective supranational control over international peace and security. Despite the impressive credentials of its authors and a massive promotional effort throughout the world in support of their proposals, this normative response at the dawn of the nuclear age produced only the faintest resonances in the United States and elsewhere, and such thinking was quickly and completely marginalized as a world order alternative by the geopolitical passions associated with the East/West rivalry.

There were other international jurists in the first decade or so after World War II who definitely believed that a new world order was coming into being, and that to be acknowledged as a historical reality, it needed only to be identified, described, and named by a reputable scholar. Among international lawyers, perhaps the bravest and most influential attempt to do for the mid-twentieth century what Grotius did for the early seventeenth century was that made by C. Wilfred Jenks in *The Common Law of Mankind*,[24] a work that undoubtedly deserves fresh consideration forty years after its initial publication. Jenks interpreted the global setting as exhibiting a convergence of normative trends with respect to the social content of law that created the prospect of transcending ideological and civilizational differences, both of which he discounted as superficial and propagandistic.[25] As with Clark and Sohn, the Jenks view did not take significant hold even in academic circles, given the societal preoccupations with the Cold War agenda in this period.[26]

## G. VISIONARY DISLOCATION AND THE COLD WAR

Unfortunately, as is evident, history did not cooperate with a reflective consideration of underlying normative tendencies that contained the range of plausible alternatives for the future. The world was riven by ideological and geopolitical tensions that became unbearable during periods of international crisis by the end-time implications of nuclear weaponry. These conditions assumed a deadly reality as a result of a critical dependence on weapons of mass destruction as the lynchpin of "containment," a reliance expressed by

24. C. Wilfred Jenks, The Common Law of Mankind (1958).

25. For an important world order critique of Jenks' approach, especially as neglectful of the values consequences of public order differences, see Myres S. McDougal and Harold D. Lasswell, *Ideological Differences, in* Studies of World Public Order 3–41 (1960).

26. *See also* F.S.C. Northrop, The Meeting of East and West (1944).

the doctrine of nuclear deterrence. Indeed, what followed was a prolonged eclipse of Grotian expectations of an "emergent world order" that embodied a cosmopolitan ethos, underscored by an anxious concern about whether civilizational, and even human, survival were any longer reasonably ensured, given the risks of geopolitical collapse. Could a durable world order be based for very long on a doctrine with the acronym MAD (Mutual Assured Destruction), often also called by its nickname"the balance of terror?" Many influential commentators on the passing scene became alarmed about the human condition. Jonathan Schell gave the most eloquent expression to these anxieties in *The Fate of the Earth,*[27] and the British social historian, E.P. Thompson, wrote an extraordinarily powerful essay about the serious moral consequences for a civilization that is preparing to inflict nuclear catastrophe on its enemy should stability break down. Thompson identified this posture as one of "exterminism," which he powerfully argued was deeply corrupting for a society even in the fortunate event that it is never called upon to carry out its threat; in other words, the preparation is itself morally corrupting, and suggestive of an outmoded and excessive attachment to a world order system that is essentially anachronistic.[28]

The 1970s reinforced this dark mood by its emphasis on ecological danger, dramatized by the Club of Rome study, *The Limits to Growth,* which rested its argument on the challenge of an unresolved "global problematique," to wit, that interrelated trends of population growth, food supply, pollution, and resource availability were producing a deepening crisis of sustainability for industrial civilization.[29] *Limits* refrained from offering any kind of social or political critique or world order solution, but its printouts and graphs strongly implied that anything less than a fundamental adjustment in Western lifestyle within a matter of years would result in a tragedy of catastrophic proportions that would cause unprecedented human suffering. The contentions of *Limits,* derived from the outcomes of an elaborate computer program devised by systems analysts working as a team at MIT, created for a time a new species of technocratic authority to bolster its sensationalist analysis of the existing global situation. But it also encouraged a backlash, consisting of various forms of criticism of method and inferences drawn, centered on the contention that the

27. JONATHAN SCHELL, THE FATE OF THE EARTH (1988).

28. THE FATE OF THE EARTH, *supra* note 27; *see also* E.P. THOMPSON, BEYOND THE COLD WAR: A NEW APPROACH TO THE ARMS RACE AND NUCLEAR ANNIHILATION (1982).

29. DONELLA MEADOWS ET AL., THE LIMITS TO GROWTH (1972).

dramatic conclusions of *Limits* were a result of "cooking" the data in various ways that overstated the dangers. The graphs and tables in the Club of Rome study did suggest that the basic trends could be depicted with precision and confidence and, when the dire, predicted consequences failed to materialize as the time of collapse passed, the whole approach was discredited. This sequence facilitated the re-emergence of a basic posture of ecological complacency, and suppressed the sense that environmental decay would provide the objective conditions for transition to a more regulated and centralized form of world order than had been provided by the Westphalian solution during the past three-and-a-half centuries. In retrospect, one kind of exaggeration led to another kind; ecological complacency seemed as unwarranted, given the realities, as had the earlier ecological gloom and doom.

The realization of an ecological emergency suggested the existence of a world order crisis of the sort depicted so vividly by Garrett Hardin through his image of the "tragedy of the commons."[30] In its essence, this historical tragedy arose when the common pasturelands of England were overgrazed. when each sheep or cattle owner maximized the size of his herd without regard for the sustainable population of the sum total number of animals belonging to all owners, the rational pursuit of private interests destroyed the collective interest. Hardin analogized this development, which led to the destruction of the commons and the enclosure movement, to the jeopardy of the global commons: the interests of the whole were unprotected under conditions where carrying capacity was being exceeded, suggesting a threat to human well-being, especially for future generations. If such a diagnosis had managed to shift the locus of control over transnational market forces to the establishment of effective mechanisms of environmental control at regional and global levels, then the preconditions for a Grotian Moment would have arguably come to exist, even if only during a brief window of opportunity in the early 1970s when concern about ecological vulnerability was at its height. A few attempts were made to treat this context as a world order circumstance with system-transforming potentialities.[31]

30. GARRETT HARDIN, THE TRAGEDY OF THE COMMONS (1968).

31. *See* RICHARD FALK, THIS ENDANGERED PLANET: PROSPECTS AND PROPOSALS FOR HUMAN SURVIVAL (1972).

## H. RESTATING THE CASE FOR A GROTIAN MOMENT IN AN ERA OF GLOBALIZATION

But something additional has been happening during the last several decades that relates to this main narrative line. It is difficult and controversial to specify this phenomenon, but it relates to the cumulative impact of the transnational rise of financial markets, the mobility of capital, the integration of production, the erosion of territoriality for most economic activities at the technological cutting edge, along with the ethos of the internet, which leads to non-spatial loyalties as its most ardent adherents displace "citizenship" with claims of "netizenship."[32] The role of the state has been caught up in this partially concealed maelstrom—which itself embodies a dynamic associated with the activities of the transnational corporation and the shift in economic power from national banks and reserve systems to rootless traders with minimal accountability to any specific political community, and a behavioral pattern dominated by the relentless pursuit of profits. This overall reframing of world order is now generally being discussed beneath the rubric of "globalization," one of those buzzwords we often deplore because of its infuriating slipperiness, yet depend upon, because it calls attention to an essential pattern of policy and action that challenges earlier modes of comprehension based on statist categories. "Globalization" in some ways functions the way such words as "paradigm" and "paradigmatic" did a decade or so earlier.[33]

So far, this dynamic of globalization has rested its normative case for acceptance on the promises of liberal economics and the benefits claimed for sustained economic growth on a quasi-global scale. This economistic outlook turned ideological after the Cold War ended, and has been fashioned into the world's first truly global ideology that rests on consumerism as promoted and reinforced by the global media, including now the internet, which is likely to provide us with a world shopping mall and business and banking centers by early in the next century and threatens to make netizens of us all, whether we like it or not. This process of globalization is so powerful because it has been reinforced by *several complex associated developments*:

32. For a helpful overall conceptualization, see IAN CLARK, GLOBALIZATION AND FRAGMENTATION: INTERNATIONAL RELATIONS IN THE TWENTIETH CENTURY (1997).

33. For a skeptical view as to the significance of these developments, see PAUL HIRST AND GRAHAME THOMPSON, GLOBALIZATION IN QUESTION (1996).

- the weakening of organized labor and the apparent disappearance for the present of "dangerous classes" that had earlier provided the necessary political basis for the social contract between labor and business that improved overall living standards while moderating corporate profits—in effect, a social contract that held for more than a century.[34]

- the collapse of socialism as an ethical challenge to capitalism and the acceptance of the amoral logic of the market as further minimizing claims arising from the social agenda of welfare and job security;

- the disappearance of serious geopolitical rivalry and a compensating attentiveness to global economic relations and, with it, the rising pressures of "competitiveness' ";

- the promotion of market-oriented constitutionalism as a major foreign policy goal of the United States, giving rise to the espousal of "enlargement" as the only feasible path to peace—this hypothesis of "democratic peace" rests on the empirical and conceptual claim that democracies do not engage in wars against each other; and

- the undermining of political support for global public goods, such as the financing of the U.N., environmental protection, and humanitarian assistance, partly as a result of the discipline of global capital with its pervasive stress on liberalization and privatization, and its dislike of public sector solutions.

Does this pattern of developments that constitute globalization amount to a newly emergent world order? Will the role of the state, especially the security role, be sufficiently diminished to justify the overall portrayal of transition, in the sense of a Grotian Moment, a passage from a statist world order to one that is economically and otherwise connected on regional and global levels to qualify as an emergent post-statal reality? And if so, what kind of juridical account will provide a bridge to link the persisting statist realities with the

34. As analyzed in John Gerard Ruggie, *At Home Abroad, Abroad at Home: International Liberalisation and Domestic Stability in the New World Economy*, 24 MILLENNIUM 507–26 (Winter, 1995); the role of dangerous classes is to be found in IMMANUEL WALLERSTEIN, AFTER LIBERALISM 252–71 (1995).

distinctiveness of this emergent globalism? Grotius himself was from the northern portion of Europe where the pressure and incentives to rethink and challenge medievalism, especially its universalist pretensions, were greatest. Is it the United States, Asia/Pacific, or Africa that is best situated to provide the nurturing of observation and experience that will produce an authoritative reformulation of world order capable of providing a normative consensus to guide decisions and policy formation in the next century?

There seems present an objective set of circumstances that does now constitute a Grotian Moment in the following sense: part of the Grotian contribution was to prefigure a new normative order that could apply to states claiming sovereignty, territorial supremacy, inter-state equality, and the divine right to rule, and repudiating any willingness to defer on vital normative issues to the earlier medieval framework of Christendom and *res publica* as interpreted and implemented by the Roman Church. The foundation of authority rested upon the universalism embodied in the precepts of natural law, which were then hierarchically arranged to reflect the local/global structures of medieval internationalism.

We currently confront in this era of economic and cultural globalization a more profound normative vacuum: the dominating logic of the market in a world of greatly uneven social, economic, and political conditions and without any built-in, reliable means to ensure that continuing global economic growth does not at some point and in certain respects cause decisive ecological damage. As we approach the year 2000 there is a mood of downsizing indifference to larger issues of human well-being and collective betterment, a state of affairs described journalistically as a severe case of "compassion fatigue." We seem mostly to be in the grip of dangerous indifference to many instances of severe human suffering in a cybernetic context in which we are aware of ongoing human ordeals in real time and are also subject to the manipulations of an advertising-laden media with its single-minded message: "leave it to the market, stupid!" This is also the rallying cry of many governments these days, as well as the outlook of the Bretton Woods institutions of the World Bank and International Monetary Fund.

This double set of circumstances—system change and normative vacuum—has been described by the German sociologist Ulrich Beck in a challenging fashion:

> The West is confronted by questions that challenge the fundamental premises of its own social and political system. The key question we are now confronting is whether the historical symbiosis between capitalism and democracy that characterized the West can be generalized on a global scale without exhausting its physical, cultural, and social foundations. . . . And should we not . . . come to the conclusion that we have to rethink, indeed reinvent, our industrial civilization. . . . Are not new social contracts waiting to be born?"[35]

Beck also emphasizes the extent to which this process of globalization has involved a transition from one social epoch to another as an unplanned and essentially apolitical development that came about without being consciously promoted. By noting that such a transition "contradicts the democratic self-understanding," Beck expresses the widely accepted, although rarely reflected upon or made explicit, view that fundamental social change can only come about legitimately if it is the result of democratic participatory debate, dialogue, direct action, and reflection.[36] Is the democratic self-understanding, which is by no means present throughout the world, a component of achieving legitimacy for the next world order? To the extent that an affirmative response is made, the Grotian challenge needs to be reformulated and extended in the following manner: the existing framing of world order requirements cannot adequately safeguard widely shared human values unless explicitly directed to address certain broad concerns:

- ensuring the revenue base to support global public goods in connection with a strong and effective U.N., an environment program capable of protecting the global commons, and the various mechanisms needed to ensure respect for fundamental obligations to uphold human rights as set forth in widely ratified treaties;

- providing for participatory rights for the peoples of the world and their official and unofficial representatives on matters of fundamental global policy by way of democratic organs of governance that provide meaningful access for appropriate citizens'

35. Ulrich Beck, Anthony Giddens and Scott Lash, Reflexive Modernization: Politics, Tradition . . . Modern Social Order 1.
36. *Id.* at 3.

associations and other transnational networks, thereby restricting the orbit of influence currently exercised by the WTO and Group of Seven;

- negotiating a series of new transnational social contracts that establish effective regulatory authority on behalf of those victimized by capital and monetary flows—social criteria of need in addition to economistic criteria of profits and return on investment as the basis for allocating resources and revenues; and

- establishing reliable mechanisms of accountability that impose potential responsibility on those who act on behalf of states, international institutions, market forces, and transnational social actors. An International Criminal Court with broad powers of investigation and effective procedures to ensure implementation in a consistent manner is established and allowed to operate without being subject to political controls. According to the proposal for an International Criminal Court now under formal consideration, the Security Council must authorize any initiative by the tribunal, which means that each of the permanent members has a veto over any proposed criminal investigation, and would presumably block action taken against itself or close allies.

Positing these normative goals is a way of reintroducing a normative architecture to offset the prospect of a future world order that reflects mainly economistic priorities. But it must also be realized that states, as the main actors in international life, can no longer be counted upon as the principal agency for achieving normative adjustments. There are two important conclusions that follow:

- the state system has already been significantly eroded in its problem-solving credibility, especially by the rise of global market forces; in these altered circumstances, even leading states have been far less able to fulfill their basic territorial responsibility to provide security and welfare for their own citizens or to participate effectively in fashioning a new normative framework that is capable of regulating transnational economic activities; and

- under these circumstances, a new normative order will almost certainly not evolve from the primary agency of the state; the state appears to have lost its creativity and autonomy as a political form; the European Union is one exploration of another source of agency, although it was originally established by intergovernmental cooperation and is currently stymied in its further evolution by various expressions of nationalistic resistance, elites being far more globalized and economistic than citizenries in most countries of contemporary Western Europe; there is also the possibility that the state could be reoriented to become more reflective of people-driven priorities, or at least more expressive of an equilibrium between globalization-from-above and transnational social forces, or globalization-from-below.[37]

## I. THE GROTIAN MOMENT OR STEPPING INTO THE NORMATIVE ABYSS

In summary, a haunting question rises to the surface. Do we have the receptivity as an intellectual community to acknowledge a Grotius if her ideas are being disseminated among us? Waiting for Grotius resembles waiting for Godot unless social forces can provide a supportive and receptive climate. At present, these forces seem insufficiently crystallized to recognize that a Grotius for the emergent globalized world order has arrived on the scene, even if equipped with treatise in hand to offer the global village a comprehensive normative account that could help bridge past, present, and future.

Grotius was "heard" in the seventeenth century because the Enlightenment project of the Renaissance was already well underway and the Protestant Reformation had taken place in the North of Europe; religious authority was in definite retreat and finally neutralized by the barbarity of the Thirty Years' War, the event that galvanized Grotius into normative, conceptualizing action, paving the way, although not explicitly, for modernism and secularism, and the ascendancy of science.

There is an assemblage of disparate contemporary social forces that might welcome a Grotius, especially if she came from elsewhere than the West: the networks of transnational social groupings that have shown up at U.N. conferences on world issues such as environment, population, women, human rights, and stirred things up; the

37. This distinction is explored in RICHARD FALK, ON HUMANE GOVERNANCE: TOWARD A NEW GLOBAL POLITICS (1995).

displaced workers and the poor in the West; the sectors of international society that fail to attract investors and those that are oriented around a religious outlook and are not likely to relate comfortably or successfully to a world order scenario that seeks to restructure world order on the basis of the primacy of the economistic world picture.

In my view, at this point, I am quite sure that a genuine Grotian response would be either accidentally or deliberately lost in the noise of the global media and internet, and evoke only sporadic interest at the margins of influence, and inconclusively even there, because of the absence of any coherent understanding of the transitional reality.

So my overall conclusion is confusing in its meaning, and is elusive even for me: "Yes, after all, due to the cumulative and multidimensional character of globalization, we are objectively at a Grotian Moment, but not because the Cold War has ended, i.e., not as of 1989, but rather because the discipline of global capital has been able *fundamentally* to restructure state/society relations in dangerous and often cruel ways, but also in some beneficial and hopeful ways.

"But no, we do not yet act as if we—as a civilization or series of civilizations—realize this Grotian need for a responsive normative framework; we have been lulled to ideological sleep by a mixture of consumerist allurements and a deadening market-driven ideological consensus; the ambiguity of "the Grotian Moment" can be expressed by a 'yes,' immediately followed by a 'no.' "

But such an end-point has an uncomfortable postmodern deconstructive ring that can be understood as either an expression of despair or as a counsel of quietism. This is not intended. The outcome of the dynamics of struggle to control the transition to some variant of geogovernance will realize the hopes and expectations of some actors. Withdrawing from the struggle is to lose by default to either the economistic globalists or one or another extremist backlash, whether religious or nationalistic. As Immanuel Wallerstein expresses the imperative for bold imaginative risk-taking: "We are in effect being called upon to construct our utopias, not merely to dream about them. Something will be constructed. If we do not participate in the construction, others will determine it for us."[38] And hopefully, the utopias constructed will serve as the inspiration for new forms of

38. Immanuel Wallerstein, *The Inter-state Structure of the Modern World System*, *in* INTERNATIONAL THEORY: POSITIVISM AND BEYOND 87, 106 (Steve Smith, Ken Booth and Marysia Zalewski eds., 1996).

political action, a recovery of moral and political vision, and an overall clarification of the normative choices so as to make it easier for the next Grotius to fill what now is being experienced as a normative abyss.

# CHAPTER II

# WORLD ORDER: TOWARD EQUILIBRIUM BETWEEN INTERSTATE LAW AND THE LAW OF HUMANITY

## A. CONCEPTUALIZING THE CONTEMPORARY FAILURES OF WORLD ORDER

The notion of world order is situated between interstate law and the law of humanity, although not necessarily at all in the middle. The interstate is presumably the past, a time when clearly the interstate dimension dominated our understanding of international law, but not the more distant past when states in the modern sense didn't exist. Perhaps, then, we should associate the period of the interstate with "the modern" and the law of humanity with "the postmodern."

The law of humanity is associated with the future; it is more a matter of potentiality than of history or experience. It is prefigured, and to some extent embodied, in the substance and theory of the international law of human rights. Its formal reality has been established through the primary agency of states and qualifies as a domain of interstate law. But the historical potency of the international law of human rights is predominantly a consequence of its implementation through the agency of civil society.

This agency of civil society needs to be understood in two senses. First in the transnational nongovernmental sense, typified by Amnesty International and the various regional watch groups—that is, voluntary associations of citizens using information about abusive behavior on the part of states, exerting influence to obtain compliance, and, failing this, to disclose information about abuses that challenges the legitimacy of the accused state. Here, the preoccupation is with the well-being of the individual human being and, as such, satisfies one aspect of the law of humanity. (In contrast, interstate law is preoccupied with the interests of the state as promoted by its official representatives.)

There is a second dimension of the agency of civil society in relation to the law of humanity: it is the activation of peoples to pursue their emancipation from oppressive structures of governance, social movements legitimated by the aspirations embodied in interstate law. The movements of emancipation in Eastern Europe (as, for instance, Solidarity in Poland and Charter 77 in Czechoslovakia) were sustained, in part, by the realization that their most fundamental grievances had already been validated by the state that was offering such blatant resistance. In this kind of setting, the law of humanity is buried in the forms of interstate law, but must be exhumed, and made operative, by the militancy of civil society.

World order, then, is a composite reality, reflecting the persisting influence of states on its normative order, yet also exhibiting the effects of voluntary associations and social movements that are motivated by the law of humanity and situated in civil society. The global spread of political democracy, with its roots in constitutionalism, makes those persons within the territorial space controlled by the sovereign state increasingly aware of their political, moral, and legal option to appeal to broader communities in the event of encroachment on their basic human rights.

The character of the law of humanity is not self-evident. It could mean law that is enacted by and for the peoples of the world, as distinct from the elites who act in law-making settings on behalf of states. Such a usage would correspond to "the rights of peoples," the innovation associated with the efforts of the radical Italian parliamentarian Lelio Basso that led to the establishment in the mid-1970s of the Permanent Peoples Tribunal in Rome. Such an innovation is itself explicitly conceived to be a counter-institution intended to expose the abuses of states and the deficiencies of international institutions, and to provide civil society with its own autonomous voice. The formalization of this voice by way of legal instruments (for instance, The Algiers Declaration on the Rights of Peoples [1976]) and acts (for instance, the various decisions of the Permanent Peoples Tribunal) constitutes the substance of the law of humanity so conceived. In this sense, then, states are not regarded as appropriate agents for the development of the law of humanity, and it depends on civil society to establish new forms of law-creation and law-application.

It is also necessary to distinguish the law of humanity from the phenomenon of globalization, although there are some connections that will be noted as well. Interstate law presupposed the autonomy of the territorial state, although such a presupposition was always a legal fiction given the hierarchical reality of geopolitics. During most of the period of the ascendancy of the state, the largest part of humanity was excluded from its protective structures, associated for convenience sake with the Peace of Westphalia (1648), and subordinated within the frame of one or another variety of imperial geopolitics. That is, the interstate system was primarily a regional system centered in Europe, and only because the region projected its power globally did the illusion arise of a world system. Ironically, it is only in recent decades, with the collapse of colonialism, that interstate law became an encompassing global reality. The irony arises because, at this historical point of climax for interstate law as a framework of formal membership, the realities of interdependence and integration undermine the presupposition of autonomy, rendering partially obsolete the claims of interstate law.

There is a certain confusion that follows from distinguishing the law of humanity as "the other" in relation to interstate law. During the modern period, the ideology of the state included the claim that such a system of distinct sovereignties upheld the well-being of humanity, that interstate law was the best vehicle by which to achieve the objectives of the law of humanity. In this regard, interstate law, with its positivist disposition, was seen as an improvement upon the naturalist approach that rested on a vague foundation of universalism that didn't correspond with the specific interests, cultural diversities, and concrete values of separate people organized on the basis of distinct national identities. That is, the state reconciled the particular with the general in a satisfactory manner so long as territoriality approximated economic, social, political, and cultural reality. Of course, here too, adequacy depended on fiction as illustrated by the terminology of nation-state, a juristic conception of nationality that often obscured the presence within state boundaries of several ethnic groups with separate, often antagonistic, psycho-political conceptions of national identity. The state-fracturing impact of the right of self-determination when extended to "peoples" (as in Article 1 of the Human Rights Covenants and in the post-1989 practice relating to the former Yugoslavia and Soviet Union) has exploded once and for all the misleading pretension of designating states as "nation-states."

But, arguably, the erosion of territoriality has undermined the major premise of interstate law and its derivative claim to operate as the guardian of human well-being. This erosion can be understood from different angles: matters of vulnerability—the state has lost the capacity to uphold security in light of nuclear weaponry and long-range delivery systems; matters of environmental protection—the state cannot safeguard its territory from the adverse effects of extraterrestrial behavior, nor can it by its own efforts maintain the global commons (oceans, atmosphere); matters of economic viability—the state, even if well endowed and large, can no longer provide an adequate framework for economic activity, and is gradually being superseded by an array of international regimes and by the regionalization and globalization of capital markets and corporate and banking organizations. In these three types of erosion, the well-being of humanity requires law to operate on a regional, or global, scale that corresponds to the scope of operations. It is here, however, that interstate realities persist, and the law of humanity is mainly in the dreaming (or pure aspirational) phase. Interstate law provides what control there is in relation to war/peace and environmental issues and, except for the European Union, with respect to transnational economic activity. Thus, the inability of interstate law to rise to these challenges and the failure of the law of humanity to take effective shape is one way to express a critical view of world order; the deep structural quality of these criticisms also helps explain why even such momentous historical occasions as the end of the Cold War and the reunification of Europe can have only a superficial relevance to an enquiry into prospects for the emergence of the law of humanity in an effective form.

There is, in fact, a historically aggravating circumstance associated with the end of the Cold War, the seeming disappearance of strategic and ideological conflict, and the focus upon world economic policy. Global security frameworks, based on interstate activities, had been devoted mainly to the containment of strong states; international law provided an underpinning, prohibiting recourse to aggression and validating collective security arrangements by way of either alliances or international institutions. There were many problems, including the difficulty of differentiating claims of self-defense from those of aggression and the unwillingness of dominant states to forego interventionary diplomacy, but the interstate undertaking was coherent and, since World War II, quite successful in the North, but it depended on the prevention of projections of military force across acknowledged international boundaries (the Gulf War). With the new situation of international relations there arises a preoccupation with the weak state, namely, the implosive realities of states that cannot maintain their own internal order in relation to either interventionary forces within their immediate region or secessionist tendencies of distinct ethnic groups within their larger national population. The ordeal of Bosnia (or Somalia) is illustrative, with acute and prolonged human suffering arising from systematic criminality or from total breakdown of governmental capacity. Interstate legal forms can validate "humanitarian intervention" under either statist or international institutional auspices, but the challenge of implementation can be overwhelming, especially in those cases where no sufficient strategic interest exists to provide the requisite political will to act effectively or where no geopolitical consensus among leading states can be formed. In the process, despair and anger emerge, as we are aware of the inability and unwillingness to protect victims of abuse. Often only civil society initiatives are helpful in these settings, and then in ways that do not address the underlying conflict, as by providing humanitarian relief on a daily basis and seeking to identify and strengthen reconciling and democratically oriented social forces. The Helsinki Citizens Association has been playing an unheralded, but genuine, role in trying to build civil society coalitions that continue to seek alternatives to the violent polarization of Bosnian political space in terms of ethnic and religious enmity.

To some small extent environmentalism, as an expression of transnational civil society, has brought to bear the perspectives of humanity, encouraging and influencing states to establish regimes capable of protecting the global commons. Such transnational influence, as exerted by the Cousteau Society and Greenpeace and a coalition of other transnational associations, is responsible for safeguarding Antarctica from mining and developmental activities. The modality of the counter-conference, as evident at the Earth Summit held under U.N. auspices in Rio during June of 1992, has also been challenging interstate complacency about environmental issues from the perspectives of the urgencies of humanity, but without any capacity to enact directly or indirectly appropriate protective law in relation to the dissemination of toxic substances, global warming, or ozone depletion. Civil society performs a role as critic of interstate law, but is incapable at this stage of providing a real alternative. Such limitations on the influence of civil society are even more apparent in relation to war/peace issues and to transnational economic activity. Note that the argument from a world order perspective operates on two levels:

first, the eroding capacities of interstate law to provide effective action and creative solutions; and second, the failure of a more responsive law of humanity to evolve, and the inability of transnational social forces expressive of civil society to fill the normative vacuum. I would depict the post-Cold War world order crisis by reference to this combination of circumstances.

## B. STRENGTHENING THE LAW OF HUMANITY: AN URGENT CHALLENGE TO AN EMERGENT GLOBAL CIVIL SOCIETY

There are strong market-driven tendencies to constitute an effective system of global dimensions that operates to promote world trade and investment, that protects the flow of strategic resources from South to North, and that guards the North from threats mounted by the South. There are a number of policy arenas in which this phenomenon of globalization-from-above can be observed: the responses to threats against strategic oil reserves in the Middle East; the efforts to expand the GATT framework; the coercive implementation of the nuclear non-proliferation regime; the containment of South-North migration and refugee flows; the criminalization of "terrorist" violence of a revolutionary character and discretionary status of counter-revolutionary terrorism; patterns of interventionary diplomacy that flow only North-South; the "reforming" of the United Nations by concentrating authority in the Security Council and in the IMF/World Bank (while downgrading Southern priorities: eliminating the U.N. Center on Transnational Corporations, marginalizing the General Assembly, UNCTAD, UNDP, UNESCO); and the reliance on the G-7 summits to set world economic policy despite the nonrepresentation of eighty percent of the world population. The implications of globalization-from-above would tend to supplant interstate law with a species of global law, but one at odds in most respects with "the law of humanity."

Transnational social forces provide the only vehicle for the promotion of the law of humanity, a normative focus that is animated by humane sustainable development for all peoples—North and South—and seeks to structure such commitments by way of humane geogovernance (that is, governance protective of the earth and its peoples that is democratically constituted, both in relation to participation and accountability, and that is responsive to the needs of the poorest twenty percent and of those most vulnerable, e.g., indigenous peoples). To suggest the political dynamics associated with these conceptions, I propose the terminology of "globalization-from-below" to identify these transnational democratic forces, and their implicit dedication to the creation of a global civil society that is an alternative scenario of the future to that of the global political economy being shaped by transnational market forces. The hopes of humanity depend, in my view, upon the capacities of globalization-from-below to challenge effectively the prevailing dominance of globalization-from-above in a series of key arenas that can be identified in very general terms as the U.N. (and other international institutions and regimes), the media, and the orientation of states. Each of these arenas is complex, and needs to be deconstructed in several stages to identify the actual sites and stakes of political struggle. My argument in this essay is that law provides these agents of global civil society with one instrument of potential influence, and that the grounding of law so conceived is what is meant by "the law of humanity."

## 1. The Law of Humanity Already Contained in Interstate Law, But Not Yet Actualized

There exists in the corpus of interstate law *latent* recognition of important ingredients of the law of humanity, making the latter function as a normative catalyst, and not necessarily as an innovative and idealistic alternative. This generally unappreciated potentiality of interstate law can be illustrated by brief reference to four instances.

### *Articles 25 and 28 of the Universal Declaration of Human Rights*

There exists agreement among international law specialists that the Universal Declaration has been incorporated into positive international law, but many provisions are simply ignored by human rights organizations as well as by others. Article 25 confers the right upon every person to an adequate standard of living, while article 28 confers an even more far-reaching right: "Everyone is entitled to a social and international order in which the rights and freedoms set forth in this Declaration can be fully realized." Even transnational democratic social forces that adhere to the mandate of global civil society have been silent about such *legally binding* promises by states. It seems desirable to break the silence, to speculate as to the shape of such "a social and international order," and to insist that market forces be held accountable for upholding such standards within their sphere of operations and that states undertake to fulfill such legal expectations. That is, there already exists in interstate law lip service to the basic ethical demands of the law of humanity (treating each person on earth as a sacred subject), making the implementation of interstate law in this respect equivalent to the enactment of the law of humanity.

### *Article VI of the Treaty on the Non-Proliferation of Nuclear Weapons*

No international agreement has been given a higher priority in recent years than the NPT, especially by the geopolitical leaders of the state system. Article VI commits existing nuclear weapons states "to pursue negotiations in good faith" to terminate the nuclear arms race, to achieve nuclear disarmament, and, most dramatically of all, to conclude "a treaty on general and complete disarmament under strict and effective international control." It is obvious that this part of the non-proliferation bargain has been ignored by the nuclear weapons states. Is it not time, especially with the end of bipolarity, for the countries of the South to insist on the implementation of article VI as part of a reciprocal arrangement to forego nuclear weaponry that alone accords with international justice? Should not peace groups that participate in transnational activities coordinated their commitments to nuclear abolitionism to insist in the year 2000 that the nuclear weapons states begin finally to implement Article VI of the NPT?

### *The Nuremberg Principles*

The idea of holding leaders accountable for crimes of the state was put into practice after World War II in the form of prosecutions of German and Japanese officials at Nuremberg and Tokyo; subsequent trials also held accountable all those in society who carried out the blatantly criminal policies of these states, including corporate officers and medical professionals. The Nuremberg promise was to treat this experience as the first step in the development of an international law of personal responsibility that would bind all countries in the future, and would not be applied only to a defeated power. This promise was given legal credibility by being adopted in the binding form of The Nuremberg Principles, first by General Assembly Resolution 95[1] in 1946, and then in 1950 by authoritative formulation by the International Law Commission. But given the belligerent practices of all of the victorious powers in World War II since 1945, it is reasonable to conclude that the Nuremberg promise has been broken, although there have been recent moves under U.N. auspices to revive a Nuremberg process of some kind in relation to Saddam Hussein and to those in the former Yugoslavia associated with "ethnic cleansing" and the systematic rape of Bosnian women.

The forces of civil society have not been oblivious to the relevance of this Nuremberg experience. It was in the political consciousness of Daniel Ellsberg, who explains that a reading of the Nuremberg Judgment convinced him of his personal obligation to release the Pentagon Papers during the latter stages of the Vietnam War, and, more recently, of Mordecai Vanunu, the Israeli nuclear engineer who released "secret" information about Israel's nuclear weapons program, who was convicted in Israeli military courts of "treason," and is currently being held in jail. Both Ellsberg and Vanunu have been acknowledged by global civil society in the form of awards of the "alternative" Nobel Peace Prize, the Right Livelihood Award. There have also been a series of "Nuremberg Actions," violations of domestic law to highlight criminal preparations by states for aggressive wars by the development and deployment of such allegedly first-strike nuclear weapons systems as the Trident Submarine and the D-5 warhead.

### *The Preamble and Articles 1 and 2 of the U.N. Charter*

The celebrated opening words of the Preamble "to save succeeding generations from the scourge of war," represent a basic commitment to find ways to resolve conflict other than through warfare, yet U.N. practice, especially recently (as in the Gulf War and Somalia), discloses a disposition by states to endow the U.N. with a war-making role, to militarize the approach to security within the framework of the U.N., and to downgrade, if not eliminate, the search for justice in the relations of states and respect for the dignity of each person in economic and social relationships. Here again, unexploited normative opportunities exist for civil society initiatives to bring to fruition the empty words of obligation accepted years ago by representatives of the leading states, and never repudiated or even questioned.

## 2. Additional Civil Society Initiatives Needed to Realize the Law of Humanity

Realization of the law of humanity requires some independent visionary initiatives, especially to satisfy certain structural needs of world order given the scale and scope of international activities. This theme needs detailed discussion, and can only be introduced here in a preliminary fashion. An emphasis on geogovernance is beginning to be acknowledged in establishment circles that are primarily tied to the interstate world: for instance, in the call of the Stockholm Initiative of April 22, 1991, for the constitutional renewal of the United Nations from the perspective of global governance; in the 1992 report of the U.N. Secretary-General, Boutros Boutros-Ghali, *An Agenda for Peace,* with its emphasis on a U.N. collective security process that is more independent of geopolitics than at present and on a strengthening of capabilities for preventive diplomacy that seem more feasible than efforts to resolve conflict after fundamental breakdowns in order have occurred; and in the proposal of Brian Urquhart to establish a U.N. Volunteer Force (outlined in the June 10, 1994 issue of the *New York Review of Books,* with further commentary in the July 15, 1993 issue) that could engage in peacekeeping operations (under the "exclusive authority" of the Security Council and "the day-to-day direction of the Secretary-General"), without present degrees of dependence on U.N. member states, especially the leading ones.

To promote the law of humanity, geogovernance must become a more organic part of the outlook for transnational social forces. There are two circles of emphasis, both associated with the interplay of functional or practical argumentation on behalf of global arrangements with normative argumentation on behalf of a humanely oriented sustainability.

There exists a strong distinct case for geogovernance as adapted to the specific realities of *environmental protection* and of *global market operations.* The prospects for voluntary adaptation of consumptive patterns and of technological choices in a manner that locates the primary financial burden in the North depends on having a much stronger institutional capability to set and implement environmental standards for the states and for the global market. Such a possibility could not even be put on the agenda of the 1992 Earth Summit, as states and market forces resisted such moves in the direction of environmental geogovernance. Only a concerted demonstration of commitment and need as part of the agenda of globalization-from-below could hope to fashion the interstate political will to establish an equitable, yet effective, form of environmental geogovernance. Legal specialists, to serve the cause of the law of humanity, need to work out the institutional forms in helpful detail so that the process of negotiation can be encouraged on the basis of specific plans.

The regulation of the global market is even more difficult to achieve without the successful political mobilization and intervention by civil society forces. As matters now stand, the G-7 states are committed to sustaining the regulatory vacuum on the global level. The abolition of the U.N. Center on Transnational Corporations was expressive of this anti-regulatory disposition. Civil society is beginning to awaken to its responsibilities on these matters. The Permanent Peoples' Tribunal, at its Berlin session of 1988, investigated charges that IMF Structural Adjustment Programs were encroaching on the rights of the peoples in the Third World; the International Peoples' Tribunal to Judge G-7, held in Tokyo just before the G-7 summit of July 1993, issued a comprehensive indictment of the manner in which market forces currently operate, including the continuing practices of shielding money stolen from peoples by dictatorial leaders in secret overseas bank accounts and of allowing banks and corporations to choose tax and regulation havens in places such as the Cayman Islands and the Bahamas. At present, civil society forces need mainly to expose the abuses arising from the regulatory vacuum and to resist globalizing initiatives (NAFTA, GATT) that neglect the well-being of the most vulnerable social sectors. The wider task of filling the regulatory vacuum will be a crucial challenge to champions of an emerging law of humanity.

The other set of structural needs involves the redesign of international institutions, especially the United Nations, so as to give greater weight to global civil society perspectives. Again, this is too complex a matter to be discussed here in appropriate detail. What is needed, to put it briefly, is the weakening of geopolitical and market leverage on all phases of U.N. activities, with mechanisms for greater participation both by countries in the South and by transnational social forces committed to the promotion of human rights and democratization.

Reform of the Security Council has received attention recently. There are statist and market pressures to give the two financial superpowers, Germany and Japan, permanent seats in the Security Council, and some reluctant willingness to give some populous states in the South—India, Brazil and Nigeria are most often mentioned—second-class permanent membership (presence, but without a veto) as part of a statist bargain. The orientation of global civil society would go further, insisting on setting aside a permanent seat for "a moral superpower" (as designated by a panel of Nobel Peace Prize winners), another for a representative of the most economically deprived states (as determined by reference to UNDP indices), a third for a representative of global civil society (as selected by a panel of alternative Nobel Peace Prize winners), and a fourth to represent the world assembly of indigenous peoples.

Other steps of structural reform are needed as well: reasserting the role of the General Assembly; establishing independent sources of U.N. revenue, possibly by imposing a transaction tax on international financial operations or on the taking of resources from the global commons; and generalizing the commitment of states to accept the compulsory jurisdiction of the World Court and increasing the authority and binding effect of "Advisory Opinions." There are many more such initiatives that should be promoted by advocates of the law of humanity.

Efforts illustrative of more specific legally delimited initiatives that are also important at this stage include: the World Court Project that is being promoted by transnational groups to implement the 1996 World Court Advisory Opinion as to the status under international law of threats or uses of nuclear weaponry; and a draft convention to monitor and eliminate the international arms trade that has been prepared by citizens' associations composed of lawyers and is being promoted transnationally.

## C. A CONCLUDING NOTE

Realizing the law of humanity is a complex, multifaceted, yet indispensable task. The main promotional energy will have to come from civil society, although one goal of transnational politics is to make states, mainstream political parties, and global market forces more receptive to the claims and values asserted by the advocates of the law of humanity. These advocates need to push their efforts strongly in two critical settings: the U.N. and the media. The U.N. is an ambiguous entity; its Charter can be read as substantially embodying the law of humanity, yet much of the practice of the Organization embodies the most regressive features of interstate law, including deference to market forces, discretionary reliance on violence by geopolitical actors, and extreme selectivity and double standards in enforcement activity. Similarly, the media, especially in the atmosphere of democratic canons of legitimacy, is supposed to pursue truth without biasing its presentation for the sake of state or market, yet the reality of media operations (reinforced by patterns of ownership) is an acceptance of voluntary censorship to protect controversial statist undertakings from scrutiny and of refusal to delve deeply into most deformations wrought by the market in light of advertising revenues and the managerial orientations of media executives. The U.N. and the global media are two sites of struggle, or battlefields, wherein the prospects of global civil society and the law of humanity are likely to be determined in the years ahead. The challenge is certainly formidable, but the opportunity is present to a historically unprecedented degree. Existing knowledge validates neither pessimism nor optimism, making the pursuit of the vision that corresponds to our values the most sensible course of action. And who is to say that its realization is less likely than the emancipation of Eastern Europe seemed a decade ago?

# PART II

# SUBSTANTIVE CONCERNS

# CHAPTER III

# THE UNITED NATIONS, THE RULE OF LAW, AND HUMANITARIAN INTERVENTION*

In building on its first fifty years, can the U.N. advance the cause of peace and justice in the years ahead? What role does law play in relation to these prospects? At first glance, the ending of the East/West rivalry between the two superpowers and their respective blocs should have opened wide the gates of opportunity. But instead one finds a climate of skeptical assessment based on the disappointing U.N. response to a series of disconcerting challenges to peace and security in the post-Cold War world: Somalia, Bosnia, and Rwanda.[1]

These conflicts, situated within the territorial limits of sovereign states that are full members of the United Nations, have given prominence to a new series of controversies relating to the viability of humanitarian diplomacy and humanitarian intervention. In a sense, the agency of civil society has become both problematic and emancipatory, in different respects, but at the same historical moment. The negative aspect of this agency relates to the violence and extremism of ethno-nationalist forces which, when fully mobilized, are generative of cruel political movements with a high potential for genocidal activity, justified as part of the crusade for a secure and pure ethnic state. The United Nations, regional institutions, and leading states have been challenged by such outbreaks of ethno-nationalist violence in the last several years, and have sought to respond in the spirit of human solidarity, but have done so ineffectively.

The positive aspect of the agency of civil society is associated with the rise of transnational social forces committed to the promotion of

*Portions of this chapter appeared as an article in a symposium edited by Saul H. Mendlovitz and Burns H. Weston: Richard Falk, *The United Nations and the Rule of Law*, 4 TRANSNAT'L L. & CONTEMP. PROBS. 611–42 (1994).

1. Particularly in retrospect, the U.N. "success" in the Gulf War seems both anomalous (nonrecurrent) and partial (restoring Kuwaiti sovreignty, but leaving Iraq's brutal authoritarian state intact).

a more equitable, peaceful, environmentally safe, and humanly decent world. These forces have sought to exert influence on the United Nations, and have been active on the ground in efforts to mitigate the impact of ethno-nationalist violence and to promote various inter-ethnic frameworks of reconciliation and tolerance.

More generally, voluntary civic dimensions of international life are being organized in more effective ways from the perspective of exerting influence on the United Nations. This was evident in relation to the 1994 U.N. Conference on Population and Development held in Cairo where women's groups, in particular, were remarkably successful in reconceptualizing the normative guidelines relative to population policy, superseding the focus of demographers on making available the technical means to reduce fertility by the more humanistic stress on improving the education, health, and social status of women, especially girls.

This Cairo experience prefigures the perspective taken in this chapter. It finds that the most encouraging, albeit precarious, emergent trend is associated with increasing democratic empowerment within the various arenas of the United Nations, and argues, in particular, that the domain of U.N. operations of peace and security, which has been generally neglected by grassroots activism, would benefit greatly from an increased attention.[2]

To grasp the rationale behind such a conclusion, it is helpful to consider the broader U.N. experience with respect to the rule of law. My intention is to view the past with a rearview mirror so as to make corrections that will encourage movement toward the points of destination dictated by the proclaimed goals of the United Nations and its membership that were reaffirmed during 1995, its fiftieth anniversary year: peace, justice, development, and sustainability. These goals are sometimes fused under the single label of "sustainable human development."

It needs to be acknowledged that the outlook for progressive development of the United Nations is rather dismal as of 1998. Governmental perspectives are generally disinterested or adverse. The more promising settings for the extension of governance involve global economic activity (World Trade Organization) and regionalism (European Community, Asia Pacific Economic Forum).

2. Such an outlook may be overly optimistic as it overlooks a statist backlash that is likely to curtail use of U.N. conference arenas by civil initiatives. For this reason, it is problematic to project an "emergent trend" into the future.

And then there is the ambiguous effort to reorient NATO evident in the last stages of the Bosnian War, and more particularly, in its central role in the implementation of the Dayton Peace Agreement. Is this an expedient and anomalous role for military organizations such as NATO, or does it represent a trend toward relying on regional security capabilities to enforce humanitarian law and goals?

## A. SCOPE OF INQUIRY

The scope of inquiry undertaken here is limited to the role of law in relation to the operations of the United Nations, that is, law as a constitutional frame and as authoritative guidance with respect to contested action.[3] This emphasis is further narrowed by considering only the relation of law to the peace and security activities of the United Nations. This is generally the most controversial and challenging domain of U.N. activity, but it also provides the public with a litmus test of the effectiveness of the organization as a whole with respect to protecting the global interests of the peoples of the world. This criterion for assessing the U.N. as a success or failure is generally adopted by the media, and is reflected in the attitudes of leaders who appraise the U.N. in terms of its perceived capacity to contribute to the peace and security of societies victimized by aggression, and more recently, by its response to other severe breakdowns of order.

Understanding the role of law in these settings, including its limits and unused potential, is thus indirectly an inquiry into the link between effectiveness and legitimacy as it bears on the operations of the United Nations, particularly those of the Security Council.[4] To illustrate by reference to a concrete instance, the functioning of the Security Council in response to Iraq's conquest of Kuwait in August

3. This conception of law reflects the influence of the New Haven School of jurisprudence. *See, e.g.*, HAROLD D. LASSWELL AND MYRES S. MCDOUGAL, JURISPRUDENCE FOR A FREE SOCIETY: STUDIES IN LAW, SCIENCE AND POLICY 203–06 (vol. 1, 1992); for the clearest, comprehensive exposition of this New Haven School in the setting of international law, see LUNG-CHU CHEN, AN INTRODUCTION TO CONTEMPORARY INTERNATIONAL LAW: A POLICY-ORIENTED PERSPECTIVE (1989).

4. Such preoccupations embrace chapters VI and VII of the Charter as well as a variety of extensions of its activities, such as the establishment of an international criminal tribunal for the prosecution of persons responsible for grave breaches of international humanitarian law in the former Yugoslavia since 1991. *See* S.C. Res. 808, Feb. 22, 1993; *cf.* James C. O'Brien, *The International Tribunal for Violations of International Humanitarian Law in the Former Yugoslavia*, 87 AM. J. INT'L L. 639 (1993); Theodor Meron, *War Crimes in Yugoslavia and the Development of International Law*, 88 AM. J. INT'L L. 78 (1994).

of 1990 elicited a range of responses; those preoccupied with short-run effectiveness tended to be indifferent to rule of law considerations, while those more concerned with institutional effectiveness over time were generally distressed by this indifference.[5] In an important sense, this longer term concern supports a U.N. that is in the short run mindful of legitimacy as well as effectiveness, goals that are not always easily reconcilable.[6]

Dominant states alone possess the capabilities to ensure U.N. effectiveness but, in exchange, their governments have tended to insist on control over operations and a wide range of discretion in relation to the scope of the mission, thereby compromising U.N. legitimacy. Such a compromise cast a shadow upon the U.N. response in the Gulf War, especially during the aftermath of Desert Storm when the Kurds in the North and the Shi'ia (so-called "Marsh Arabs") in the South were exposed to brutal and unchallenged repression by Saddam Hussein because Washington evidently decided on its own not to risk the collapse of Iraq as a unified state by lending support to resistance activities that might move in separatist directions. This pattern of geopolitical indifference to human suffering made the organization appear, especially to observers from non-Western countries, to be an extension of U.S. foreign policy rather

5. For a perceptive expression of this latter concern, see Burns H. Weston, *Security Council Resolution 678 and Persian Gulf Decision Making: Precarious Legitimacy,* 85 AM. J. INT'L L. 516 (1991); see also the contributions in THE GULF WAR AND NEW WORLD ORDER: INTERNATIONAL RELATIONS OF THE MIDDLE EAST (Tareq Y. Ismael and Jacqueline S. Ismael eds., 1994).

Of course, the distinction between short-run and long-run is polemical to some extent as those who stress effectiveness would argue that legitimacy would follow automatically if, and only if, the U.N. can fulfill its substantive mandate in situations, as and when these arise, to protect the victims of aggression. This line of reasoning conflates the short run with the long run; further, those who share Franklin Roosevelt's view that the U.N. system will succeed only if its most powerful members can work together to keep the peace, functioning as an alliance for peace in the manner that enabled victory in World War II, would not regard concerns about legitimacy to be treated as something separate from the capacity to respond effectively whenever challenges to the peace arise. Legitimacy, then, is basically, in this view, an outgrowth of effectiveness. Little else matters. Such an orientation is not harmful if the U.N. is acting only in cases that involve responses to aggression. But if the organization becomes a vehicle for geopolitical designs, then a constitutional framework of constraint provides an essential shield for smaller states. The overall issue of legitimacy is usefully considered in David Caron, *The Legitimacy of the Collective Authority of the Security Council,* 87 AM. J. INT'L L. 552 (1993); see also the early groundbreaking article by Inis Claude, *Collective Legitimation as a Political Function of the United Nations,* 20 INT'L ORG. 367 (1966).

6. Such mindfulness does not imply a mechanical attitude toward constitutional and other legal constraints, but it does insist upon a high degree of fidelity to "the spirit" of the law or, in the sense of the New Haven School, to the relations between policies promoted and values at stake.

than an institution serving the shared purposes of the membership as a whole in the manner specified by the U.N. Charter.[7]

This core issue of constitutionality in peace and security actions has several additional dimensions that need to be addressed. There is the question of double standards and selective action (failing to treat equals equally) that became especially salient over the years in relation to repeated Israeli uses of force beyond its borders, but also in other settings where strategic relationships overrode minimal adherence to Charter constraints: the Turkish intervention and continuing occupation of a part of Cyprus and the Indonesian invasion and annexation of East Timor. There is also the crucial set of issues regarding respect for sovereign rights versus a less statist definition of peace and security surrounding controversies about humanitarian assistance, especially the bearing of such undertakings on the Charter's article 2(7) duty not to intervene in matters essentially within "the domestic jurisdiction" of member states, which is an aspect of the broader question of sovereign rights in relation to U.N. claims to exert control over issues arising internal to state boundaries.

There is the further question, largely unexplored in the scholarly literature, as to whether when the U.N. uses force or authorizes its use, its mandate should be more tightly constrained by law than is the case for comparable action by states governed by the traditional law of war as set forth mainly in the Hague and Geneva Conventions.[8] And finally, there is the matter of whether the latent potential already contained in the existing framework of United Nations law could be used to facilitate a process of global reform without reliance on formal Charter amendments, or whether it is essential or more beneficial to alter or replace this framework by amending the Charter.

7. Note even the Secretary-General's oblique remark referring to the Gulf War experience and the decades of frustration during the Cold War: "Never again must the Security Council lose the collegiality that is essential to its proper functioning, an attribute that it has gained after such trial." BOUTROS BOUTROS-GHALI, AGENDA FOR PEACE 45 (1992). This impression of geopolitical appropriation was reinforced by the way the war was fought, by the nature of "the peace" imposed, and by the abandonment of segments of Iraqi population vulnerable to Saddam Hussein's wrath until public pressures mounted.

8. *See* ADAM ROBERTS AND RICHARD GUELFF, DOCUMENTS ON THE LAWS OF WAR, (2nd ed. 1989), for a convenient collection of relevant documents associated with the statist framework of the law of war; for an important critique of this framework, see Chris Jochnick and Roger Normand, *The Legitimation of Violence: A Critical History of the Laws of War*, 35 HARV. J. INT'L L. 49 (1994). The challenge here is to promote a distinctive framework for U.N. uses of force in peacekeeping modes that is heavily weighted toward the protection of civilian society and the restoration of peace, and is far more restrictive in relation to claims of military necessity than is the current international law of war.

What is not addressed in this chapter, although it is an aspect of the U.N. relationship to the rule of law, is the lawmaking role of the United Nations, which includes its extraordinary range of contributions to the creation of a normative architecture for the conduct of international relations over the course of the last fifty years. Closely related to this direct contribution to the development of international law and less appreciated in academic literature, is the role played by the U.N. in nurturing transnational democratic initiatives, the manifold expressions of the voluntary and spontaneous actions of citizens and their organizations and associations that are being generated by civil society.[9]

Whether it be pressure to implement human rights or the framing of relief operations and humanitarian aid along safer lines amid the wartime rigors of civil strife, the existence of international humanitarian law in the form of a framework of written law consisting of rules and standards backed by the authority of the United Nations is crucial to the work of these activists who function outside the domain of intergovernmental relations.[10] These transnational relief and humanitarian agencies need to define their own operations, often under emergency circumstances, in relation to whatever political and military authorities are exerting effective control by reference to a mutually acceptable framework of rights and duties.[11] The U.N. is providing, through its sponsorship of lawmaking treaty negotiations and its official conferences on the major global challenges, the basis for the progressive development of international law in response to

9. *See* RICHARD FALK, EXPLORATIONS AT THE EDGE OF TIME: THE PROSPECTS FOR WORLD ORDER (1992), for discussions of the relevance of international law to the growth and development of transnational democracy. A central argument of this book is that transnational democratic empowerment is breaking the bonds of territorial politics, and facilitating the emergence of a global civil society.

Generally, this grassroots activity has been discussed in a U.N. context by reference to nongovernmental organizations (NGOs). I follow here Saul Mendlovitz's lead in seeking a better political language to depict the phenomenon. The terminology of NGOs, with its stress on nongovernmental, reinforces the idea that governments are primary, while initiatives by peoples and citizens groups are secondary. A more neutral vocabulary leaves the issue where it belongs, for the reader to decide.

10. For impressive overviews, see GEOFFREY BEST, WAR AND LAW SINCE 1945 (1994); for relevant texts and materials, see THE LAWS OF WAR (W. Michael Reisman and Chris T. Antoniu eds., 1994), ROBERTS AND GUELFF, *supra* note 8.

11. *See especially*, Jennifer Leaning, *When the System Doesn't Work: Somalia 1992*, *in* A FRAMEWORK FOR SURVIVAL: HEALTH, HUMAN RIGHTS, AND HUMANITARIAN ASSISTANCE IN CONFLICTS AND DISASTERS 103–20 (1993) (other chapters are also relevant). *See* PROGRAM ON HUMANITARIAN ASSISTANCE, THE MOHONK CRITERIA FOR HUMANITARIAN ASSISTANCE IN COMPLEX EMERGENCIES (pamphlet, World Conf. on Religion and Peace, Feb. 1994).

the rapidly evolving priorities and values associated with commitments to achieving a just and sustainable world order. This development has involved the formulation of declaratory and aspirational goals, as well as more contractual obligations, perhaps most centrally, the prohibitions placed upon uses of force that cannot be authoritatively justified within the scope of individual or collective self-defense. Such contributions to the wider rule of law in world society is indicative of a general disposition by the U.N. that should also be favorable to respect for law in its own operations, and thus invites queries as to why the Organization has done so much better when it projects its law-oriented influence beyond the orbit of its own activities than when it acts itself.

It is also relevant in this wider sense to take note of U.N. contributions to lawmaking and law application by way of the activities of the International Law Commission and the International Court of Justice.[12] Both organs of the U.N. have played major roles in the enunciation and development of international law across a wide range of subject matters. As well, law-declaring and lawmaking resolutions of the General Assembly, the status of which has been a matter of persistent debate among international law specialists, have exerted a definite, although uneven and controversial, influence on the growth of law during the past half century.[13]

For those skeptical of this quasi-legislative role of the General Assembly one need only refer to such achievements by way of widely endorsed resolutions that have been indispensable to the articulation of the evolving right of peoples to self-determination. As mentioned earlier, the Universal Declaration of Human Rights has paved the way for the extraordinary dynamic of law-making in the human rights field, and its increasing linkage to matters of peace and security. Also notable has been the acceptance of the Nuremberg Principles by the U.N. General Assembly, and then by the world as a whole. The Declaration on Principles Governing the Friendly Relations Among States provides the best overall summary of the legal framework governing the relations among sovereign states.[14] These quasi-legislative

12. These activities are usefully surveyed in Oscar Schachter, *United Nations Law*, 88 AM. J. INT'L L. 1 (1994).

13. *See* Richard Falk, *On the Quasi-Legislative Competence of the General Assembly*, 60 AM. J. INT'L L. 782 (1966); *see also* JORGE CASTANEDA, LEGAL EFFECTS OF UNITED NATIONS RESOLUTIONS (1970), and nuanced discussion in ROSLYN HIGGINS, PROBLEMS AND PROCESS: INTERNATIONAL LAW AND HOW WE USE IT 24–28 (1994).

14. U.N.G.A. Res. 217 A (III), 95 (I), and 2625 (XXV), respectively. For convenient texts, see BASIC DOCUMENTS IN INTERNATIONAL LAW AND WORLD ORDER 298–301, 140, 108–13 (Burns H. Weston et al., eds., 2nd ed. 1990).

acts have had a variable impact on international behavior that depends on a range of actors, including nongovernmental actors representative of voluntary civic associations, especially those of a transnational character, that seek to promote effective implementation or, as the case may be, encourage disregard.[15]

In the mid-1990s there is a definite crisis of confidence in existing world order capacities that arises from the vulnerability of world society to genocidal forms of ethno-nationalism, as recently manifest in Rwanda and the former Yugoslavia. Implementing the Convention on Genocide has not engaged the strategic concerns of leading states, and this circumstance has minimized responses organized by way of the United Nations. In the context of peacekeeping, the U.N. role has been marginalized, a mixture of diplomatic initiative and relief operations, but with the unfortunate characteristic of impartiality as between the perpetrator and victim of ethnic cleansing and other war crimes. Somewhat inconsistently with this reluctance to be drawn more deeply into the quagmires of intense civil strife, is the move by the Security Council to establish an *ad hoc* tribunal dedicated to the indictment, apprehension, and prosecution of all those responsible for serious war crimes, including political and military leaders, in the former Yugoslavia. This undertaking has been subsequently extended to include Rwanda. It remains to be seen whether these U.N. roles of peacemaker and enforcer of legal accountability can be combined successfully in relation to Bosnia.

It also is uncertain whether the challenge of such depraved political behavior will give rise, more than fifty years after Nuremberg, to an International Criminal Court that represents an addition to the institutional resources of the United Nations and a step forward in subordinating the immunities of sovereignty to procedures of global

15. *Compare*, for instance, the dismal fate of the "authoritative" definition of agression, U.N.G.A. Res. 3314 (XXIX)(1974), BASIC DOCUMENTS, *supra* note 14, at 224–26, *with* the initially aspirational role of the Universal Declaration of Human Rights, which, as argued here, may be the most influential legal document in the last half-century. It is not necessarily the obligatory character of the text that counts nearly as much as whether a politics of implementation is successful, which may depend on whether the network of transnational citizen associations gives its intense support. This so-called informal sector of the international legal order (in contrast to the formal sector, which relates to the direct and indirect activities of states and intergovernmental actors) is increasingly demonstrating a capacity to influence law-making procedures. The case of indigenous peoples is especially notable in this regard, particularly their effort during the last decade to secure a Universal Declaration of the Rights of Indigenous Peoples. For useful discussions, see Symposium, *Contemporary Perspectives on Self-Determination and Indigenous Peoples' Rights*, TRANSNAT'L L. & CONTEMP. PROBS. (vol. 3, Spring 1993), especially contributions by Dalee Sambo (at 13–49) and S. James Anaya (at 131–64).

accountability. As of now, the International Law Commission has produced a draft statute that puts the proposed Court under the authority of the Security Council, and hence subject to geopolitical control through the veto power held by its five permanent members. If such a Court comes into being at all, even as currently proposed, it will reflect the vigorous campaign of the NGO community that has made this proposal a high priority.[16]

What is evident, above all in light of Bosnia and Rwanda, is the importance of overcoming a global vulnerability to genocide.[17] A legalist approach is not able to achieve such goals on its own. Other steps must be taken, as well, if the United Nations is to serve the peoples of the world, including the creation of some kind of independent peace enforcement capability that is financially autonomous.[18] Whether transnational democratic forces can focus on this challenge and generate pressures to produce global reforms is, at best, uncertain at this point. What seems definite, however, is the corrosive effects of this inability and unwillingness by the established global order to respond vigorously to the fundamental moral and legal challenge directed at the United Nations by genocidal politics.

## B. ORIENTING CONSIDERATIONS

The Charter of the United Nations is suffused with a commitment to strengthening the rule of law in human affairs. In its Preamble a pledge is made "to establish conditions under which justice and respect for obligations arising from treaties and other sources of international law can be maintained. . . ." Such a wording recognizes that

16. There exists a variety of resisting postures by several states, including the U.S., as of mid-1995.

17. This vulnerability existed during the Cold War, but it was obscured by the bipolar character of geopolitics, which had a tendency to impose minimum order and restraint within respective blocs. As such, bipolarity denied the right to self-determination to many peoples and nations, but also inhibited the outburst of genocidal variants of ethno-nationalism. There were exceptions (earlier genocide in Burundi, Rwanda; Indonesia in East Timor; Cambodia during the regime of the Khmer Rouge) to geopolitical control. What is now evident, especially in response to Bosnia, is that even the geopolitical heartland of Europe is now susceptible to genocidal politics, and that still no major incentive exists to prevent such behavior.

18. *See* Richard Falk, *Meeting the Challenge of Genocide in Bosnia: Reconciling Moral Imperatives with Political Constraints,* and Saul Mendlovitz with John Fousek, *The Crime of Genocide: Prevention and Punishment: A Proposal for Enforcement, both in Genocide, War, and Human Survival* (Charles Strozier and Michael Flynn eds., 1996). For valuable general perspective, see LEO KUPER, THE PREVENTION OF GENOCIDE (1985); GENOCIDE: CONCEPTUAL AND HISTORICAL DIMENSIONS (George J. Andreopoulos ed., 1994).

international law in peace and security issues will only flourish under certain "conditions." These are not specified, but they presumably relate to the absence of serious tension and distrust among leading states and the removal of fundamental grievances associated with poverty, repression, exploitation, and domination. Such conditions call for a transformation of the characteristic modalities of statecraft, if not the structure of international society. In effect, to establish such conditions posits at the very outset of the Charter a world order challenge that heretofore has certainly not been met, and has only rarely been noticed.

This broad world order goal is reaffirmed as a "Purpose of the United Nations" in article 1(1) where it is undertaken to resolve international disputes "in conformity with the principles of justice and international law." The General Assembly, in article 13(1), is assigned the task "to initiate studies and make recommendations" for the purpose of "promoting international cooperation in the political field and encouraging the progressive development of international law and its codification." After fifty years it is useful to inquire into the extent to which this mandate to promote the rule of law has been carried forth into practice, and to identify areas of disappointment.

It is necessary to assess the extent to which the United Nations as a political actor is a creature of geopolitics, and the degree to which this political identity is necessarily in conflict with the rule of law. It is mistaken to assume an inherent conflict between geopolitics and respect for international law. When international law reinforces the political will of dominant states, it is likely to be invoked to support global policy initiatives. This was done insistently by the U.S. government during the hostage crisis with Iran (1979–81) and throughout the Gulf Crisis (1990–91). But when a reasonable interpretation of international law inhibits the preferred policies of strong states on matters of high priority, then the law will tend to be cast aside or ignored by its violators as has been the case on occasions involving contested uses of force without a U.N. mandate in circumstances where no credible basis for claims of self-defense existed. In light of the response to Iraq's aggression against Kuwait, the failure to challenge in 1975 Indonesia's aggression, annexation, and subsequent abuse of the indigenous population of East Timor is an especially revealing instance of selectivity and double standards in the application of Charter prohibitions, exhibiting deference to geopolitical considerations.

Another notable instance of defiance of the legal authority of the U.N. system arose in the 1980s when the U.S. government refused to adhere to an adverse World Court decision of 1986 that legally condemned its direct and indirect military efforts to overthrow the Sandinista government in Nicaragua.[19] These contrasting patterns of compliance or defiance depend on many contextual factors, including the outlook of leaders, especially their view of whether the promotion of international law contributes to or interferes with the achievement of central foreign policy goals at the level of state action, and whether in a context of controversy central or marginal questions are at stake. A main purpose of this chapter is to consider the degree to which the primacy of geopolitics has over the last several decades tarnished the U.N. record with respect to the role of international law, with what results, and whether it seems at all feasible in the future to rely upon legal procedures and standards to contain some of the arbitrary features of geopolitics.

In the background of this inquiry are two broad world order concerns that condition the contemporary operative roles of law: first, the emergence of a series of challenges that overwhelm the problem-solving capacity of even the most powerful and activist sovereign states; such challenges include environmental issues such as climate change, ozone depletion, and reductions in biodiversity, as well as transnational flows of disease, drugs, refugees, pollutants, crime, information, and communication.[20] More exotically it also encompasses concerns about protecting the earth against asteroids and meteors capable of inflicting catastrophic damage, but supposedly capable of being deflected through missile intercept systems developed and operated on the basis of a concerted human effort enlisting transnational cooperation. In other words, an effective international legal order cannot be realistically achieved by states acting on their own, and in practical terms this often means relying on the United Nations system for regulatory activity of global scope. Of course, global regulatory arrangements can be negotiated outside of the U.N.,

19. *See* Military and Paramilitary Activities in and against Nicaragua (Nicaragua v. U.S.), I.C.J. Rep. 1986; the U.S. intervention of December 1989, in which the head of state of Panama was removed and another American military base was installed, is another prominent example of lawlessness, again undertaken in the name of freedom and democracy.

20. Of course, the perception of this challenge is not new, but surfaced in a prominent way back in 1972 with the publication of the Club of Rome's *Limits to Growth* study. Donella Meadows et al., The Limits to Growth (1972). *See also* The Blueprint for Survival (Edward T. Goldsmith ed., 1972). My own contribution to this earlier surge of concern is Richard Falk, This Endangered Planet: Prospects and Proposals for Human Survival (1972).

giving rise to special regimes possessing notable autonomous features. The mutation of GATT into the World Trade Organization is an important recent example. Paradoxically, the U.N. system is a statist organization, constituted and constrained by states, and only able to act effectively when leading states can act in concert and are willing to provide the resources and commitment needed to carry out the mandate.[21]

Second, and even more fundamental, the state has itself lost ground in relation to the projection of its authority, directly and indirectly. This is particularly true with respect to global economic forces associated with the movement of money and the activities of corporations and banks. Such a power shift has placed even the strongest and richest states in increasingly passive roles when it comes to foreign economic policy. Such passivity is expressed by the absence of any serious regulatory initiatives on the part of states with respect to global economic activity. Even the laundering of monies derived from organized crime or stolen from the treasuries of poor countries by corrupt political leaders has been kept generally protected, by secret bank accounts, from any serious regulatory scrutiny. The United Nations is a prism through which states express their perceived interests, but these interests are conditioned by the mix of pressures mounted against governments, political parties, and elected leaders. An independent media and organized labor have not proved consistently effective in correcting these abuses. Unless leading states are "resituated" more autonomously in relation to the global marketplace, the U.N. is likely to continue its pattern of deference, adapting itself increasingly to a central role as an instrument to promote global economic interests by way of upgrading such market-driven financial institutions as the IMF and World Bank, while notably backing off from modest regulatory efforts that had been earlier underway (for instance, terminating the Centre for Transnational Corporations in the early 1990s).[22] More insidiously, perhaps, the Security Council may exhibit an order of priorities with respect to peace and security

21. On the growing tendency of economic globalism to eliminate discretion in governmental policymaking, see Thomas L. Friedman, *When Money Talks, Governments Listen*, N.Y. Times, July 24, 1994; Colin Hines and Tim Lang, *Free Trade is a Dangerous Drug*, The New Statesman, July 23, 1993. This is also a theme of the Global Civilization Project, an undertaking of the World Order Models Project; for its latest report, see RICHARD FALK, ON HUMANE GOVERNANCE: TOWARD A NEW GLOBAL POLITICS (1995) (especially chapter VI).

22. For a more detailed analysis of this tendency toward the marketization of the state from this perspective, see Richard Falk, An Inquiry into the Political Economy of World Order (June 1994)(paper presented at Portrack Seminar, Dumfries, Scotland).

by reference to issues of global economic policy that are being set by non-accountable and largely invisible global market forces.

## C. THE CHARTER AS CONSTITUTIONAL FRAME

The establishment of the United Nations was an elaborately negotiated process. The process was crystallized in a foundational document of a treaty character: the U.N. Charter that was signed in San Francisco on June 26, 1945, by delegates representing the fifty-one founding governments. With such a diverse membership establishing the United Nations, and considering the status of members as sovereign states, it might have been supposed that the textual language of the Charter would be construed strictly, but constitutional documents, while generally accorded a nominal hallowed status, tend to be opportunistically interpreted in accordance with the prevailing political will even in communities that maintain high standards of governmental accountability.[23] Such has been the case with the Charter, especially with respect to peace and security, suggesting that the role of the United Nations is being shaped by the changing configuration of geopolitics more than it is a reflection of its own internal diplomacy as governed by statist membership rules. Perhaps such a result was or should have been foreseen, and intended, at least by some of the drafters of the Charter, given the idea of permanent membership and veto power in the formal structure of the Security Council.

A rationale for opportunistic interpretation of the Charter has been given in terms of presumed major purposes, especially the presumption that the founding membership of the United Nations above all wanted the organization to be in a position to respond effectively in the event of a threat to or breach of the peace. Such a presumed priority has been prominently relied upon by the West in efforts to sidestep the Soviet veto during the Cold War years. The contractual element of a Soviet veto was never directly challenged or abridged,

23. There have been many discussions of the extent to which original intentions and text were circumvented in the setting of the U.S. Constitution early in the history of the republic with respect to the conduct of diplomacy. See particularly the passage in Edwin S. Corwin's classic study to the effect that the real meaning of the foreign affairs distribution of powers in the Constitution was "left for events to resolve." EDWIN S. CORWIN, THE PRESIDENT: OFFICE AND POWERS 170–71 (4th ed. 1957) *as quoted and discussed in* BRADFORD PERKINS, THE CAMBRIDGE HISTORY OF AMERICAN FOREIGN RELATIONS: THE CREATION OF A REPUBLICAN EMPIRE, 1776–1865 70, 54–80, 117 (1993).

but its blocking impact was limited to the extent feasible and perceived as desirable by various interpretative devices. First of all, the Soviet absence from the Security Council during the early stages of the Korean War (1950) was not then allowed to prevent "decisions" despite the clear language in article 27(3) that decisions required ". . . the concurring votes of the permanent members."[24] Second, recognizing that such an interpretative tactic depended on the unusual and unlikely contingency of a Soviet boycott of all Security Council proceedings (specifically, occasioned by the U.N. failure to credential the Peoples Republic of China as the proper representative of China), an occurrence that was not at the time thought likely to recur, and which indeed the Soviet Union quickly ended. Given the complex experience of the Korean War, the Western majority resorted to what was expected to be a more enduring device to circumvent the prospect of a Soviet veto, namely, the celebrated Uniting for Peace Resolution, which in effect conferred a residual responsibility upon the General Assembly to recommend action, including uses of armed force, in the event that the Security Council was stalemated in a situation of threat, breach of the peace, or act of aggression.[25]

The assumptions created by the Korean War were that the Soviet side in the Cold War would be associated with Charter-breaching uses of force, and that a more empowered U.N. would serve Western interests in relation to containment.[26] Underneath this view was the political confidence that positions favored by the West would be supported by decisive margins in both the Security Council and General Assembly, and that it was only Soviet obstructionism that would seek to prevent a vigorous U.N. role. As developments ensued, this early expectation about the U.N. was misleading in two central respects. First, the dynamics of decolonization led by the late 1960s to an atmosphere in the General Assembly that was adverse to Western

24. For a spirited defense of this interpretative flexibility, including the appropriateness of departing from the plain language, see Myres S. McDougal and Richard N. Gardner, *The Veto and the Charter: An Interpretation for Survival, in* McDougal and Associates, Studies in World Public Order 718–60 (1960).

25. U.N.G.A. Res. 337 A (V), 1950, in Basic Documents, *supra* note 14, at 181–82. In effect, this resolution provided a constitutional ground for elevating the General Assembly into a residual Security Council, thereby rewriting the Charter in a fundamental, yet possibily justifiable, way.

26. For a seminal analysis that holds up exceedingly well in retrospect, see Myres S. McDougal and Harold Lasswell, *The Identification and Appraisal of Diverse Systems of Public Order, in* McDougal and Associates, *supra* note 24, at 3–41; there is a danger here of uncritically validating self-serving interpretations of contested and dubious initiatives as became the case in relation to the Vietnam War and other extravagances of the Cold War era.

positions on a number of critical issues associated with Third World advocacy of a new international economic order and in relation to the struggle for self-determination. Second, the United States and its allies found themselves quite often resorting to force on behalf of legally controversial claims (that is, other than as in Korea within the clear mandate of self-defense), perhaps most prominently in Indochina and in relation to the insulation of Israel's various claims to strike militarily across borders from any operational U.N. response.

As a result, the Uniting for Peace Resolution was not used in the partisan manner anticipated as the West became as threatened by the potential empowerment of the General Assembly as by the Soviet bloc. In a sense, the intended Charter equilibrium based on the veto was restored, but at the cost of creating the appearance of an ineffectual U.N., that is, an organization that was so consistently split in relation to most peace-threatening developments as to be unable to protect states that were victims of aggression or to provide a reliable mechanism for responding to threats to the peace. Yet this experience of gridlock was always implicit in the veto, which was part of an effort to ensure Soviet membership and participation after World War II in an organization where their view of policy would almost never prevail if a serious East/West conflict took shape.[27] In this sense, the U.N. was structured from the outset to be a universal instrument of geopolitics, rather than as a creature of law or a mechanism serving one geopolitical faction against its rival, or as an institution that acted on the basis of what a majority of member states favored. This U.N. orientation reflected Franklin Roosevelt's conviction that only the maintenance of the anti-Fascist alliance that prevailed in World War II (joining East and West) could reliably keep the peace by collective action after 1945.[28] The outbreak of the Cold War, then, doomed this conception of effectiveness for the Organization, and led to its marginal role with respect to peace and security, with the Korean War representing an anomaly more than a precedent. In this respect, the emphasis on effectiveness that had earlier led to the Uniting for

27. Less obviously, the veto ensured each of the five permanent members of the Security Council of the capacity to block any U.N. initiative, thereby reconciling sovereignty with the status of being a great power. That is, the *political* prospect of being outvoted was one service of the veto, but the *statist* prospect of retaining discretion was its more fundamental role.

28. For illuminating discussions of Roosevelt's thinking on these issues, see WILLARD RANGE, FRANKLIN D. ROOSEVELT'S WORLD ORDER (1959).

Peace Resolution was implicitly cast aside in favor of a more textually conservative commitment to universality and geopolitical consensus.[29]

For this reason, the end of the Cold War and the Iraqi challenge in the form of blatant aggression and annexation of a U.N. member in 1990 posed such an attractive opportunity to foster "a new world order" along neo-Wilsonian lines of collective action on behalf of a victim of aggression. Without going over once more the familiar debate on the Gulf War, it is evident that U.N. response, although effective in dislodging Iraq from Kuwait, thereby reversing aggression, nevertheless remains confusing and ambiguous as a precedent. Several reasons can be enumerated: the Charter commitment to peaceful settlement was not carried out convincingly, and for many, not in good faith, hence, resort to war seemed premature, given the possibility of achieving comparable results with respect to the restoration of full Kuwaiti sovereignty by means of a combination of sanctions and diplomacy; the mandate to wage war delegated almost unlimited discretion to the American-led coalition, and this meant the addition of war goals not authorized by the Security Council, such as the removal of capabilities to produce weapons of mass destruction; a "peace" of sorts has been imposed that has both failed to protect the peoples of Iraq against abuses by their own government or from the extensive suffering produced by international sanctions that are continuing several years after the ceasefire.[30]

It can be argued that, in the Gulf War, the Security Council *has done what it was meant to do*, namely, provide an arena at the global level to fashion and implement a geopolitical consensus to the extent that is possible at a given time. The Soviet collapse, the strategic significance of Gulf oil, the perceived threats to Israeli security, concerns about the proliferation of nuclear weapons, as well as the specific diplomatic skills and militarist orientation of the Bush presidency

29. A comparable result occurred in relation to disputes with the Soviet Union about its financial responsibility for peacekeeping missions that were authorized by General Assembly initiative, in the face of a Soviet vote in opposition. For background discussion, see ROBERT E. RIGGS AND JACK C. PLANO, THE UNITED NATIONS: INTERNATIONAL ORGANIZATION AND WORLD POLITICS 36–41, 112–30 (2nd ed.); *see also* RUTH B. RUSSELL, THE GENERAL ASSEMBLY: PATTERNS/PROBLEMS/PROSPECTS (1970) and JOHN G. STOESSINGER AND ASSOCIATES, FINANCING THE UNITED NATIONS (1964).

30. For more elaboration of these legal objections, see Richard Falk, *Reflections on the Gulf War Experience: Force and War in the UN System*, in THE GULF WAR AND THE NEW WORLD ORDER 25–39 (Tareq Y. Ismael and Jacqueline S. Ismael eds., 1994); *see also* Weston, *supra* note 5. For useful overall independent assessment, see OMAR ALI, CRISIS IN THE GULF: AN INDEPENDENT IRAQI VIEW (1993).

combined to provide the geopolitical foundations for an effective response in relation to limited goals under the auspices of the United Nations. The cost of effectiveness in constitutional terms required that the Security Council acquiesce to the U.S. demand for almost total operational control over the modalities of response. It was this combination of a wide U.S. strategic agenda and the acquiescence of other states that created the impression that the Security Council lacked autonomy and was appropriated by the U.S. government to give a global community "cover" to what was in its essence a traditional exercise in great power diplomacy.

In retrospect, the U.S. government seems to have been shortsighted in its approach. It could have seized the occasion of such outright aggression by Iraq to build confidence in the institutional capacities of collective security much in the manner that George Bush described when trying to build support for an effective response in the first several months after the Iraqi attack of August 2, 1990. Subsequent developments in Somalia, Bosnia, Haiti, and Rwanda have confirmed the need for a more autonomous mechanism for collective security, as well as revealed the unwillingness of the United States to bear the leadership burdens associated with effective responses. At this point in international history the U.S. government and public opinion do not view breakdowns of internal order, however severe, as generally engaging strategic interests sufficiently to warrant either American casualties or major budgetary commitments.

The reversal of the U.S. commitment in Somalia during 1993 has turned out to a decisive moment, disclosing that it was not possible to restore peace and order in the face of determined indigenous opposition without incurring serious human costs in the form of casualties, that "blue helmets" did not on their own ensure an acceptance by warring factions of the U.N. presence, and that, without genuine consent by indigenous forces, the intrusion of peacekeeping missions even of a mainly humanitarian cast could be provocative in the target society and unpopular in the intervening society. At the same time, having built expectations about the post-Cold War potentialities of the Security Council, the public response has been itself self-contradictory, combining low levels of engagement with an increasing public mood of disillusionment. This mood reached a climax in 1994 when the permanent members of the Security Council refused to support even a modest operation in Rwanda to protect the Tutsi majority, to the extent possible, from further massive genocidal abuse.[31]

31. The following *Economist* cover stories, each accompanied by a lurid visual image, express this mood of disillusionment with the United Nations as a source of peace and security:

This geopoliticizing of the Security Council is a matter of degree. The United States exerted its influence in 1992 to induce the imposition of limited sanctions upon Libya in circumstances where Libya had posed no credible threat to the peace. At issue was Libyan obstruction of the investigation of the Lockerbie terrorist incident of several years earlier in which a direct Libyan connection has never yet been convincingly demonstrated.[32] Libya's resort to the World Court to uphold its sovereign rights to refuse the extradition of two individuals sought for questioning in such circumstances as embodied in the Montreal Protocol was rebuffed by a majority decision deferring to the Security Council, thereby declining the opportunity to establish a doctrine of limited judicial review.[33] Such a geopoliticizing of the Security Council is also reinforced by the failure of members to mount a formal and public challenge, for instance, by seeking an advisory opinion from the International Court of Justice to establish guidelines that might identify limits upon the right of the Security Council to delegate uses of force to states.

Instead of such a move toward constitutionalism, what has emerged from the Gulf War is the sense that the U.N. will be used, other than for the sake of relief, only when geopolitically useful, especially to provide a "law-laundering" service, that is, to provide a kind of legitimizing mandate for what is, in its essence a unilateral, or at best, a use of force by a coalition of likeminded states.[34] This type of selectivity was revealed in stark manner in relation to Haiti where, during 1993–94, the effort to restore Jean-Bertrand Aristide to power had been frustrated by the refusal of the Haitian military clique

*Shamed Are the Peacemakers,* THE ECONOMIST, Apr. 30–May 6, 1994, at 15–16; *Who Will Save Rwanda?,* THE ECONOMIST, June 25–July 1, 1994 at 19–21. This bleak assessment of U.N. peacekeeping roles may not last very long. To some degree, it has already been superseded by the seemingly bloodless and effective restoration of a democratically elected government in Haiti, although the latter development as of November 1994 remains uncertain in character and effects and there are ample reasons to be concerned about the impact of this instance of humanitarian intervention even if Jean-Bertrand Aristide is able to remain in control of the government. *See* Allan Nairn, *Occupation Haiti: The Eagle is Landing,* THE NATION, Oct. 3, 1994, at 344–49 and Allan Nairn, *Our Man in FRAPH,* THE NATION, Oct. 24, 1994, at 458–61. *See also* Joanne Landy, *Magical Thinking About Intervention in Haiti,* 8 PEACE AND DEMOCRACY NEWS 11–13 (Summer 1994).

32. S.C. Res. 731, *adopted* Jan. 21, 1992.

33. See Libyan publications that raise objections from an international law perspective: IBRAHIM ANANI ET AL., THE INTERNATIONAL LEGAL ORDER AT THE CROSSROADS: THE SECURITY COUNCIL AND THE LOCKERBIE AFFAIR (1992); LOCKERBIE CASE AND THE FUTURE OF THE INTERNATIONAL LEGAL ORDER (no author or editor given)(The Islamic World Studies Center, 1992).

34. As will be argued in a later section, there are constitutional as well as geopolitical reasons for a cautious response to internal war appeals for U.N. intervention.

to step aside. The U.S. government was timid about risking a second Somalia, but at the same time was unwilling to accept the outflow of Haitian refugees. The Clinton administration also came under increasing pressure from domestic groups led by the influential Black Caucus not to repatriate these refugees forcibly to Haiti. Such a combination of circumstances in the summer of 1994 led officials in the U.S. government to talk about "the inevitability" of intervention, and in that setting to seek and obtain a blank check approval ("all necessary force") from the Security Council in advance, giving to a prospective intervention a kind of U.N. blessing and making it more acceptable to the American people. Such a U.N. cover helped lessen international perceptions of external action in Haiti as one more exercise in interventionary diplomacy by the United States, which had historically played a role as the traditional overlord in the region.[35] What is manifest in the Haitian setting, regardless of what eventually happens, is the extent to which a response to the severe denials of democracy and abuses of human rights is incidental to a set of domestically driven pressures in the United States that alone explain why the toleration of the Haitian military was no longer an acceptable option.[36]

The U.N. Charter, as the credible foundation of Security Council action, has been seriously compromised by these recent developments in the peacekeeping area. There is a lack of consistency in practice, a failure to articulate principled lines of distinction identifying when a U.N. response is appropriate and when not, and a reliance on unrestricted mandates given to coalitions of states led by the United States. The Security Council is widely perceived as a geopolitical instrument, one that is currently dominated by the United States at a time when American leadership is *domestically* driven and seemingly confused about appropriate peacekeeping roles in situations where no strategic interest is perceived to be at stake. Despite this fundamental deficiency, the U.N. Security Council, with the United States at the lead, deserves some credit for continuing to support

35. N.Y. Times, July 22, 1994; S.C. Res. 940, *adopted* July 31, 1994; also relevant is Editorial, *A UN License to Invade Haiti*, N.Y. Times, Aug. 2, 1994.

36. At this writing, the interventionary option has pushed aside the Haitian military and firmly restored Father Aristide to power with minimal bloodshed. The initial motivational basis for these acts seemed closely tied to a concern about Haitian refugees. *See* John J. Miller, *One Answer to Haitians' Crisis: Let Them In*, Wall St. J., Aug. 2, 1994, which contains the following disturbingly accurate observation on the evolution of U.S. policy toward the military takeover in Haiti: "So desperate are some people to block the flow of Haitians, they are lobbying for a U.S. invasion of Haiti . . . " *id.*

major relief efforts that have mitigated human suffering, and saved hundreds of thousands of lives in Somalia, Bosnia, and Rwanda.[37]

Furthermore, constitutional memories are short. It remains possible, and I would contend, desirable, to encourage a more constitutionally oriented approach to the activities of the Security Council, thereby softening the current impression of its services as a geopolitical rubber stamp. Even such enhanced constitutionalism would be only a matter of degree for the near future. The U.N. cannot hope to mount a major response depending on military capabilities without engaging the shared priorities of the permanent members of the Security Council, or at least not seriously challenging strongly held oppositional views. In the last several years China has frequently abstained or even gone along on crucial Security Council votes, despite manifesting a degree of opposition to the U.N. approach, possibly because it has been the recipient of diplomatic side-payments (e.g., reduced pressures on human rights, preferential trade arrangements) and possibly because its economic growth seems tied to positive relations with leading states.

The main hope to achieve enhanced constitutionalism remains a genuine rearticulation of strategic interests by an American president in such a manner as to incorporate neo-Wilsonian goals, a posture in contrast to President Bush's purely expedient embrace of such an approach for the sole purpose of mobilizing public support for a proactive response by the U.N. to Iraqi aggression back in 1990. Another line of possibility might be opened up if the General Assembly or the non-permanent members of the Security Council were to insist upon guidance from the International Court of Justice with respect to the more controversial applications of the provisions of Chapter VII of the Charter. A final possibility would be an initiative taken by the Secretary-General, possibly consisting of nothing more than an increased use of his pulpit to call for such constitutionalist moves as a way of strengthening the U.N. in its fiftieth anniversary year, or to lay the groundwork for a stronger, more respected, reconstituted United Nations in the twenty-first century.

## D. REWRITING THE SOCIAL CONTRACT

Overall, participation by states as members of the United Nations is voluntary and limited by certain assurances; the most important of

37. For generalized arguments in support, see Jarat Chopra and Thomas G. Weiss, *Sovereignty Is No Longer Sacrosanct: Codifying Humanitarian Intervention,* 6 ETHICS & INT'L AFF.

these is the article 2(7) commitment by the organization not "to intervene in matters which are essentially within the domestic jurisdiction of any state." Even textually there are loopholes within this provision, starting off with the word "essentially," but extending to the clause of the provision that affirms that deference to domestic jurisdiction "shall not prejudice the application of enforcement measures under Chapter VII." Because the U.N. has been acting under Chapter VII in recent humanitarian emergencies despite the absence of a threat to the peace dimension, the protected area of internal political life has been continuously and uncertainly eroded, a process endorsed by the last two Secretaries-General that did not elicit formal objections from the membership.[38]

This basic social contract between states and the U.N. is also being rewritten by the rise of human rights as a matter of global concern. Increasingly, severe abuses of human rights are viewed as a sufficient basis for protective action under U.N. auspices. The internationalization of human rights is necessarily at odds with a commitment to respect the territorial supremacy of sovereign states, especially if the scope of human rights is enlarged to include a "right to democracy" as understood by the West.[39] In this regard, the claim of many Asian countries that the U.N. is being used for interventionary purposes under the mantle of "humanitarianism" becomes more understandable even if the argument is often cynically invoked by authoritarian governments seeking to deflect criticisms of their abusive domestic practices.[40]

The issue posed for the United Nations in its fiftieth year was delicate and crucial. There is little question that, in an interdependent world in which countries have universally accepted the commitment to observe human rights, the notion of domestic jurisdiction should

95–117 (1992); *see also* Thomas G. Weiss, *UN Responses in the Former Yugoslavia: Moral and Operational Choices*, 8 ETHICS & INT'L AFF. 1–22 (1994).

38. *See* discussion in Richard Falk, *Human Rights, Humanitarian Assistance, and the Sovereignty of States*, *in* A FRAMEWORD FOR SURVIVAL: HEALTH, HUMAN RIGHTS, AND HUMANITARIAN ASSISTANCE IN CONFLICTS AND DISASTERS 27–40 (Kevin M. Cahill ed., 1993).

39. *See* Thomas M. Franck, *The Emerging Right to Democratic Governance*, 86 AM. J. INT'L L. 46 (1992) for an influential argument along these lines.

40. The Bangkok Declaration, Final Declaration of the Regional Meeting for Asia of the World Conference on Human Rights, Bangkok, Mar. 29–Apr. 2, 1993, A/CONF.157/ASRM/8, Apr. 7, 1993; *see* Ken Brown, *Rights Issues Aside, Asia Deals Rise*, N.Y. TIMES, Aug. 1, 1994, (discussing the increasing willingness of the U.S. government to overlook the abuse of human rights in deference to market considerations).

be viewed flexibly, subject to a process of continuous reinterpretation.[41] Nevertheless, there are several genuine concerns that arise out of the recent U.N. approach.

First, double standards accentuate the geopolitical character of the organization; China and Indonesia, despite severe violations of human rights, are not subject to interventionary pressures, whereas Cuba, accused of far less serious human rights violations, has been subject to illegal economic coercion for years, although not directly by the United Nations.[42] What are the criteria? Why are the Kurds being protected in Iraq, but not in adjacent Turkey? Of course, in part, this selectivity reconfirms the geopolitical character of the Security Council, exemplified by a pattern of responses associated with the perceived interests of the U.S. government and its main partners in the Security Council. It is to be expected, as these interests are currently perceived through a realist prism, that selectivity rather than principled action is descriptive of the Security Council flow of decision. As already argued at the end of the prior section, a more suitable calculus of strategic concerns would include strengthening the rule of law aspects of U.N. operations, thereby increasing respect for the organization.

Second, an ideological conception of political legitimacy has emerged from the outcome of the Cold War, which appears to privilege market-oriented and secular constitutional orders. Thus, Peru's market orientation and Algeria's anti-fundamentalist stance spare these governments from any U.N. response based on the abridgement of fundamental human rights. In light of the stability of many Pacific Rim countries that adhere to soft authoritarianism rather than constitutional democracy, it seems provincial to associate political legitimacy exclusively with Euro-American political forms. From the perspective of world peace and sustainable development, the case for political pluralism remains strong.

Third, and most significant, a stricter view of the domestic jurisdiction core of the social contract that relates members to the United Nations seems to identify a practical outer limit for U.N. effectiveness, given current world conditions and recent U.N. disappointments. Intervening for essentially humanitarian purposes, that is, in

41. *See* McDougal and Lasswell, *supra* note 26.

42. For critique and review of U.S. economic coercion against Cuba, see UNITED STATES ECONOMIC MEASURES AGAINST CUBA (Michael Krinsky and David Golove eds., 1993).

settings where permanent members do not perceive strategic interests, is likely to be ineffectual, and thus discrediting. The rapid reversal of the commitment by U.N. forces in Somalia underscored this vulnerability of a U.N. undertaking of humanitarian character and has contributed greatly to widespread disillusionment with the overall capacities of the organization. This disillusionment has reached its most anguished expressions to date in relation to Bosnia and Rwanda where it is confirmed by now that the U.N. would not act even to stop palpable genocide, despite flagrant flaunting of agreed guidelines adjusting relations between the U.N. peacekeeping forces and the combatting parties.[43]

In these settings, the constitutional basis for an effective U.N. response is abundantly present, but the geopolitical mandate is generally not supported at the levels required for effectiveness. The ideological and economic stakes are currently seen by the political leadership of powerful countries as small, remote, and antagonistic compared to the costs and uncertainties of acting, especially given the domestic preoccupations of the leading countries, and their past failures within the domain of interventionary diplomacy even when strategic stakes were present and massive commitments made and sustained for years. A partial exception to this generalization arises if strong domestic pressures can be mobilized in response to a deterioration of life circumstances in a given country. This response may have an ulterior motive as seemed to be the case in relation to Haiti during the early 1990s. The outflow of refugees from Haiti and the policy dilemma posed for the U.S. government (unwilling to either forcibly repatriate or admit refugees) seemed mainly responsible for generating in Washington the political basis for a pro-democracy intervention.

But even where some geopolitical backing is present, the social contract based on respect for territorial sovereignty should not be lightly cast aside. Interventionary diplomacy, whether directly under U.N. mandate or delegated to hegemonic states, has a poor record when it comes to benefitting the peoples living in the target society, and often inflicts heavy destruction without accomplishing its supposed objective.[44] There are almost no successful interventions on the

43. *See, e.g.*, Susan Sontag, *Godot Comes to Sarajevo*, N.Y. Rev. of Books, Oct. 21, 1993, at 52–59.

44. For example, Panama has not yet benefitted politically or economically from an allegedly humanitarian U.S. intervention carried out by brute force in 1989.

cheap, yet the motivation to act "surgically" and rapidly is politically overwhelming.

The Gulf War model of inflicting one-sided casualties in a battlefield encounter, thereby gaining ardent public support for contested uses of force, aggravates the problem, and is not a relevant option in the Bosnia class of cases. In these instances, the goal of political restructuring to eliminate the genocidal leadership generally requires that the intervening side credibly display a readiness to embark upon an invasion and prolonged occupation of the offending country, quintessentially the pattern that led to success in Germany and Japan after World War II.

More recently, and far more inconclusively, the Vietnamese invasion of Cambodia in 1979 dislodging the Khmer Rouge did, after more than a decade, help create a peace process for the country that included establishing democracy. This goal, brokered and initially implemented by the U.N., was made far more difficult by the survival of the Khmer Rouge as a political actor and by the authoritarian orientation of Prince Sihanouk, the dominant political personality on the Cambodian scene. Note that such anti-genocidal interventions were in each instance *incidental* to the true rationale for recourse to war, which involved reactions to menacing aggressive policies that threatened core interests associated with the power, security, and economic well-being of the intervening states.

In effect, the U.N., regardless of the moral and legal attractiveness of the cause, is not able at this stage of its existence to act effectively in response to humanitarian crises that arise from unresolved political conflict unless there are also present strong perceived geopolitical interests. If the U.N. is entrusted with such missions mainly as a reaction to public pressures, often reflecting in recent years media-generated pressures (especially the CNN factor), it is likely to fail if seriously challenged in the target society, thereby causing the organization to fail in its mission and lose face. This assessment is reinforced by the refusal of major states to encourage the formation of a U.N. enforcement capability, constituted by volunteers, that could respond on the basis of the severity of the human deprivation rather than being dependent on the ad hoc motivations and geopolitical priorities of leading members.[45]

45. *See* proposals by Kai Bird, *The Case for a U.N. Army,* THE NATION, Aug. 8–15, 1994 at 160–64; Brian Urquhart, N.Y. REV. OF BOOKS, June 10, 1993 and May 12, 1994; and some hint of suggestions in AGENDA FOR PEACE, *supra* note 7, at 24–27.

In some sense, respecting the domestic jurisdiction constraint on U.N. competence acknowledges this limiting set of circumstances as a current reality, and conveys more accurately a commitment to the discharge of a relief function, which can be performed successfully by the Security Council in such humanitarian settings. Institutional modesty along these lines would help avoid false expectations about U.N. contributions to humanitarian crises laden with a heavy political content. Such clarity might help set the stage for the sort of global reforms that would be needed to make the U.N. capable of doing more on its own, enabling the sort of responses required by a more comprehensive agency designed on behalf of a peoples-driven system of global security.[46]

## E. RETHINKING THE RELEVANCE OF INTERNATIONAL HUMANITARIAN LAW

Ever since the U.N. engaged in peacekeeping activities that included the use of force, questions have arisen about the applicability of international humanitarian law. From a positivist perspective, it would seem that the U.N., because it is not a state, was not a party to The Hague and Geneva Conventions made for and by states to regulate interstate combat. In practice, the U.N. has been dominated by the U.S. government in those few security undertakings that have emphasized enforcement and combat. This U.S. influence has meant two things: adherence to international law guidelines when it comes to *purely* humanitarian matters such as treatment of prisoners and of the wounded, and a very wide, self-serving, discretionary latitude when it comes to the choice of weaponry and tactics in battlefield situations, which has meant adopting combat patterns that minimize U.N./U.S. casualties even at the cost of heavy civilian casualties for the other side. Such an impact of U.N. military efforts on the civilian population is especially pronounced in recent civil war settings where no clear distinction can be drawn between what is military and what is civilian.

This second element has not received much attention, but in both the Korean War and the Gulf War airpower was relied upon in a

46. Part of the argument in the prior section is that global security in the post-Cold War setting is market-driven, and it relies on the contrast between the Gulf War and Bosnia/Rwanda as primary world order texts for the comprehension of the U.N. role. For a prescriptive analysis of how to achieve U.N. enforcement capabilities, see Robert Johansen, *Reforming the United Nations to Eliminate War*, 4 TRANSNAT'L L. & CONTEMP. PROBS. 455–502 (1994).

manner that inflicted enormous civilian casualties. The Korean air war was carried out in a particularly destructive fashion by bombing dams that released floodwaters and directly attacking villages and towns in the countryside.[47] In Somalia, the use of helicopter gunships to attack General Aideed's followers in their strongholds in south Mogadishu caused heavy civilian casualties, and turned many Somalia citizens into opponents of the U.N. effort. When the U.N. delegates to others the operational command over the use of military power, it also has effectively ceded complete control over the choice of tactics and weaponry relied upon. Operationally, the implementing states can and do specify the tactical significance of military necessity in an expansive way without Security Council scrutiny . Not so incidentally, the humanitarian law of war has also been generally unsuccessful in constraining states with respect to battlefield behavior.[48] The rules and standards that qualify as international humanitarian law are generally vague and ambiguous, enabling legal challenges to be easily evaded. In other words, it is exceedingly difficult to refute a claim of military necessity made under wartime conditions. This is especially so as the claimant state, that is, those who act on its behalf, need only possess a reasonable, good faith belief that the guidelines of military necessity were consistent with the battlefield actions taken.

The fundamental critical point is the contention that, when the U.N. has recourse to force, it should be authorized only as an utter last resort, and then in a *special* more restrictive way: as a waging of peace, not war. Surely, this follows from the overriding U.N. commitment "to save succeeding generations from the scourge of war."[49] Even in the operative provisions of Chapter VII, the Security Council has no authority to wage war as such, but only the right to undertake military "action" and "force" as specified in article 42 in the event that diplomacy and "provisional measures" (including economic sanctions) as indicated by articles 40 and 41 are found, after a suitable deliberative process, to be "inadequate."

47. On tactics of the Korean War and its devastation of civilian society, see GABRIEL KOLKO, CENTURY OF WAR 404–11 (1994); *see also* WALTER G. HERMES, TRUCE TENT AND FIGHTING FRONT (1966) and ROBERT FRANK FUTRELL ET AL., THE UNITED STATES AIR FORCE IN KOREA 1950–53 (1961).

48. See extensive analysis along these lines by Best, *supra* note 10.

49. For a penetrating analysis of this presumed need for U.N. "super violence" to mitigate statist violence, see Toshiki Mogami, *The United Nations and Non-violence, in* GLOBAL TRANSFORMATION: CHALLENGES TO THE STATE SYSTEM 412–38 (Yoshikazu Sakamoto ed., 1994).

This refusal to authorize the organization to wage war is a distinguishing and precious component of the U.N. framework, appropriately seeking to ensure that U.N. peacekeeping takes on a different character than that of traditional alliances (such as NATO during the Cold War) that aggregate a number of states to an agreed resort to war in the name of collective self-defense under specified treaty conditions.[50] If the U.N. in major peacekeeping contexts has taken on all of the aspects of traditional warmaking, with the additional prerogative of being the agent of organized global society and, hence, not necessarily bound by a law evolved by and for states, such an exemption would result if the traditional statist framework of constraint embodied in the humanitarian law of war is regarded as not being applicable, leaving those who act under a U.N. mandate without any legal liability in the event of violations of the laws of war. Of course, some kind of accountability might still result from voluntary patterns of adherence by U.N. forces and by media exposure of violative behavior.

The argument being made here is that the U.N. should be held to a far more rigorous set of standards than those that have governed states during wars, yet such standards have not even been formulated and do not exist in any authoritative form. This absence explains, in part, why the discussion of such issues has been generally framed in terms of an extension of the existing law of war to U.N. operations.[51] The position being advocated here is partly contractual (the spirit and letter of the Charter), partly pragmatic (the success of the U.N. in the peace and security field depends, especially in relation to internal conflicts and deprivations, on the favorable attitudes of the domestic population and their representatives, including in most settings on some degree of consent), and partly principled (the significance of rejecting war as a legitimate social institution, and hence, of placing strong constraints on the use of force).

What is needed, yet difficult to achieve, is the articulation of a new framework of U.N. humanitarian law that would establish legal

50. For discussion of the debate on the post-Cold War role and identity of NATO, whether it can be transformed into an agency of regional security now that Europe lacks an external threat, see Charles William Maynes, *Bye Bye Bosnia: Misperceptions Fuel the Urge to Do Something, Anything in the Balkans,* Washington Post, Aug. 6, 1995; part of this debate is whether to leave NATO as it was, in case Russia reemerges as a threat to Europe in the event that a new ultra-nationalist leadership takes control in Moscow. For helpful overall assessment of regional prospects and roles, see Bjorn Hettne, *The New Regionalism: Implications for Development and Peace, in* The New Regionalism 1–49 (1994).

51. The ICRC held a conference in Geneva (June 22–24, 1994) and issued a subsequent report on "UN Peacekeeping and the Humanitarian Operations" that explores this theme under the rubric of the applicability of humanitarian law to U.N. uses of force.

limits on the discretion to use force under U.N. auspices, a treatymaking process that sharply narrows "military necessity" and would certainly exclude reliance on certain weaponry (weapons of mass destruction, landmines) and tactics (strategic bombing, indiscriminate artillery, civilian targeting). Such a treaty would have to be reinforced by special, appropriate training given to those who exercise command and wear blue helmets, and most probably, will not prove feasible without the creation of a voluntary force that assumes the distinctive burdens associated with waging peace in the prescribed ways.[52]

Of course, there are problems aside from the implicit challenge directed toward the option of geopolitical appropriation (that is, the availability of the U.N. to sanitize resort to war when the essence of decision is a statist assessment of national interests as in relation to Haiti and may also raise the opposite issue of the sufficiency of political will as in the case of the continuous U.N. dithering display in relation to Bosnia over the course of several years).[53] The central logistical objection to what is being advocated here is that for the foreseeable future the implementation of collective security will depend heavily on the availability of military capabilities provided by the permanent members of the Security Council, and this dependence would not be overcome in circumstances of major challenge even by the establishment of a U.N. volunteer army, which at best is unlikely to produce a force larger than 20,000. The pressure to use such a force in circumstances where it was unlikely to be sufficient could easily lead to a loss of credibility, as could the opposite failure of preserving its credibility by conditioning its availability on high prospects of success even when the challenge posed was severe, embodying genocidal behavior.

As the Gulf War and the Korean War show, much larger scale military commitments may be needed to address challenges of outright aggression across international frontiers. Such considerations do, indeed, limit the short-term prospects for waging peace in an appropriate manner, yet it would still be possible in most circumstances to circumscribe the mandate of the Security Council in much more specific and constrained language and to activate the Military

52. Not necessarily more risky for the U.N. force, as its presence is less likely to alienate the civilian population at the scene of the conflict.

53. In 1994, the U.S. government sought and obtained Security Council authorization to use force in relation to the internal situation in Haiti similar to what was received in the Gulf War context, namely, "all necessary force."

Staff Committee, according less discretion to the main agents of a U.N. operation when it comes to the use of force and insisting upon a far greater institutional role for the Security Council by way of collective management of the means and ends of combat.

In this event, the skeptical argument of opposition contends that the main states, if unable to shape the U.N. operations that they fund, would then act on their own outside the U.N. framework, claiming such statist prerogatives as "collective self-defense," the right to protect nationals abroad, and reviving claims to act in spheres of influence. In this event, the U.N. role will be further subverted and moved back to the margins of world politics. Such a possibility surely exists as recent patterns of American, French, and Russian coercive diplomacy with spheres of influence have exhibited. Yet even in the present climate of reluctance to support autonomous U.N. peacekeeping, it seems possible to strike a somewhat better "world order bargain" between leading states and the Security Council on the use of force than existed in either the Korean or Gulf War, thereby producing a dynamic balance between setting limits on the use of force, yet allowing governments to protect the well-being of nationals serving under a U.N. command, legitimizing specific uses of force, yet constraining its scope and character.

Two sets of recommendations are being proposed. The more drastic requires a rethinking and a restructuring of the use of force by the U.N. along more minimalist lines. Such a project presupposes the creation of a U.N. volunteer force that is not merely a U.N. army, but rather an autonomous military capability that is specifically designed and oriented to achieve its goals of restoring peace as nonviolently as possible, but not necessarily as impartially as possible.[54] To move in this direction will undoubtedly depend on mounting considerable pressures from the grassroots beneath the banner of strengthening the United Nations in terms of capability, credibility, and priorities.

More modest, and more immediate, would be a change of attitude toward peacekeeping, already prefigured in the criticisms of the Gulf

54. Indeed, it has been the failure of the U.N. to take sides in the face of genocide that constitutes the essence of its humanitarian failure in Bosnia, as well as in Rwanda. *See* David Reiff, Slaughterhouse: Bosnia and the Failure of the West (1995); Alain Destexte, *The Third Genocide*, 97 Foreign Pol'y 3–17 (Winter 1994–1995). In part, this failure by the U.N. is "caused" by the absence of political will on the part of its leading members. In this sense, the U.N. is set up to fail: it has been given insufficient means to take sides, yet its mandate places it so close to the commission of atrocities that it may be seen as complicit if it adopts and retains a posture of impartiality.

War as too unilateralist and by the avoidance of militarist approaches in more recent U.N. peacekeeping operations due to combat-avoiding initiatives by field commanders and U.N. officials (e.g., UNCTAC in Cambodia, UNPROFOR in former Yugoslavia). Of course, the problematic aspects of combat avoidance in the face of a genocidal challenge expose anew the U.N. to the charge of ineffectuality, the failures of weakness.

## F. MOVING TOWARD GLOBAL GOVERNANCE: ACTIVATING LATENT LAW WITHIN THE U.N. FRAMEWORK

With the disappearance of bipolarity, and the generally unsatisfactory and limited effects of unipolarity (given the subjective and objective reality of U.S. withdrawal from a position of assertive leadership), calls for global governance from transnational social forces grow more persuasive and insistent.[55] At the same time, the anachronistic entrenched interests of major members, exhibiting a statist resolve to retain control over the military dimensions of power, presently inhibit any dramatic enhancement of U.N. capabilities in the peace and security field. It is widely assumed that a prior step would be action to make the Security Council permanent membership more reflective of the distribution of power and influence in the 1990s, but even here differing ideas of suitability and feasibility appear to place obstacles along the path of formal action.[56] U.N. procedures by way of amendment (as distinct from by way of deviant

55. The limited relevance of unipolarity recalls the debate about U.S. decline and overstretch triggered in the 1980s by the publication of PAUL KENNEDY, THE RISE AND DECLINE OF THE GREAT POWERS: ECONOMIC CHANGE AND MILITARY CONFLICT FROM 1500–2000 (1987); *see also* EDWARD N. LUTTWAK, THE ENDANGERED AMERICAN DREAM (1993); for a partial response in the earlier setting, see JOSEPH S. NYE, JR., BOUND TO LEAD: THE CHANGING NATURE OF AMERICAN POWER (1990); in retrospect, the robust claims that "a unipolar moment" existed in the aftermath of the victory in the Gulf War hardly lasted beyond its utterance in the spring of 1991; a strong reformist call for global governance is contained in "Common Responsibility in the 1990s: The Stockholm Initiative on Global Security and Governance," 36–42 (Apr. 22, 1991); this direction of policy recommendation is presented in more comprehensive form in COMMISSION ON GLOBAL GOVERNANCE, OUR GLOBAL NEIGHBORHOOD (1995); for a less institutional focus on the character and emergence of global governance, see the various contributions in GOVERNANCE WITHOUT GOVERNMENT: ORDER AND CHANGE IN WORLD POLITICS (James N. Rosenau and Ernst-Otto Czempiel eds., 1992); for more emphasis on global market forces, see RICHARD FALK, ON HUMANE GOVERNANCE: TOWARD A NEW GLOBAL POLITICS (1995); along these lines, see also JEREMY BRECHER AND TIM COSTELLO, GLOBAL VILLAGE OR GLOBAL PILLAGE: ECONOMIC RECONSTRUCTION FROM THE BOTTOM UP (1994).

56. For instance, should financial capabilities and economic stature be the main qualification for permanent membership? Or willingness to contribute to U.N. peacekeeping as evi-

practice) are cumbersome, allowing existing permanent members to veto any modification in the Charter that erodes their influence.

Deeper than these procedural obstacles are attachments to sovereign prerogatives, especially with respect to the use of force by larger countries. Globalization is bypassing the state along a variety of dimensions, and reorienting its role and outlook. The leading states do, however, retain their predominance in relation to violent conflict, and perform valuable functions in safeguarding the world economy against certain types of disruptive challenges. There is a reluctance by governments and their leaders to compromise this capability by building up the autonomous capabilities of the United Nations to provide peace and security to the peoples of the world (rather than for the market). It is mainly not, as is so often claimed, a matter of money; it is an expression of political will, a resistance by military and political bureaucracies at the level of the state to the loss of their control over security functions. This resistance also reflects an unwillingness by leading states to de-instrumentalize the Security Council (that is, to weaken its utility as an instrument of geopolitics). The U.S. government seems especially opposed at this time to the emergence of a more autonomous U.N. with respect to the politics of global governance. In the regional setting of Europe it is Germany that is now proposing a regional security focus to supersede statist security and the United Kingdom that most vigorously resists.[57]

One possible opening, especially in light of this resistance, is to build upon what Dorothy Jones calls "the declaratory tradition of international law."[58] That is, to encourage and rely on growing democratic, civil society pressures to implement the enacted, yet latent, elements of international law.[59] These elements include Chapter VII provisions in the Charter designed to make collective security collective, the constitutional provision for recourse to the World Court for Advisory Opinions in situations of contested legality, the reliance on the Nuremberg Principles to impose greater accountability upon those who act on behalf of the state, the duties imposed by the United

denced by prior contributions? Or representativeness to give decisions a greater semblance of legitimacy?

57. *See* Michael Lindenmann, *Germans Outline Plans to Draw EU Nations Closer on Defence*, FIN. TIMES, June 8, 1995, at 2.

58. See Dorothy Y. Jones, The Declaratory Tradition in Modern International Law in Traditions of International Ethics (Terry Nardin and David R. Mapel, ed., 1992) 42–61.

59. Richard Falk, The World Order Between Insterstate Law and the Law of Humanity: The Role of Civil Society Institutions, lecture transcript, International University of Peoples' Institutions for Peace, Rovereto, Italy, July 29, 1993. See also chapter 2.

Nations Covenant on Economic and Social Rights, and the call in article 28 of the Universal Declaration of Human Rights for an international order capable of providing all persons with a standard of living sufficient to meet elementary human needs as specified elsewhere in the document.

Undoubtedly most relevant of all to the concerns of this project is the implementation of the Genocide Convention.[60] This most fundamental claim of international law imposes a legal duty on ratifying states to act so as to prevent the commission of the crime of genocide. Although each situation is distinct, there seems little doubt that the genocidal features of the violence in Bosnia, Rwanda, and possibly Burundi, engage this duty to act. Further, that support for humanitarian intervention under the aegis of the U.N. provides a reasonable format within which to take all necessary preventive steps, although there is no assurance that the undertaking would be successful, an uncertainty that pertains to all enforcement endeavors.

The argument here is not a matter of all or nothing. It is contending that treating the legal duty to prevent genocide as a serious claim on resources would be a constructive, and feasible, step. The empirical record suggests that a small effort by the U.N. in Rwanda at the crucial time might have saved hundreds of thousands of lives from slaughter, and that a greater U.N. presence in Burundi would likely have deterred a spread of inter-ethnic killing. Bosnia, at this stage, is more problematic. In retrospect, at the time when ethnic cleansing, systematic rape, and death camp conditions for refugees became firmly documented, the anti-genocide duty should have prompted efforts to deter the Serbs and Croats by all politically feasible means, including threats of serious bombardment. Quite possibly such interventionary initiatives would have failed, risking an expansion of the magnitude of genocidal activity and posing a policy choice of withdrawal or escalation for U.N. forces. Unless a political foundation is laid for such endeavors the prospect for success in the more complex Bosnian-type setting is poor. The overall experience of interventionary failure (Vietnam, Afghanistan, Lebanon) is certainly relevant here.

At this stage of public consciousness governments are not treating this legal duty to prevent genocide as a serious political obligation. In this respect, the prospect of anti-genocide enforcement by the United Nations for the foreseeable future will depend upon the mobilization of public pressure of a sort that has not previously been

60. *See* references, *supra* note 18.

evident, or upon the perceived overlap between the prevention of genocide and the pursuit of geopolitical goals. For instance, if Western interests in the Middle East coincided with a fragmented Iraq or a weakened Turkey, it would offer the Kurdish peoples in the two countries a measure of increased protection against genocidal dangers.

The contention put forward here is that there lies dormant in *existing* international law the foundations for a greatly enhanced system of global governance, but these latent potentialities are unlikely to be activated by leading governments unless prodded by mobilized and focused social forces associated with transnational democratic initiatives. The plausibility of such a mobilization is established by reference to the impressive NGO role in relation to the implementation and extension of human rights (for instance, with particular reference to women and indigenous peoples), the implementation of international humanitarian law standards in situations of civil strife, and the establishment of environmental standards globally, as well as regionally, during the 1980s with respect to human rights provisions and procedures of the Helsinki Accords.[61] There are several projects along these lines that manifest a new transnational professional commitment by lawyers and some of their associations, exerting pressure on the U.N. to modify geopolitics in the direction of geogovernance.[62]

## G. CONCLUSION

This chapter has tried to steer a course between cynicism (given the cruel potency of geopolitics, expressed as much by withdrawal and indifference as by assertiveness and devastating interventionary warfare) and naive legalism (the daunting tendency of optimistic legal specialists to assume that formal obligations and actions by the United Nations are inherently benevolent and constructive). In this navigational space, always precarious, there are nevertheless real policy directions that might over time, and under the pressure of

61. For general line of advocacy, see Richard Falk, *In Search of a New World Model*, 92 Current History 145–49 (1993).

62. This distinction is at the center of the outlook developed in the latest phase of the World Order Models Project (WOMP), especially in chapter 1. *See* Falk, *supra* note 9. Such specific undertakings include the World Court Project and the effort to establish an International Criminal Court.

circumstances, contribute to an improved capability and legitimacy for the U.N. Security Council in the peace and security sector of its operations.

One theme has been the false closures on the relevance of law to the operations of the United Nations attributable to the primacy of geopolitics in the setting of peace and security. This primacy has reduced the constitutional stature of the organization in two principal, seemingly opposed, directions: making it overly responsive to the priorities of its most powerful member, while making it underresponsive to challenges of a humanitarian character that do not engage perceived strategic interests. Both clusters of responses, varied by the specifics of context in relation to particular cases, share a realist conception of what is strategic. Within this conception a calculus of interests is made that does not accord any distinct value to engendering respect for law as both internal guide to the operations of the U.N. and to shaping the interaction between the U.N. and states.

Henry Kissinger and Zbigniew Brzezinski, two arch-proponents of realism as writers and policymakers, have recently published books that may indicate more receptivity to the central contention made here: the U.N., on balance, will be more effective to the extent it becomes more legitimate, and it will gain in legitimacy, again on balance (there are exceptions), to the extent that its reputation for constitutionalism improves.

Kissinger, in his long book *Diplomacy*, contends, somewhat unconvincingly, that in the end the U.S. government has in recent decades actually pursued a neo-Wilsonian foreign policy, by which he means that the orientation of government has been shaped more by values than by interests.[63] I think the Kissinger argument that realist assessments are a mask that hides normative preoccupations is vastly overstated, but it does suggest that an American president need not be afraid to clarify national interests through an incorporation of the legal and moral dimensions of world order.

Brzezinski contends that America's prospects to sustain leadership in the world will disintegrate quickly unless animated by some core moral convictions.[64] Here, too, such a perspective could encourage a more principled, less opportunistic, relationship to the United Nations and its future.

63. *See* Henry Kissinger, Diplomacy 804–35 (1994).

64. *See* Zbigniiew Brzezinski, Out of Control: Global Turmoil on the Eve of the 21st Century (1993).

Such outlooks, when considered against the ups and downs of the U.N. in recent years, strongly shift the spotlight to the specific responsibility of the United States as the unchallenged leading member of the organization in these early post-Cold War years. With respect to shaping the identity of the U.N. in matters of peace and security it remains, unfortunately, a unipolar world. The implications of such unipolarity underscore the importance of political leadership, the willingness to articulate a vision and build support for it. The last several presidents, including the present occupant of the White House, have been most disappointing in these respects. Of course, this prospect has become further complicated by the efforts of the Gingrich Congress to cut back the U.S. role in the United Nations by placing financial and other constraints on the level of U.S. participation.

If we cannot look to political officials for leadership, can we look elsewhere? The bloc system of the Cold War era seems to have induced a posture of passivity on the part of other important states on global policy issues, including the future of the United Nations. Not only passivity, but an unhealthy attitude of dependence on the United States to take the lead has been a prominent feature of U.N. activities in the 1990s. It is important for the future of the United Nations that other countries exert influence and provide capabilities. Perhaps the rightist lurch of American political life, with its anti-U.N. posture, will at last stimulate other governments to invest more of their political energy and material resources to make the U.N. work better on behalf of the peoples of the world.

The greatest creativity in this period continues to come from informal and voluntary initiatives rooted in civil society, most evident locally and transnationally.[65] Yet this agency of change, which has been so significant in relation to the promotion of human rights, humanitarianism in war, and the protection of the environment, has never been effectively focused on the United Nations as a framework for achieving peace and security.

Perhaps the plight of the world, as well as the lost opportunities of this period after years of dangerous strategic stalemate, will open up the U.N. as an arena for transnational social forces. Possibly, a modest beginning would be a citizens' monitoring effort that issued a report each year on the degree to which the Security Council upheld the U.N. Charter in its undertakings and adhered to the imperatives of international law. Possibly, such an initiative, if well done,

65. These developments are analyzed in FALK, *supra* note 91.

could attract more activist energies, and even induce governments here and elsewhere to lengthen their time horizon beyond immediate public impact, as well as alter their understanding of the scope of interests at stake.[66] Part of the realist affliction is to conceive of foreign policy in a statist calculus, despite the integrative tendencies that are making business, finance, and trade evolve according to a regionalist and globalist calculus. A more globally and regionally situated realism would lead to an increased realization that an increasingly effective and autonomous United Nations could make the next century more secure, more prosperous, and more peaceful.

66. There are some tentative moves in this direction, but nothing has materialized yet.

# CHAPTER IV

# THE COMPLEXITIES OF HUMANITARIAN INTERVENTION: A NEW WORLD ORDER CHALLENGE

## A. FRAMING AN INQUIRY

The interplay between the actualities of interventionary diplomacy and juridical support for norms of nonintervention are an integral feature of a world of sovereign, yet unequal, states pursuing diverse goals. The juridical stress on sovereignty, reinforced by spatial notions of territorial supremacy within fixed boundaries, provides the doctrinal underpinnings of noninterventionism, while the effort to project power and influence beyond territorial sovereignty, virtually a definition of what distinguishes a great power from an ordinary state, creates the geopolitical pressures that result in intervention in the internal and external affairs of weaker sovereign states.

Part of the complexity traditionally associated with interventionary diplomacy is its confounding and varying admixtures of politics, morality, and law. These admixtures exist whether or not the particular intervention is characterized as "humanitarian," although by so describing an intervention the moral/legal justification is given additional importance. The political dimension is preoccupied with the decisive issues of effectiveness and acceptability, managing the means/end relationship between commitment and outcome and assessing the acceptability of the interventionary claim in various arenas of decision and assessment. It is also crucial to decide whether the overall interest of the intervening state, including its reputation for effective and legitimate action, is promoted by the effort to influence behavior by coercive means in a foreign country and whether sufficient resources can and should be brought to bear to achieve the interventionary goals within a reasonable amount of time given the level of existing support.

The moral dimension is preoccupied with vindicating the claim that the use of force is essential and proportionate, that it benefits the peoples of the target society as well as serves the values (and interests) of the intervening state, and that it contributes to the global common good.[1] The legal dimension is preoccupied with invoking and establishing precedents and legal argumentation about rules and standards in support of or opposition to a particular interventionary undertaking.[2]

The subject matter of intervention evolved as an incident of Westphalian world order, in which states were the only legitimate actors enjoying rights of territorial supremacy and in which there were no external legal constraints on governmental decisions to use force as an instrument of statecraft. The more recent practice pertaining to interventionary diplomacy has exhibited the impact of several new elements, although the centrality of states remains, as they alone have the military capabilities and political disposition needed to fashion the sort of policy that is likely to be identified as "interventionary."[3] The most significant new element is the role played by the United Nations and regional entities, especially in Europe, in interventionary settings, but the character of the U.N. role is ambiguous overall and from case to case. Particularly confusing is the uncertainty to which a United Nations Security Council decision involves a genuinely collective and community interventionary judgment guided mainly by considerations of public good and the degree to which such a decision is little more than a legitimating rationale for uses of force that would be otherwise more widely viewed as "illegal" if undertaken by a state on its own or in coalition with other states. Also relatively

1. These perspectives may not point in the same direction: the 1986 U.S. air strike against Libya in alleged retaliation for Libya's complicity in terrorist actions against U.S. targets was and remains inconclusive from these viewpoints. It is not assured that Libya was involved in the specific terrorist incident that served as the factual basis for the interventionary claim, and it was not clear that the targets chosen were either appropriate or proportionate, and yet the attack did not arouse any strong adverse reaction, partly because Libya had previously and blatantly acted in a provocative manner with respect to international terrorism and partly because the U.S. use of limited force was widely, but not uniformly, accepted as a reasonable way to compel Libya to change its behavior, which seems to have happened in the period subsequent to the attack; for a series of skeptical assessments of the American claim, see E.P. Thompson, Mary Kaldor et al., Mad Dogs: The U.S. Raids on Libya, (1986).

2. *See* Myres S. McDougal & Florentino P. Feliciano, Law and Minimum World Public Order (1961) on the process by which claims to use force are validated in international law.

3. Russia, although no longer a global presence of the sort associated with the Soviet Union at the height of the Cold War, is nevertheless, since 1989, an uncontested interventionary actor in "the near abroad," the region comprised of those formerly independent states that had previously been republics in the Soviet imperial system.

new is the emergence and magnitude of an array of transnational civil initiatives that seek to mitigate the suffering of the people living in the target societies and of those participating in any warfare that results. The International Committee of the Red Cross, established already in the middle of the nineteenth century, in reaction to the horrific battlefield conditions of the Crimean War, is suggestive of this nongovernmental role that has been expanding in interventionary contexts, especially those expressly described as humanitarian. What is also relatively new are legal constraints on the use of force as an instrument of statecraft and the formal prohibition of all forms of coercion that possess an interventionary character.[4] How to evaluate this normative innovation in the status of force remains controversial: are we dealing mainly with a change in discursive reality such that what has mainly changed is language, not behavior, with major states still retaining on a behavioral level a discretionary option to use force? A middle position contends that the discursive change alters behavior by legitimating challenges directed at uses of force that did not previously exist, affecting over time subtle moves away from reliance on force, thereby affecting in subtle ways the balance of considerations entering into the enactment by government of their national security approach.

A final development of the last half century is the emergence of a highly articulated international law of human rights, backed up psychologically by ideas about governmental and individual accountability for their gross violation. Cumulatively, new expectations about conformity to minimal human rights standards generates interventionary pressures, especially given the capacity of TV to create real time awareness on a global basis of many types of inhumane behavior.

This complexity of the interventionary phenomena has a number of contradictory effects. It has become more difficult to identify who is responsible for what. The state continues to dominate interventionary diplomacy, but often operates indirectly, by reliance on the authorizing mandate of one or more layer of institutional authority at regional

4. There is a long list of familiar legal authorities here starting with the Pact of Paris (also known as the Kellogg-Briand Pact) of 1920; article 2(4) of the United Nations Charter is the basic contemporary rule of prohibition; it is enlarged upon in relation to the prohibition of intervention by states. *See* Declaration on the Inadmissibility of Intervention in the Domestic Affairs of States and the Protection of their Independence and Sovereignty, U.N.G.A. Res. 2131(XX), Dec. 21, 1965; these fundamental ideas are integrated in the Declaration on Principles of International Law Concerning Friendly Relations and Co-operation Among States in Accordance with the Charter of the United Nations, U.N.G.A. Res. 2625(XXV), Oct. 24, 1970.

and global levels. Such indirectness of mandate both dilutes and disguises the role of the state to some extent, somewhat undercuts certain anti-interventionary criticisms, and also shifts part of the responsibility for failure to achieve interventionary goals to the wider institutional frameworks, especially that of the United Nations.[5] Further, the nonintervention norms and prohibitions on the use of force are somewhat at odds with the contemporary view that the occasion of human rights abuse provides legal and moral grounds for disregarding the sovereign rights of states.[6] Given this complexity, it is hardly surprising that the subject matter of interventionary diplomacy has consistently given rise to controversy and inconclusive results, particularly in constitutional democracies that claim a moral advantage and legal validation for their foreign policy initiatives partly because of the domestic accountability of political leaders by way of free and periodic elections and legislative checks.[7] In discussing the reluctance of the Bush Administration to get involved on the ground during the early stages of the war in Bosnia, then Secretary of State James Baker recalled a few years later that "the American people would not have stood for such a commitment for even three days!"[8] Such a perception of a citizenry skeptical about an interventionary policy operates as both a definite check on a proposed intervention that is not clearly based on widely acknowledged strategic interests or national security considerations. Of course, when such lines of justification are powerfully present, then the passions of the electorate can act, on occasion, as a spur to intervene. Such an observation seems particularly applicable to the United States, the sole surviving superpower in the post-Cold War period and the country most inclined to avoid a realist public accounting of its interventionary

5. This reliance has caused a rather meaningless debate as to whether the U.N. has "failed" because of the dismal outcomes in several recent peacekeeping tasks or that the U.N. has been made into a scapegoat by leading member states. *See* DAVID REIFF, SLAUGHTERHOUSE: BOSNIA AND THE FAILURE OF THE WEST (1995).

6. See typical argument along these lines in Jarat Chopra and Thomas G. Weiss, *Sovereignty Is No Longer Sacrosanct: Codifying Humanitarian Intervention*, 6 ETHICS & INT'L AFF. 95–117 (1992).

7. This is not to say that the moral/legal status of an intervention is the primary ingredient of its acceptability; generally, far more relevant is the sense of interests at stake in relation to prospects for success at acceptable costs; as the Gulf War suggested, the level of domestic support rose dramatically when a quick and easy victory resulted, whereas the early popularity of the Korean and Vietnam Wars dropped as the costs rose, the war dragged on, and the prospects for victory diminished.

8. Observation made during an informal meeting with the faculty of the Woodrow Wilson School, Princeton University, Apr. 1994.

claims, partly, no doubt, because of its own anti-colonial heritage, its recent championship of international human rights including the right of self-determination, and its tendency to disguise its selfish motivations for overseas actions.[9]

A further stage-setting factor is the extent to which geopolitical pressures to intervene have become much less credible on realist grounds since the end of the Cold War.[10] This development reinforces the normative impact of the collapse of colonialism and the participation in global politics of the ex-colonies as independent states whose leaders remain generally suspicious of *any* interventionary claim. To circumvent such resistance within the setting of the United Nations it is necessary to formulate interventionary arguments in a manner that effectively obscures great power aspects. The rise of "humanitarian" rationalizations is an effort to reconcile the proactive impulse to intervene with the normative inhibitions on the use of force for geopolitical purposes given the present historical setting.

There is a further general observation. To the extent that intervention (aside from countries intervening in the affairs of their neighbors) is the exclusive work of great powers its feasibility as a policy option is often shaped by the nature of the governing structure in the intervening state. If the state is authoritarian, it generally needs less public support at home when embarking upon intervention, and is less interested in mounting an elaborate justification, beyond deflecting international reactions and positing its security concerns. Such a state can also reverse course more readily as it has not mobilized its citizenry in such a way as to be entrapped in their expectations. If the state is democratic, it must persuade the citizenry of the merits of an interventionary policy, especially, as is usually the case, if resistance is expected in the target society, if casualties are anticipated as a distinct possibility, and if there is no assurance of a rapid

9. There are two contradictory lines of interpretation. One regards the United States as a self-maximizing intervening power with little sense of moral scruple. For a powerful articulation of this view, see GABRIEL KOLKO, CENTURY OF WAR 412–51 (1994). The other sees the United States as unwilling to act coercively in foreign policy until it is first convinced of the moral correctness of its position. An influential formulation of this view can be found in HENRY KISSINGER, DIPLOMACY (1994).

10. Geopolitical factors remain relevant in some settings. Islamic challenges in key Middle East countries may yet create a new geopolitical climate favorable to intervention should the pro-Western orientation of the governments in Saudi Arabia, Turkey and Egypt be seriously threatened; also, one could imagine a number of scenarios involving a resurgent and assertive Russia, possibly aligned with China, that would raise the geopolitical stakes in the outcome of various internal struggles for power.

end to hostilities. Once the public is persuaded, however, the termination of an intervention is often politically problematic as it may involve an acknowledgment of failure that has cost the lives of citizens. The United States has assumed much of the interventionary role during the Cold War and since its conclusion, and has a particular need to rest its policy on a firm platform of public acceptance, a position that was greatly solidified during the long ordeal prompted by the definitive interventionary experience of this era, namely the Vietnam War.

Historical memory is also of crucial relevance, as is its definitive construction. Everyone knows how governmental attitudes toward national security policy and resultant international behavior in the West were shaped after 1945 by "the lessons of Munich," and associated fears about "appeasement" and lack of military preparedness, supporting a learning experience by leaders and publics alike that it is important to confront early expressions of aggressive behavior even in marginal settings to avoid later having to deal with a much more central challenge to the established world order. Such a process of social learning was further reinforced in the American case by the lost innocence at Pearl Harbor that disrupted the reassuring national belief that an ocean on either coast made the United States permanently secure in peacetime. This realization of vulnerability to surprise attack by distant enemies was further reinforced by revolutionary technological developments associated with the means of waging war: by nuclear weaponry above all, but also by missiles, guidance systems, and the advent of sophisticated submarines and long-range bomber aircraft.

Twenty-five years later, the "Vietnam syndrome" imparted a quite different message, namely, that it is not worth the effort to address challenges in marginal arenas when the consequence is military frustration leading to serious division and demoralization in the core country and its allies, as well as magnifying suffering and devastation in the target society. Since the Vietnam War literally every American political leader, regardless of party or ideological orientation, has attempted to rally public support for recourse to military action in a manner that would erase the Vietnam syndrome from public consciousness once and for all, thereby removing one source of reluctance to use force in pursuit of national interests. In contrast, those opposed to interventionary diplomacy, especially those who felt harmed or betrayed by the Vietnam War, have continued to regard the Vietnam syndrome as a useful cautionary inhibition upon interventionary impulses.

But such a preliminary assessment is lacking in historical specificity. Although interventionism has been a pervasive feature of international relations, its specific forms vary with the times, and it needs to be so understood by reference to the global setting. The central argument of this chapter is that interventionary diplomacy during the Cold War reflected the bipolar character of geopolitics inducing patterns of intervention that were based primarily on maintaining or disrupting ideological affiliations, especially in countries where geopolitical affinities were ambiguous and contested, and the risks of escalation seemed manageable.[11] It is revealing that the most globally dangerous instances of intervention, as well as the most serious and sustained outbreaks of violence and threats of wider war, occurred in relation to countries divided along ideological lines (Vietnam, Korea, China, Germany) or in countries situated geographically close to one or the other superpower (Afghanistan, Cuba).

Since 1989, the geopolitical pressures to intervene have weakened in most settings, while humanitarian pressures to intervene have strengthened, but their character is fundamentally different. Both types of intervention have proved problematic given current realities about the capabilities needed for an effective intervention and the extent and character of support required to achieve the requisite political will to sustain an interventionary effort until its goals are reached. The failure of geopolitical interventions is associated mainly with their inability to overcome indigenous nationalist forces of resistance, particularly when reinforced diplomatically and militarily by counter-interventionary capabilities, whereas the failure of humanitarian intervention arises mainly because of the relatively shallow commitment on the intervening side, simplifying the tactics of resistance even without counter-interventionary support.[12]

11. In essence, interventionism on the periphery was encouraged while avoided at the core; thus, serious confrontations occurred in Vietnam, Korea, Afghanistan, but not in Eastern Europe or Central America; the tense moments occurred in circumstances of uncertainty as in the Cuban missile crisis or with respect to access to Berlin; governing elites in Moscow and Washington both learned that testing the will of their adversary in such settings was dangerous and should be avoided.

12. It is a revealing, if inconclusive, hypothetical inquiry to wonder whether the outcomes in Vietnam and Afghanistan would have been different if the intervening superpower had not faced counter-interventionary responses; the Gulf War can be usefully analyzed from these perspectives. The prospect of strategic encounter would have led both sides to be far more cautious, probably discouraging Iraq from ever going ahead with its campaign to annex Kuwait by military conquest; as the conflict unfolded, there was no counter-interventionary ally for Iraq to call upon, but there was also a disposition on the intervening side to avoid efforts at

Closely related to this shift in the justifying discourse is an apparent change in political backing. The geopolitically oriented interventions represent the outgrowth of an assessment of strategic interests by government leaders who then mobilize public support for an interventionary policy, whereas humanitarian interventions characteristically result from societal pressures, recently enhanced by a more globalized media, that finally compel a reluctant political leadership to act against their sense of the national interest, but to limit commitments to the extent possible. Among the limiting approaches in this recent period that intends to defuse societal pressures to act while avoiding an open-ended interventionary commitment has been the transfer of formal responsibility to the United Nations. Because interventionary diplomacy, especially if lacking strong geopolitical motives and sufficient capabilities, is likely to fail, the reputation of the United Nations in the field of peace and security has declined, temporarily at least. Much of this decline has been related to the perceived failures of the U.N. to respond to humanitarian emergencies in such countries as Somalia, Rwanda, Burundi, and most of all, Bosnia. This failure has been reinforced by the transfer of primary responsibility from the United Nations to NATO, itself a complex, multi-faceted process, an aspect of an approach adopted to induce the parties to agree finally, if precariously, upon a peace plan. The contrast between NATO's willingness to engage Serb resistance militarily, and the U.N. reluctance to do so, has encouraged the view of U.N. ineffectuality. And, in a crucial sense, even NATO's role was overshadowed in the peace process by the essentially unilateral character of the United States diplomacy, epitomized by virtually locking up the three Bosnian leaders in a military base in Dayton, Ohio, until they finally reached an agreement. In effect, there exists now a repertoire of diplomatic tools and modalities for addressing humanitarian challenges, but none offer any strong promise of consistent success, and even the peace in Bosnia remains controversial as to humanitarian effects.

Finally, because states continue to be guided by a rather narrow conception of self-interest that does not extend to the well-being of foreign societies and their peoples, their unwillingness to intervene

the political restructuring of Iraq. So confined, the Gulf War was decided on a defined desert battlefield where the realities of military superiority could be brought quickly to bear; post-ceasefire efforts to protect the Kurds or to induce the collapse of Saddam Hussein's regime have had far less success.

effectively in circumstances of great human urgency increasingly encourages independent grassroots initiatives to undertake humanitarian missions. An outstanding example of this expanding role is *Medecins sans Frontieres.* More to the point, the agents of humanitarian intervention are now often actors other than governments, especially transnational citizens associations, operating on a political logic that is shaped almost exclusively by moral considerations, largely an ethos of responsibility and solidarity, that is very different than the statist outlook that guides most governments when they are engaged in humanitarian missions. Of course, such generalizations need careful qualification. For instance, there is a series of governments of middle size, most notably those of the Scandinavian countries, Canada, and the Netherlands, that act in a more genuine humanitarian spirit and subordinate *their* statist character to an identity shaped by the humanitarian imperative. At the same time, the capabilities and outlook of these transnational forces should not be romanticized. Some of these transnational actors are funded and otherwise dependent on one or more governments, and thus lack real independence. Also, if conflicts cross the threshold of large-scale violence, nongovernmental actors generally lack the financial, diplomatic, and logistical means to address directly the core of the conflict or may even be unable to gain access to the participants.

The present status of interventionary initiatives is, then, shaped by several realities:

- intervention in almost any foreign society is likely to entail important risks of failure for the intervening side;
- geopolitical factors may persuade leaders to take such risks, but humanitarian concerns are unlikely to do so even if backed up by strong political pressures;[13]
- to defuse political pressures to alleviate human suffering without adopting a major interventionary commitment has encouraged reliance upon the United Nations;
- disillusionment with this pattern is likely to produce, at least temporarily, a reduced role for the United Nations, and greater

13. The Gulf War discloses the relative priority of these two classes of concerns, providing an illustration of a massive geopolitical response and a minimal humanitarian response.

reliance on regional actors, dominant states, and instances of an outright refusal to act at all;

- humanitarian concerns have also been stimulating significant transnational initiatives of a non-governmental character;

- the combination of media attention and the evolution of a human rights culture provides a coherent rationale for "humanitarian intervention" (that is, serious expectations that severe abuses of human rights, including acute economic and cultural deprivations, are matters of international concern that justify interventionary action and overcome otherwise restraining considerations associated with nonintervention commitments and attitudes); and

- this combination of developments in the last several years, especially in light of the human ordeal that has accompanied the dissolution of former Yugoslavia, has caused profound disillusionment with the capacity of the collective will in international society to protect vulnerable peoples against severe forms of abuse and suffering arising either from governmental aggression (Bosnia, Chechnya, East Timor, Tibet), or acute ethnic strife (Bosnia, Rwanda, Burundi) or from governmental collapse (Somalia).

What should we learn from this dismal experience? How shall the interplay between interventionary diplomacy and international law be interpreted in light of both doctrinal formulations and the practice of states, international organizations, and transnational citizens' associations? What is the legal standing of various claims of humanitarian intervention by different types of actors (states, international institutions, NGOs)? How can the role of international law be strengthened without raising expectations too high? How can the constraining impact of geopolitics be acknowledged without undermining the relevance of international law?

## B. CONCEPTUAL AMBIGUITIES

Intervention is notoriously ambiguous as a legal term of art. It is used journalistically to describe all forms of influence projected primarily by governments of states (but more recently by other political actors as well) in their "interaction" with one another. Generally, the term intervention has been reserved for situations in which a powerful state uses forcible means, characteristically including the use of military capabilities, to alter the policies or governing structures of weaker states. In geopolitical terms, intervention has been used to maintain traditional spheres of influence within the region of a powerful state, and more widely during the Cold War when the entire Third World became an arena for competitive interventionary diplomacy of the two superpowers.[14] The United States has frequently intervened over the course of many decades in the Caribbean and Central America to uphold its traditional control within this neighboring region—an interventionary pattern early formulated as a precept of foreign policy (The Monroe Doctrine), although its interventionary character was somewhat disguised in each particular instance by lofty claims of protecting democracy and rescuing the people of a target society from an abusive government, and by invoking rather flimsy contentions of regional authorization. In the last several years, interventions in Grenada, Nicaragua, Panama, and Haiti have all been justified in such humanitarian terms with varying degrees of credibility.

But are each of these instances properly regarded as interventions from the perspective of international law? When a government gives its clear and uncoerced consent to the initiative of another country it is removing a large part of the interventionary taint, but of course ambiguities surround the authority to invite intervention and the genuineness of the invitation. And more recently the contention is that, when the people of the target country seek protection from their own government, their approval of interventionary action is equivalent to consent and has the effect of removing, or at least qualifying, the interventionary taint.[15] Also, as in Haiti, the essentially unilateral move of the U.S. government to restore the elected government to

14. Regional politics is quite distinct, in many instances, from global geopolitics; Egypt's intervention in Yemen, Iran's intervention in Dhofar, and India's intervention in Bhutan and Sikkam were connected mainly with hegemonic ambitions of regional scope.

15. For influential formulations along these lines, see W. Michael Reisman, *Sovereignty and Human Rights in International Law,* 84 AM. J. INT'L L. 866 (1990); Reisman, *Coercion and Self-Determination: Construing Article 2(4),* 78 AM. J. INT'L L. 642 (1984); Anthony D'Amato, *The Invasion of Panama Was a Lawful Response to Tyranny,* 84 AM. J. INT'L L. 516 (1990); but compare the very strong opposing argument of Sarah A. Rumage, *Panama and the Myth of Humanitarian Intervention in U.S. Foreign Policy: Neither Legal Nor Moral, Neither Just Nor Right,* 10 ARIZ. J. INT'L & COMP. L. 1 (1993).

power was undertaken after sustained brutality by a military regime that had usurped power from the elected civilian leadership and with the blessing and collaboration of the United Nations Security Council.[16] Given the view of the International Court of Justice in the *Lockerbie* case—that there is no review of Security Council action within the formal scope of its authority—it would seem that any initiatives endorsed by the United Nations are effectively immunized from interventionary accusations of a legal character, at least as mounted *within* the United Nations.[17] Even the manifestly unilateral intervention by the United States in Grenada in 1983 was allegedly regionalized by reliance on the mandate of a previously unknown political actor, the Organization of Eastern Caribbean States. In a sense, such reliance on multilateral authorization is both an acknowledgment of respect for prohibitions on unilateral intervention and a dubious manipulation of this prohibition through the use of a multilateralizing fig leaf. When the Soviet Union relied on similar tactics to mask its unilateralism in Eastern Europe during the Cold War, the interventionary pretexts of "invitation" or Warsaw Pact authorization were dismissed in the West as such crude deceptions as to be even unworthy of rebuttal.

What, then, should be deemed to be intervention from the perspective of international law? Consent can be coerced or manufactured, public approval can be claimed or highly contingent and unreliable. It is impossible to be too rigorous in abstract legal terms about the doctrinal contours of interventionary practice. Whenever an external agency is acting coercively to alter the governing structure or orientation of a sovereign state, then an interference with sovereign rights is occurring such that a challenge of some sort is being directed at unconditional nonintervention norms. But if the governing process has collapsed or is widely perceived as engaged in massive and gross violations of human rights amounting to "crimes against humanity," especially if there is a genocidal element present, then the moral and legal requirements for intervention are surely satisfied, especially if

16. For analysis, see Richard Falk, *The Haiti Intervention: A Dangerous World Order Precedent for the United Nations*, 36 HARV. INT'L L. J. 341 (1995).

17. Obviously, it is still possible to challenge the legality of U.N.-sponsored initiatives by reference to the constraining principle of "domestic jurisdiction" embodied in article 2(7) of the U.N. Charter, but what seems unlikely is that such challenges can be successfully mounted before the ICJ, given its current reluctance to review judicially the acts of the Security Council; the World Court is not bound to respect its own precedents, and so would technically be capable of taking a different approach to contested Security Council action in the future. *See* article 59 of the Statute of the International Court of Justice.

the humanitarian concerns are not intertwined with economic and strategic interests as would be the case if the target country were an important oil supplier, the site of foreign investment or a military base, or located in a geographically sensitive place. A well-founded humanitarian claim to act can be explained either as an exception to the prohibition on nonintervention or a suspension of such a prohibition in light of either the illegitimacy of the territorial government or the existence of anarchic conditions of brutality and chaos.

Let us consider, then, situations in which there is widespread acceptance among governments and in the public that the proclaimed goal of coercive action is to alleviate suffering of the people in the target society that arises from either the breakdown of government (the so-called "failed state" problem) or by policies pursued by government that are violative of the fundamental human rights of part or all of the society. In such settings, we speak generally and appropriately about "humanitarian intervention." Actually, because of the interventionary taint, especially in ex-colonial regions, other less evocative terms of art are generally relied upon by the supporters of coercive initiatives, e.g., "humanitarian assistance," "humanitarian operation," and "humanitarian diplomacy." Problems of this sort cannot be properly dealt with by semantic evasions. The essence of these projects is to cross international borders and act within a country, allegedly to help people who are there in a condition of acute distress. It is interventionary in this fundamental sense, and for this reason the terminology of humanitarian intervention remains with us. Of course, underneath the political language relied upon by various participants in the discussion of policy responses to humanitarian emergencies of various sorts exist controversies that arise from different factual assessments and different perceptions as to the mix of motives attributed to the intervening actors. As already mentioned, the range of actors participating in such an undertaking includes humanitarian NGOs and international institutions, as well as states.

## C. THE JURISPRUDENTIAL PREDICAMENT

Most of the international literature on intervention ignores geopolitical pressures and constraints. Such a failure has several serious consequences for our capacity to understand and act in specific situations. Part of the neglect of geopolitics is a matter of apologetics, and part a matter of wishful thinking.[18] The apologetic part overlooks the extent to which interventionary claims are exclusively mounted by powerful states that have often in the past put forward self-serving rationalizations for their questionable uses of force to coerce weaker countries with what appears to be an anti-humanitarian net effect. A recent controversial instance would be the economic coercion maintained by the United States against Cuba for several decades in the form of sanctions. It is rather strange but those international law specialists who think of themselves as realists when describing the predominance of power in international society tend still to talk as if the most powerful states in the world can be taken at face value when they purport to act as altruistic agents of change with respect to the assertion and implementation of humanitarian claims.[19] Neither international relations nor practice lends much support to such a benevolent role for great powers, nor, it should be added, does the evidence support the opposite view that geopolitically motivated action will never confer humanitarian benefits. Conclusions either way are persuasive to the extent that their assessment is particularized by reference to the characteristics and effects of particular interventionary claims. But there should be no illusions about the independent weight that is to be accorded humanitarian factors.

When Vietnam invaded Cambodia in 1975, presumably mainly for security reasons, and effectively removed a genocidal regime from power, it was widely condemned, and Vietnam was called upon to withdraw by the United Nations despite the danger that, by so doing, it would revive the influence of the Khmer Rouge, and the successor Cambodian government installed as a result of the Vietnamese intervention was precluded from representing Cambodia in the United Nations. The anti-Vietnam posture was based purely on geopolitical calculations despite the extremity of opposing humanitarian considerations, namely, that it was more important to avoid the extension of Vietnamese influence and to placate China (then hostile to Vietnam) than to relieve the people of Cambodia from the grotesque burdens being imposed on their lives. Such priorities may seem extreme, but they are not anomalous when it comes to disclosing the

18. Such a distinction owes a great deal to MARTTI KOSKENNIEIMI, FROM APOLOGY TO UTOPIA: THE STRUCTURE OF INTERNATIONAL LEGAL ARGUMENT (1989).

19. Compare, for instance, the realist tone of THOMAS M. FRANCK, NATION AGAINST NATION (19??) with his support for an emergent norm entitling peoples to democratic forms of governance. Franck, *The Emerging Right to Democratic Governance*, 86 AM. J. INT'L L. 63 (1992).

relative impact of geopolitical and humanitarian claims on the behavior of leading states, and hence through their influence, of international institutions under their control.

There is another kind of geopolitical pressure operative in the years since the end of the Cold War: the *avoidance* of intervention even in the face of extreme humanitarian emergencies. The United States has been in the critical role of decisive leader with respect to the clarification of geopolitical concerns. Since its experience of encountering violent resistance in Somalia, followed by a domestic firestorm of criticism in the United States, there has operated "a Mogadishu syndrome" that has suggested that humanitarian interventions that take the form of involvement on the ground risk serious military confrontations. In reaction the United States has scaled back drastically its willingness to act directly or indirectly to restore peace and normalcy to afflicted societies except by way of applying diplomatic muscle to hasten negotiations among adversaries in Bosnia, the Middle East, and even Northern Ireland.[20] This U.S. reluctance has also expressed itself in terms of rigid limits on the duration of its commitment even to the implementation of the Dayton Agreement that it brokered, in an unwillingness to make open-ended financial commitments in such settings, and by a particularly notable resistance to desperate requests for even low-level U.N. operations to prevent the renewal of genocidal violence in Rwanda and its outbreak in Burundi. Thus, in some important sense, the geopolitics of humanitarian intervention has recently worked mainly to *discourage* action at the regional or global levels premised on responses that are reflective of attitudes of collective responsibility and compassion. It is the anti-interventionary geopolitical mood that has been as much the occasion for critical commentary as earlier it was the interventionism associated with American foreign policy, in particular, but geopolitics in general.[21]

There is also the utopian side of the ledger in these settings, with moralists and legalists naively urging governments to do what is right without any feeling for the political constraints that surround such demands. One result is frustration and bitterness that comes with the discovery that governments will not generally act in a substantive

20. It also lends support to preventive efforts as in Macedonia where a symbolic military presence under U.N. auspices has so far successfully sought to avoid any spillover of the warfare that could spread further the conflicts in Bosnia and Croatia.

21. *See* RICHARD J. BARNET, INTERVENTION AND REVOLUTION (1968); *see also*, KOLKO, *supra* note 9.

manner against their material interests to any great extent, as has been the unhappy fate of East Timor and Tibet, forcibly and brutally annexed against the clearly expressed will of their peoples. At the same time, agitation by transnational civil groups on such issues prevents the legitimation of oppressive arrangements that cannot be reconciled with minimal conceptions of self-determination and human rights. The basic compromise in these settings is to avoid substantive opposition, but engage in some sort of symbolic action that to varying degrees withholds full approval. Another utopian tendency is terrible disappointment with the role of international law, finding it impotent to overcome the torments of peoples, and entire nations, trapped in such humanitarian emergencies. Both of these effects tend to divert attention from the constructive, if modest, roles of international law, as well as from the contributions that can be made on other avenues seeking to exert political influence.

In essence, the only way to induce action in support of such humanitarian claims is to generate enough countervailing power to overcome geopolitical inhibitions; domestic protest in the United Kingdom and the United States succeeded in doing this with respect to instituting a sanctions campaign to weaken *apartheid* during the early 1980s, thereby providing the political context for an effective transnational campaign that drew upon humanitarian arguments but did not rely upon them to achieve change. In this regard, mobilized domestic and transnational pressures responsive to humanitarian emergencies can alter the geopolitical calculus to a considerable extent, especially as most political leaders are preoccupied with holding onto domestic power. A famous instance, the interpretation of which is itself a matter for continuing controversy, involved the levels of U.S. support for the early period of Israeli statehood, that is, prior to 1967 when Israel became more of a strategic partner, despite the risks that were taken that might have weakened crucial ties with oil-rich Arab countries in the Middle East. Obviously, the impact on geopolitical calculations is greatest in a democratic country such as the United States where a well-financed, deeply committed constituency that imaginatively mobilizes its resources for a sharply focused campaign and has enough of a perceived connection to domestic political balances in the United States to be a serious factor can exert pressure that will confine foreign policy within rigid parameters that make little geopolitical sense if considered purely by reference to international goals. The Cuban exile community has been remarkably effective in its efforts to maintain U.S. pressures on Castro's Cuba, despite the undermining since 1989 of geopolitical pretexts for a hostile relationship.

If international law, following the broad outlines of the New Haven approach associated with the work of Myres McDougal, Harold Lasswell, and more recently, Michael Reisman, is to be associated with some kind of conjointness between the authority to act and the capacity to implement, then the application of international law to the theory and practice of humanitarian intervention is highly problematic *in the current global setting.*[22] Recent experiences in Somalia, Rwanda, Liberia, Burundi, Chechnya, and most of all, Bosnia and Kosovo, are suggestive of both the growth of authoritative claims to act on behalf of the international community and of the absence of the capabilities to translate those claims with any consistency into outcomes that vindicate the undertaking. There is, thus, a serious gap between claim and performance with a tendency to deform the implementing policy and its agents of enactment. Does this suggest the wisdom of a higher threshold of nonintervention despite the presence of humanitarian wrongs that need to be corrected? Does it also underscore the importance of differentiating actions by states and inter-state actors, such as the United Nations and NATO, from transnational civic initiatives that are carried out by independent associations of citizens?

At issue, also, is the fundamental Westphalian question of representation. It has been useful and generally reliable to treat the constituted government as the authoritative representative of the people, the subject of international law. Furthermore, with reason, the manipulation of counter-elites to obtain invitations and mandates to intervene, which was standard Soviet practice (as in Czechoslovakia in 1968 and Afghanistan in 1979), reinforcing the view that only the legitimate, internationally recognized government has the authority to grant consent for the entry of an outside force with an interventionary mission.

But this neat Westphalian view has been eroding in a variety of respects as a result of recent practice. For one thing, if the oppressed people of a country can validate interventionary force by welcoming their own liberation, then the voice of formal governmental authority

22. See Hedley Bull's important argument that international society lacks sufficient solidarity at this time to support collective ventures for the public good on a global level such as humanitarian intervention or criminal accountability of governmental officials. Bull, *The Groatian Conception of International Society, in* Diplomatic Investigations 51–73 (Herbert Butterfield & Martin Wight eds., 1966).

can be cast aside rather abruptly; such is the implication of an alleged emergent right of democracy or the state-shattering practice of self-determination accompanying the breakup of the Soviet Union and Yugoslavia.[23] Also, if there has been a collapse of government, there is no authority to grant or withhold consent, and forcible entry can be claimed, as it has been, by reference to the objective conditions of complex humanitarian emergency. But what if those empowered to represent are also the perpetrators of crimes against humanity? These leaders are simultaneously treated as negotiating partners and potential war criminals. This is the puzzle created by the 1995 Dayton Peace Agreement. It suggests that diplomacy should be less confined to its traditional governmental parameters. Instead of treating only figures such as Karadzic and Milosevic as negotiating partners there should have been discussions with "representatives" of those peoples who did not endorse or participate in crimes of state or seek to establish states along ethnically pure lines. The feasibility of such an alternative course of action is uncertain at best. Governmental leaders, even if associated with criminal practices, may alone possess representational capacity by having sufficient control over the sentiments and capabilities of the peoples, and it would be meaningless to deny their representational authority. Such an acknowledgment of realities has led to the acceptance of both the PLO and the IRA as necessary participants in their respective peace processes, but without the Bosnian overlay of potential indictment for previous terroristic activity.

Once that overlay exists, as is the case in relation to Bosnia, it poses a fearful dilemma: the intention to prosecute those responsible for war crimes seemingly can neither be dispensed with nor implemented, and this indeterminacy imperils the move from war to peace, and makes the process appear vindictive to some, hypocritical to others. It is notable that even with the resumption of IRA terrorism in February 1996 there were no suggestions from responsible negotiating actors that perpetrators be treated as "war criminals" because in this instance, the British government has sought to protect the population by a substantive commitment rather than abandon protection and offer

23. This recent self-determination practice means that in situations other than decolonization peoples previously entrapped within a state have been acknowledged by the international community as entitled to engage in struggle to establish by an act of secession their own independent state; these developments are difficult to assess as they have also been the occasion for establishing "ethnic states" that are violently and cruelly "cleansed."

those exposed to violence the symbolic solace of a future war crimes tribunal.[24]

This issue of reconciling Westphalian notions of representation and legitimacy with post-Westphalian ideas of personal criminal accountability of agents of state power are at the very center of the difficulties surrounding the contemporary compromise between geopolitics and morality in the setting of "humanitarian intervention." The move to institute war crimes proceedings *in this instance* of Bosnia (and more casually, Rwanda) reflected the relative unwillingness of the great powers to use their capabilities directly, by way of the United Nations or through NATO to prevent ethnic cleansing in the former Yugoslavia or genocide in Rwanda, but especially in Bosnia, during the 1991–1994 period. Being unwilling to act substantively when it counted most, the political pressures to act *in some manner acknowledging the humanitarian challenge* produced a variety of symbolic gestures, including the establishment of a war crimes tribunal in The Hague, an arms embargo, sanctions against Serbia, and safe havens in Bosnia, that had a range of effects, but overall, an ambiguous, if not a perverse, impact on the underlying wrongdoing and shared the common feature of responding for the sake of humanitarian goals without devoting major resources to increase prospects that the response would be effective.

The standoff between the authority to intervene and the lack of capabilities to do so effectively raises serious questions about support for the purported legality (and even morality) of given instances of humanitarian intervention. Indirectly, as well, it suggests that, *at this stage of international society*, the doctrine of nonintervention provides a generally more constructive foundation for exerting the influence of international law than does an emphasis of the sort contained in Boutros Boutros-Ghali's oft-quoted passage in *An Agenda for Peace* to the effect that sovereignty in the sense of territorial supremacy is eroding as a principle of world order. This is not a mere jurisprudential quibble. The policy concerns here are at least fourfold, and are not altogether internally consistent:

- upholding the sovereign rights of weak states by stripping further the pretensions of legality away from interventionary diplomacy

24. Such an observation is not to be confused with an overall endorsement of the British role; indeed, Prime Minister Major's tilt toward Unionist sentiments in Ulster for domestic political gain in British elections may well have upset the balance within the IRA that had earlier opted for ceasefire combined with the prospect of all-party negotiations. On the misuse

of an essentially geopolitical character, as was the case with the Panama intervention of 1989, that is, protecting states against dubious interventionary claims even if backed by some humanitarian considerations;[25]

- avoiding punishing the victims and weakening tendencies toward reconciliation by acknowledging the inability and unwillingness of leading states and international institutions (as now constituted) of an intergovernmental character to intervene effectively for predominantly humanitarian purposes in most circumstances of acute distress;[26]

- challenging the artificial line of sovereign deference that is now drawn to give Russian intervention in Chechnya or Iraqi intervention against the Kurdish regions of northern Iraq a different, more internal legal and geopolitical status than was given to Russian intervention in Georgia, or formerly, in the countries of Eastern Europe;

- accepting the view that, despite the unevenness of international practice, it remains beneficial to maintain maximum and flexible support for the alleviation of suffering and the establishment of peace, and thus abiding a highly selective, and inconsistent, doctrine of humanitarian intervention.

This line of analysis suggests a reconvergence of authority and effectiveness in relation to humanitarian claims as evaluated in context, thereby both reinforcing sovereign rights and norms of nonintervention, but also endorsing a limited option of humanitarian intervention. Such an approach opens the way for humanitarian assistance in many, but not all, circumstances, and recognizes that the actors in the current phase of the Westphalian structure must often

by Britain of the political space during the ceasefire to pursue "the war" by other means, see Martin Woollacott, *Finding the Bone of Contention*, THE GUARDIAN, Feb. 17, 1996, at 14.

25. *See* Rumage, *supra* note 15.

26. Humanitarian interventions might become more feasible in a wider class of instances if the U.N. or a regional actor were given the financial and peacekeeping resources to act with far greater independence of geopolitical priorities, or if geopolitics was reconceived to incorporate acute humanitarian emergencies for the sake of overall global stability and investor confidence; the essence of this point is grasped by comparing the mobilization of resources to address the Iraqi challenge in the Gulf crisis with that occurring in response to the Serb challenge in Bosnia.

make tragic choices between diplomacies of interventionism and reconciliation, and that only the latter is possible in the absence of strong strategic interests on the part of major states, or the existence of a mobilized domestic constituency that is pushing humanitarian concerns onto the foreign policy agenda in a manner that overcomes a purely geopolitical assessment of interests.[27]

In advocating such a position, it is obvious that major, and likely unfortunate, uncertainties exist in relation to the adoption of a more permissive approach to interventionary options. No one can answer the "what if" questions about various recommended interventionary initiatives alleged to support humanitarian goals. Would an early minor NATO action of bombing the gun emplacements around Sarajevo have lifted the siege sooner and led to a much quicker, less devastating "peace"? Or would such action have led to a bloody Serbian retaliation against vulnerable U.N. forces (prompting their removal) or to a spread of the violence to new arenas in the Balkans?[28] Did the creation of the safe havens negligently contribute to ethnic cleansing and the containment of refugees or was it a genuine good faith effort to provide sanctuary and protection for a portion of the entrapped Muslim population of Bosnia? Clearly the inability to defend adequately several of the six safe havens contributed to the impression of U.N. impotence and irresponsibility, and probably suggested that, had the level of Serb aggressiveness been anticipated, support for the safe haven concept would not have been forthcoming. These fundamental issues are what postmodernists (in the deconstructionist mode) are fond of calling "undecidables." The vigorous debates generated reveal little about the probabilities and much about the sensibilities of participants in the debate.[29]

27. As argued, such pressures can work for or against intervention and, in normative terms, are a wild card as played in specific circumstances.

28. The retrospective claims made in light of NATO bombs bringing the Serbs to Dayton need to be tempered by the realization that their impact occurred after Milosevic had abandoned maximalist Serb goals in the war and after the military buildup of Croatia and Bosnia changed the realities on the ground; without a far more detailed analysis of causal responses at various stages of the conflict it is exceedingly difficult to draw any firm conclusions about what would have happened had bombing occurred sooner. What is clear is that the United States and other actors undertaking such earlier bombing would have had to be bureaucratically prepared in advance to cope effectively with the political fallout arising from possible failure of bombing to achieve its intended results and with possible Serb retaliatory actions.

29. To some extent the deontologically minded are drawn to positions that seem intrinsically right, acting to oppose ethnic cleansing, while the consequentially minded are drawn to positions that seem contextually sound, given likely effects of proposed actions; some combination of perspectives is probably most likely to produce results that are both responsible and responsive, but in what apt combination is impossible to codify in any useful way.

## D. MAKING HUMANITARIAN INTERVENTION HUMANITARIAN

My argument has been that, with the end of the Cold War, there has been a notable shift in interventionary diplomacy away from purely geopolitical interventionism in the direction of support for humanitarian claims to alleviate human suffering. This shift has been expressed especially strongly in U.S. foreign policy, both as directly enacted and as channelled through the United Nations and, to some extent, NATO.

From a purely normative perspective of law and morality this shift in interventionary practice is a welcome development, but it has foundered in key instances because it was based on a very shallow commitment of resources and will and underestimated the burdens associated with carrying humanitarian diplomacy out successfully. Earlier geopolitical interventions had also frequently failed because they engendered a combination of indigenous, nationalist resistance and counter-intervention organized by opposed geopolitical actors. Thus, interventionary success should never be equated mechanically with money, weapons, and even ground forces.

Interventionary experience suggests a number of conclusions with respect to humanitarian emergencies. First, the best opportunity, given available levels of capability, to avoid acute suffering is normally to become seriously engaged in a preventive mode, providing a symbolic presence and substantial economic relief, and making constructive diplomatic intermediary services available. Second, external encouragement of nationalist tendencies toward self-determination need to be balanced effectively by adequate protection of human rights.[30] Third, once battlefield results have produced a stalemate or antagonists have reached a point of disillusionment with armed struggle, outside diplomatic moves and military forces can play a valuable catalytic role in encouraging and implementing a peace process. Fourth, during the phases of most intense humanitarian emergency, in the absence of a suitable interventionary response by states and international institutions, a maximum effort should be

30. The German recognition of Croatia and Slovenia in 1991 was in this sense anti-humanitarian, even if it did support strong majoritarian claims of self-determination; ethnically or religiously mobilized majorities pose severe human rights challenges to dissident minorities, especially, as in Croatia and Bosnia, where varying interpretations of recent historical experience engendered plausible fears and established political space for opportunistic politicians to play their own minority nationalist card as Milosevic did to such devastating effect in both Croatia and Bosnia.

made to support transnational and grassroots initiatives without compromising their independence, especially those with a nonviolent, reconciling orientation. Fifth, a critical geopolitics is needed to convince those who dominate decisions about the allocation of resources that investments in conflict-prevention, human rights (economic, social, and cultural, as well as civil and political), and conflict-resolution is conducive to global stability and prosperity; whether such a critical geopolitics is presented as "a new realism" or as an abandonment of realism is not of great importance compared with altering the makeup of decisions and understanding about what counts for individual and collective well-being at this stage of international political life.

It is the contention of this chapter that these five directions of policy have been insufficiently emphasized in the years since 1989, with the consequence that there has been an unhealthy move from an initial unfounded enthusiasm for "humanitarian intervention" to a more recent unwarranted disillusionment. As a result, by and large, even allowing for some specific successes and mixed outcomes (as in Somalia), the net impact of humanitarian diplomacy has been perceived to be, and in several instances has been, anti-humanitarian. The challenge now is to rededicate our energies to increase the prospect of humanitarian interventions serving humanitarian goals.

# CHAPTER V

# ENVIRONMENTAL PROTECTION IN AN ERA OF GLOBALIZATION

## A. THE HYPOTHESIS: NEO-LIBERALISM AND DIMINISHING SUPPORT FOR ENVIRONMENTAL PROTECTION

The complex impacts of economic globalization on the prospects for environmental protection is a surprisingly neglected subject of inquiry. What is studied frequently are the specific connections, adverse and reinforcing, and quite controversial, that exist between the promotion of international trade by opening markets and the regulatory objectives of environmentalists. My concern in this chapter is with the generally ignored part of these concerns, the more structural implications, that strongly indicate that the tendencies toward economic globalization involving both integrative developments beyond the control of the state and the rise of global economic governance by way of the World Trade Organization and other multilateral frameworks, exert a generally downward pull on attempts to address various environment challenges through effective regulatory efforts.[1] In effect, I want to argue that, given the time horizons of policymakers, economic globalization and environmental protection stress fundamentally inconsistent policy objectives that could be rendered compatible only by the imposition of effective regulatory authority based on an underlying political equilibrium between the competing economistic and environmentalist constituencies. This chapter argues that such an equilibrium does not currently exist, nor is it likely to be forthcoming. As a result, the needed regulatory capacity will not be established, reflecting the relative weakness of the environmental

1. My orientation, in this respect, is broadly similar to that of JOSEPH CAMILLERI AND JIM FALK, THE END OF SOVEREIGNTY? (1992).

constituency given current world conditions. This prospect is reinforced by other related contemporary developments that are part of a deepening, but as yet insufficiently diagnosed, comprehensive crisis of public goods. Such a set of circumstances is of particular concern with respect to environmental quality because so many dimensions of environmental policy are continuing to generate data of worsening conditions and trends.[2] Whether this assessment is generally true, allowing for variations with respect to the differing characteristics of the main environmental problem areas, and if so, what might be done to improve prospects for more effective and coercive environmental regulation is of utmost importance for the future health, well-being, and security of the peoples of the world.

I realize, of course, that globalization is one of those buzzwords of the 1990s that everyone hates, yet ends up, as I do, apologetically relying upon. As slippery and easily polemicized a conception as globalization has become, it remains seemingly indispensable for the task of identifying several new, aggregative features of international reality that are not encompassed within such traditional categories of state, society or system of states, and international institution or organized international community.[3] The idea of globalization is needed to put an emphasis on the special contemporary relevance of forms of behavior and challenges that have a global scope that cannot be adequately comprehended or addressed by state-centric approaches, especially given the degree to which the state has been appropriate as a policy instrument by those whose overriding priority is to promote aggregate global economic growth.

2. See, for example, recent indications that global warming is likely to produce planetary disasters in the near future, such as the account of a presentation by Sir John Houghton, chairman of the Royal Commission on Environmental Pollution, as reported in John Vidal, *Global warming disaster "imminent,"* GUARDIAN WKLY., Feb. 25, 1996.

3. See useful discussion of globalization at the start of Andrew Hurrell and Ngaire Woods, *Globalisation and Inequality*, 24 Millennium 447–70 (1995); on its definition the authors offer:

> "The term 'globalisation' is often invoked to describe the process of increasing interdependence and global enmeshment which occurs as money, people, images, values, and ideas flow ever more swiftly and smoothly across national boundaries. It is assumed to be a process driven by technological advance which will lead to a more and more homogeneous world economy . . . ". *Id.* at 447.

See also the language used by Robert Cox: "The characteristics of the globalization trend include the internationalizing of production, the new international division of labor, new migatory movements from South to North, the new competitive environment that accelerates these processes, and the new internationalizing of the state. . . making states into agencies of the globalized world." Robert Cox, *Towards a post-hegemonic conceptualization of world order: reflections on the relevancy of Ibn Khalun, in* GOVERNANCE WITHOUT GOVERNMENT: ORDER AND CHANGE IN WORLD POLITICS 132, 145 (James N. Rosenau & Ernst-Otto Czempiel eds., 1992).

There are influential economists who take evident pleasure in pointing to earlier periods of greater internationalization of trade, measured by the extent of price differences with respect to traded goods, so as to refute the postulate of globalization as associated with distinctively contemporary conditions.[4] The argument being made here is different. It is that the increasingly globalized character of trade, finance, and investment, as reinforced by media, computerization, and advertising, has created strong regulatory imperatives that appear for various reasons to go beyond the capacity and will of states to manage, either directly on their own, or indirectly through the establishment of international regimes. So conceived, globalization poses a world order crisis of a structural and ideological character that has not existed in prior historical periods. It is not so much that the state has been bypassed by the operating logic and frameworks of globalization, as that its orientation has been deterritorialized in such a manner that it has lost, temporarily at least, much of its autonomy with respect to global market pressures and thus risks a more confrontational set of relations with those segments of its own territorial society that perceive themselves to be disadvantaged.[5]

There seems to be no adequate alternative to globalization when seeking a conceptual framework to identify the overall effects of those integrative economic tendencies that are weakening the capacity of the sovereign state to act independently and to fulfill its traditional role of protecting territorial interests. As will be discussed, the earlier preoccupation of world order thinking was that the fragmented, essentially inward-looking, nature of political authority in the world, given a society of sovereign states, worked against the protection of the global commons essentially because of a generalized reluctance of states to cooperate externally, and, more specifically, the related inability to solve the free rider problem in relation to the protection of collective goods.[6] The contemporary circumstance has evolved in a different manner, but with essentially similar difficulties with respect to environmental protection. At this point, despite drastic diversities of national situation and approach, as well as the wide range

4. Milton Friedman, *Internationalization of the U.S. Economy*, FRASER FOR. (Feb. 1989) at 10; persuasively discounted by John Gerard Ruggie, *At Home Abroad, Abroad at Home: International Liberalisation and Domestic Stability in the New World Economy*, 24 MILLENNIUM 507, 516–17 (1995).

5. This is the main theme of a collection of essays: GLOBAL TRANSFORMATION: CHALLENGES TO THE STATE SYSTEM (Yoshikazu Sakamoto ed., 1994).

6. For important study of conceptual underpinnings, see R.B.J. WALKER, INSIDE/OUTSIDE: INTERNATIONAL RELATIONS AS POLITICAL THEORY (1993); for classic conceptualization, see Garrett Hardin, *The Tragedy of the Commons*, 162 SCIENCE 1243–48 (1968).

of problems present on the environmental agenda, all governments are increasingly subject to the discipline of global capital in relation to organizing their activities and setting their priorities with respect to public expenditures and goals or, if excluded from participation in the world economy (North Korea, Cuba, Iraq) or self-excluded (Iran to some extent), are suffering immediate consequences that seem to be accentuating mass misery. So understood, governments, virtually without exception, are both ethically and politically led to the conclusion that they must gain as favorable access as possible to the global marketplace as "the only game in town." Among the impacts of globalization is the reduction of the political space or of capacity to implement divergent policy choice at the level of states, and the loss of effective supremacy by governments over those aspects of the internal or territorial domain that relate to marketized external relations.[7] This relative decline of options for the exercise of state power expresses itself in many ways, including the substantial convergence of mainstream political parties around a common neo-liberal set of perspectives.[8] This development is particularly evident with respect to the realignment of social democratic parties around the world, whether it be Labour in Britain or the Democratic Party in the United States or the Socialists in France or Japan, the regrouped Communist parties in Eastern Europe and Russia, or even the welfare-oriented governing parties in the Nordic countries. All of these mainstream political leaders have become de facto converts to neo-liberalism under a common set of historical circumstances, and all of these societies seem similarly confronted by a multi-dimensional fiscal crisis that places a premium on reduced government expenditures of public goods of all varieties (welfare, education, even culture and recreation), and definitely includes environmental protection.[9]

7. Of course, as East Asian countries have demonstrated, it is possible to combine an effective adapatation to globalization with authoritarian control over many aspects of civic life, but for disruptive impacts of globalization on the historic attempt to achieve domestic stability by balancing market against social claims, see Ruggie, *supra* note 4.

8. Whether to conceive of this homogenizing trend as primarily expressive of a decline of state power, or merely a matter of reorientation by way of externalization or internationalization, is a complex matter that is not essential to the argument of this chapter; for the former view, see CAMMILLERI & FALK, *supra* note 1; for the latter view, see GLOBAL TRANSFORMATION, *supra* note 5. Of course, as will be discussed, backlash parties and tendencies challenge this convergence.

9. It is notable that, despite its strength in governmental bureaucracies and as a pressure group, defense expenditures are generally declining in this period and would be declining further if politicians were not hiding certain welfare policies, such as preserving jobs, within the relative immunity of defense appropriations; for instance, a Pentagon aide, Daniel Donald, estimated that as much as 40% of the current defense budget is devoted to non-security,

At this point, it is fair to ask, "Why is the neo-liberal consensus a matter of great concern from the perspective of environmental protection?" My short answer, which will be discussed below in more detail, is that the costs of many forms of adequate environmental protection are not regarded as compatible with such objectives of marketization as privatization, economic growth, minimized taxation, and a non-intrusive public sector, as the state loses autonomy in relation to market forces, the latter gain greater autonomy. These tendencies are accentuated by the unevenness of material conditions around the world, which makes it difficult for some actors to feel responsible for environmental decay of a global scope and others to feel unfairly expected to bear disproportionate costs in relation to environmental cleanups. In my view, globalization's unfolding and multidimensional types of inequality, coupled to neo-liberalism, is one of the main reasons why the environmental movement has run out of steam.[10] The impact of neo-liberal priorities, especially reliance on economic growth to resolve legitimate public goods demands, was evident even before Rio, but has certainly become more pronounced since the Earth Summit in 1992.[11] The core of my argument is that globalization, as it has unfolded on this planet up to this point, is virtually forcing political leaders to embrace neo-liberalism as an orientation toward foreign economic policy, that this discourages the investment of additional public funds in environmental protection, and that it also exerts continuous downward societal pressures on jobs and personal security to an extent that significantly reduces citizen support for environmentalist priorities and policies because of the seeming opportunity costs incurred.

Whether these developments will unleash sufficient countervailing forces to produce a further reorientation of the state is uncertain, as is the possibility of such adjustment at the level of the state or even the region; to revive the domestic social contract of the welfare

essentially welfare, purposes. Lecture, Mediterranean Academy of Diplomatic Studies, Malta, Mar. 18, 1996.

10. On the historical character of globalization and its non-determined evolution, see IMMANUEL WALLERSTEIN, GEOPOLITICS AND GEOCULTURE: ESSAYS IN A CHANGING WORLD-SYSTEM (1991); Robert W. Cox, *Social Forces, States, and World Orders: Beyond International Relations Theory, in* NEOREALISM AND ITS CRITICS 204–54 (Robert O. Keohane ed., 1986).

11. One line of influential argument was that the best way to enchance environmental quality was to encourage rapid economic growth and rising living standards that would then lead to greater societal concern with environmental protection. *See, e.g.*, Gene M. Grossman & Alan B. Krueger, Environmental Impacts of a North American Free Trade Agreement (Working Paper, 1991).

state era may require, under current world integrative conditions, the negotiation of an unprecedented global social contract, an undertaking of immense complexity, and one that will arouse the ideological fury of those who believe in neo-liberal approaches. There are also possibilities of regional frameworks that might balance market and social concerns in a more mutually satisfactory manner, as has been pioneered to an extent by the European Union. Whether this kind of regional approach will induce a different kind of protectionism in light of competitive disadvantages remains to be seen. The current impact of globalization also reflects several non-structural, or less obviously structural, factors, such as the decline of organized labor, the loss of public confidence in governmental bureaucracy, the discrediting of socialist thinking, the impact of computerization and the cyberspace frontier, and the paucity of visionary political leadership in the leading states. This lessening of governmental support for environmental goals is particularly evident with respect to such difficult and serious environmental problems of global scope as the control of global warming, and indeed is readily apparent in relation to the implementation of any environmental goal that requires a North/South allocation of burdens and depends upon the establishment of institutional regulatory authority at a regional or global level that may impinge upon the freedoms of global market forces.[12] It should be noted that the same pressures are making it more difficult to maintain, let alone expand, regulatory efforts of an environmental character at governmental levels within the state.

There is another preliminary question: "could globalization in the future produce a different orientation to public policy than that generated by neo-liberalism?" The basic answer would seem to be "no," if it is accepted that an important feature of globalization in the present phase of international history is the ascendancy of market forces that are not subject to territorial delimitation and that set the priorities for government by reference to efficiency in the use of resources, profit margins, and growth rates in trade and output, and tends to regard the specific diversion of resources for non-economic goals and values, such as the elimination of poverty and the protection of the environment, as wasteful and as a burden on the world

12. The ozone diplomacy, much commented upon, is an exception made viable by a number of helpful factors: commercial substitutes, short-term health effects, agreed and irrefutable scientific data, and relatively low adjustment costs; still the evidence suggests a losing battle as each year the size of the ozone hole grows larger and lasts longer. For an upbeat account of these achievements, see RICHARD ELLIOT BENEDICK, OZONE DIPLOMACY: NEW DIRECTIONS IN SAFEGUARDING THE PLANET (1991).

economy. According to neo-liberal purists, such ends should be pursued either as a matter of philanthropic initiative or be served by the overall spillover effects of maximizing and sustaining economic growth, a set of ideas that traces its lineage back to Adam Smith's powerful notion of "the invisible land."[13]

Whether this attribution of responsibility to globalization for declining support for environmental goals is accurate or not, it doesn't by itself explain why so little academic attention has been devoted to the manifest significance for environmental protection of global economic integration in relation to trade, investment, and financial markets. My own hypothesis is that a deceptive, often subconscious, type of "realist" thinking still prevails among most academic and other expert commentators, with the effect of continuing to treat states in two misleading respects. First of all, states continue to be viewed as the only significant actor in international life, thereby overlooking the important roles played by international institutions, transnational corporations and banks, and transnational civic initiatives. Second, and even more relevant, states are wrongly still treated as if relatively autonomous vis-à-vis market forces, as well as in relation to the ideological climate within which governments shape policy. The liberal variant leads to the same result, by emphasizing the emergence of a transnational civil society in which market forces are viewed favorably as an alternative to a state-centric world.[14]

An alternative explanation for the neglect of globalization may itself be partly ideological: namely, that the neo-liberal consensus that has taken hold since 1989 is so strong, and without any obvious constructive alternatives, that it has made it unfashionable and impractical to suggest, even indirectly, that there are serious concerns about relying on the various pillars of globalization and neo-liberalism such as deregulated and privatized capital to promote growth,

13. In effect, trusting the market to send the right signals is then reinforced by the allegedly empirical argument that higher living standards generate greater societal demand for better living conditions, including enviromental protection. *See* Grossman & Krueger, *supra* note 11.

14. The word "liberal" is confusing in its reference, as it signifies both an endorsement of the market and a commitment to human betterment as an intentional undertaking. Such a fusion is evident in the quintessential report, The Commission on Global Governance, Our Global Neighbourhood (1995). One scholar sees this report "as helping to develop public consciousness of international relations away from neorealist and neoliberal concerns with system management, toward a terrain in which the moral consequences of dominant structures and practices must be faced. To this author, the articulation of alternative visions *of the big picture* in a way that links power to moral vision is one of the Report's strengths." John MacMillan, *A Kantian Protest Against the Peculiar Discourse of Inter-Liberal State Peace*, 24 MILLENNIUM 549, 561 (1995). For a more critical review of the report, see Richard Falk, *Liberalism at the Global Level: The Last of the Independent Commissions?*, 24 MILLENNIUM 563 (1995).

profits, trade, investment, and, most of all, human well-being within an international framework with as few governmental interferences as possible. Within such a framework of thought, environmental protection as a matter of governmental responsibility is then inevitably regarded, although not entirely accurately, as a burden on the posited utopia of global marketization.[15]

Closely linked to this inhibition is the reluctance of governments ever to acknowledge their own diminished autonomy and loss of capacity to uphold territorial interests, and thereby act on behalf of the well-being of their entire citizenry and in relation to the prospects of future generations. This reluctance is intensified to the extent that the government is itself dominated by those of neo-liberal persuasion, conceiving of reduced support for public goods as intrinsically beneficial for the overall evolution of society. Some useful analysis has attempted to circumvent this polarized view of the relationship by seeking to specify a middle ground in which degrees of environmental protection can be achieved within the characteristic frameworks of economic globalization, implying that polarization of approach with regard to neo-liberal priorities will not yield constructive results.[16]

Despite acknowledging the obvious practical benefits of searching for as much common ground as possible, it seems important also to face clearly the extent of the threat posed by neo-liberal thinking to the overall task of environmental protection. To encourage a more pointed dialogue on the question of neo-liberalism, I propose to violate the taboo that discourages serious consideration of how globalization is complicating what would, in any event, be an already daunting task of environmental protection facing the world as it nears the end of the most turbulent century in all of human history and prepares to embark upon a new millennium.[17] In this sense, I am

15. Even Stephan Schmidheiny concedes that there may be problems if the market sends the wrong signals with regard to "sustainability," emphasizing short-term profits rather than sustainable growth. *See* SCHMIDHEINY, CHANGING COURSE: A GLOBAL BUSINESS PERSPECTIVE ON DEVELOPMENT AND THE ENVIRONMENT (1992).

16. A particularly good example is Benedict Kingsbury, *The Tuna-Dolphin Controversy, the World Trade Organization, and the Liberal Project to Reconceptualize International Law, in* 5 YEARBOOK OF INTERNATIONAL ENVIRONMENTAL LAW 1 (1995).

17. Even with environmentally sensitive political leadership in control of governments that were not under pressure from economic globalization, the task would, in any event, be daunting, given: unevenness of perception and position, the magnitude of potential costs, the long lead time often required for adjustment, the divergencies in diagnostic and corrective assessments; to a degree, this sense of the special difficulty of meeting the environmental challenge has been embodied in emerging international environmental law in the form of "the precautionary principle."

guided by those critical canons of scholarly orientation that seek to understand problems and issues as clearly as possible even if the outcome does not fit smoothly within the framework of current policy debate, and thus risks ideological dismissal as "alienated" or "utopian."

## B. TWO RECONSIDERATIONS

More than 25 years ago, when I first became concerned about the tensions between an expanding industrial civilization and environmental stability for the planet, I was convinced that the political fragmentation associated with the state system would make it virtually impossible to achieve the degree of transnational environmental protection required to address the range of emerging problems of regional and global scope. In other words, that a world of states, each with its own self-serving rendering of historical experience and bolstered by deeply ingrained traditions of sovereignty, varying material circumstances, and wildly uneven perceptions of the character and seriousness of different types of environmental harm, was structurally incapable of meeting the ecological challenge.[18] It was then my firm conviction that only a much more centralized governance capacity would be capable of establishing and implementing the scale and extent of environmental regulation that was needed to ensure human survival, much less protect the prospects of future generations from the specter of multi-dimensional environmental decay.[19] Several supplemental factors of a contextual character appeared at the time to reinforce this conclusion, especially the short time horizons of leaders and citizens in most countries; the urgency of rapid, unhampered, development for governments with large, rapidly growing populations; the materialist character of modern civilization that measured progress and happiness mainly by reference to consumerist attainments of affluence; and, possibly most fundamental of all, a rapidly increasing world population that was being socialized by the global

18. For recent analysis along these lines, see WILLIAM OPHULS, ECOLOGY AND THE POLITICS OF SCARCITY REVISITED (1992).

19. RICHARD FALK, THIS ENDANGERED PLANET (1971); RICHARD FALK, A STUDY OF FUTURE WORLDS (1975); I tried hard to make clear that such a call for what is now described as "global governance" was not to be confused with "world government," which I opposed as a project on practical and normative grounds. For recent discussion reflecting a similar disposition toward this distinction, see Our Global Neighbourhood, *supra* note 14, at 2–7.

media to anticipate ever higher living standards based on lifestyle models prevailing in already highly industrial societies that encouraged wasteful and polluting patterns of energy use, especially in relation to transportation and housing. Part of this earlier pessimism about environmental protection was connected with the deeply modernist convictions of a generally emancipatory character that lifestyle choices, including family size, are matters of individual choice that should never be controlled by the state, and that even attempts to facilitate personal choice by way of education, family clinics, and abortions were suspect intrusions on the part of the state, and have become subjects of intense controversy.[20] This libertarian core of beliefs in modern thought and practice is closely related to the long struggle to impose limits on the absolutist claims of church and state, representing an important effort in the West to strengthen civil society in relation to competing sources of authority, and to establish the foundations for contemporary constitutionalism, including human rights.

Although most of these background features persist to a significant degree, I now believe that this earlier analysis was badly mistaken in several key respects.[21] Most dramatically, the earlier diagnosis greatly underestimated the capacity of political action in democratic societies to put environmental protection on the agenda of politicians and leaders in a substantial and responsive manner. It also literalized, and thereby falsified, the environmental danger by relying on various alarmist portrayals of resource stocks and polluting trends as measured by reference to a very specific time frame of a decade or so.[22] Also greatly unanticipated by my earlier line of interpretation was the innovative character and impressive impacts of environmental activism, both within countries and transnationally, dramatized in the 1980s by the formation and rapid growth of green parties in a

20. When China adopted a one-child-per-family approach in the late 1970s to stem its population growth, it was widely criticized for adopting authoritarian methods and some cruel results were highlighted by the media; this criticism was rarely balanced with an appreciation that China had inaugurated a vast social innovation that probably contributed greatly to regional stability and made domestic well-being more attainable for a larger proportion of the Chinese population.

21. Ken Conca offers a two-step diagnostic development that shifts from a "limits" argument to a "human impact" approach. *See* Conca, *Environmental Protection, International Norms, and State Sovereignty: The Case of the Brazilian Amazon, in* Beyond Westphalia? State Sovereignty and International Intervention 147 (Gene M. Lyons and Michael Mastanduno eds., 1995).

22. The most notorious of these was the Club of Rome report: Donella Meadows et al., The Limits to Growth (1972).

series of European countries, by the success of the militant tactics of Greenpeace in raising environmental consciousness on several crucial issues, and by the counter-conference presence of activists in official gatherings of states dedicated to environmental protection, especially the 1972 United Nations Conference on the Human Environment held in Stockholm.[23] Many of the effects of environmentalism were and are, of course, deeply disappointing to the most ardent environmentalists, but nevertheless are remarkable in view of the previous centuries of public and governmental indifference to environmental protection other than in local circumstances, and certainly beyond territorial limits and in light of the original hostility with which business and government reacted to calls in the early 1970s for environmental action as false prophecies of doom and as a menace to economic prosperity.[24] With speed and conviction, major governments overnight reallocated public resources to address serious environmental threats, facilitated the organization of several prominent global conferences, and negotiated a series of important treaties that impressively strengthened the environmental role of international law, although enforcement was left largely in the hands of states.[25] Emerging scientific confirmation of some environmental concerns helped, as did the badgering of environmental think tanks such as the widely respected Worldwatch Institute. Perhaps this rising crescendo of environmentalist sentiment during this first phase of global environmental activist success was well epitomized by a British newspaper that reported on a London conference to strengthen the Montreal Protocol on Ozone Depletion with the headline "The Greening of Mrs. Thatcher," an expression of the happy implication that if even such a dogmatic free-marketeer as Margaret Thatcher could be turned into an instant environmentalist, then the environmental movement had indeed moved into the political mainstream and the prospects for planetary survival definitely looked brighter than they had just a few years earlier.[26]

23. Possibly the most important impact of all was the degree to which mainstream political parties and international institutions were greened, partly by shifts in societal values and partly by coopting tactics that expressed concerns about losing voter support. For the range of effects on international institutions, see THE GREENING OF INTERNATIONAL LAW (Philippe Sand ed., 1994).

24. For a balanced assessment, see PHILIPPE SAND, INTERNATIONAL ENVIRONMENTAL LAW: EMERGING TRENDS AND IMPLICATIONS FOR TRANSNATIONAL CORPORATIONS (1994)(U.N. Publications, Enviroment Series No. 3); *see also* Andrew Hurrell and Benedict Kingsbury, *The International Politics of the Environment: An Introduction, in* THE INTERNATIONAL POLITICS OF ENVIRONMENT 1 (Andrew Hurrell and Benedict Kingsbury eds., 1992).

25. See useful analysis along these lines in Conca, *supra* note 21.

26. In stark contrast, however, is the opposite pattern in relation to the American Vice President, Al Gore, who was on record as a dedicated environmentalist before becoming a

But despite this earlier environmental surge, all is not well in the 1990s, and it is here that the impact of globalization comes in most evidently. As I see it, the immediate threats of environmental decay arise now more directly from the passivity of states that have been "internationalized" in their priorities and weakened in relation to the protection of territorial concerns than, as I had earlier argued, from the anti-environmentalism of strong states and the statist structure of international society. By this I mean that internationalized and weakened states, including those that are still seen as the most powerful in terms of wealth and coercive capabilities, are now constrained and conditioned by the neo-liberal discipline of global capital and certain related reinforcing developments, and are increasingly acting to minimize and discourage all public goods expenditures including those relating to environmental protection. Governments faced with fiscal, budgetary, and trade deficits, and a perceived need to promote economic growth and exports without relying on Keynesian methods, are led to remove, or at least to minimize, regulatory obstacles on private sector initiatives that had been erected during the earlier surge of environmentalist concern.[27]

There is another related development that undermines my earlier line of analysis in a manner that seems quite revealing. I had earlier believed that the kind of global governance that was needed to address environmental challenges effectively could only be established in an atmosphere of ecological crisis that would overcome societal inertia and the anticipated unwillingness of governments to diminish the extent of their territorial sovereignty. I believed then that a sense of crisis was needed to generate the intensity of pressure that could alone break the grip of the established order as concentrated in governmental institutions at the level of the state. It was my view that the state system was too embedded in rigid bureaucratic practices and beliefs to make the necessary transfers of sovereignty on the basis

national leader but felt politically obliged to downplay, if not altogether obscure, such commitments; indeed, in the 1992 presidential campaign, the incumbent, George Bush, gleefully derided Gore as "Mr. Environment," and elicited no reaffirmation of enviromentalist concerns from the Democratic Party leadership. The theme of that election was encapsulated, "It's the economy, stupid!"

27. It may be better to use the language of "reorienting" rather than "weakening" in discussing the altered role of the state; the real change brought about by globalization, in conjunction with other factors, is to make the state relatively far more responsive to global market-oriented pressures and more resistant to people-oriented territorial pressures and, in this regard, to move away from Keynesian activism in the direction of lessening regulatory burdens associated with government.

of rational calculations of enlightened self-interest and long-range sustainability, that governmental leaders would oppose vigorously and successfully, under normal conditions, the necessary relocation of political authority and capacities in international institutions, as such a process would be correctly perceived as diminishing sovereign rights and would be resisted primarily by invoking the banner of national sovereignty. But what has been occurring during the last decade in relation to economic global governance suggests that such an understanding of statist inertia and resistance to international institutionalization was partial and incomplete at best. With the creation of the World Trade Organization, the strengthening of the Bretton Woods institutions, and the various moves at the regional level associated with NAFTA and Maastricht, it is evident that leading governments and political elites, even on occasion without the genuine support of their own citizenry, have been prepared, so as to augment economic growth prospects, to accept, and even to advocate strongly, significant inroads on their independent capacity to act on behalf of purely territorial pressures. The rise of such idiosyncratic and reactionary populist figures as Patrick Buchanan and Ross Perot is precisely a consequence of their defense of territorial sovereignty and their almost lone willingness in the political arena to heed the protectionist and xenophobic pleas of workers and others displaced and threatened by globalization and the economic migrations that it induces.

In effect, economic globalization suggests that the state system is not nearly as rigid structurally as had been widely believed. If leaders are oriented toward an expanded globalizing role for political and economic authority, then the initiative for diminished territorial sovereignty may be promoted enthusiastically by governmental elites and institutions. Partly, this is a consequence of the outlook of neoliberalism and partly it reflects the perception that if economic growth and profits are the test of policy, then markets, decisional frameworks, and communities larger than the state are indispensable.

## C. ADAPTIVE ALTERNATIVES

From the perspective of environmentalist priorities, there are several adaptive responses to globalization that seem to be on the horizon of political possibility. Before discussing briefly their relative feasibility, I should make clear that globalization is not entirely negative in relation to human well-being, including the environmental agenda. As the experience of countries in East and South Asia has made clear, the mobility of capital has enabled the most rapid sustained economic development in all of history, with obvious benefit to a large proportion of large populations that had previously seemed indefinitely trapped in a spiral of poverty, population growth, and pollution. By its very nature of seeking efficient use of capital, globalization promotes a leveling up of world society, provided certain initial conditions for competitiveness are present. The plight of sub-Saharan Africa suggests, however, that if conditions for profitable return on private capital are not present, then globalization as guided by the postulates of neo-liberalism tends to polarize disparities, thereby magnifying economic and human distress. Subsidization diminishes, and capital flows predominantly to those regions and circumstances that provide stability and reassurance of rapid returns on investment. Nevertheless, as a broad historical trend, there is no doubt that globalization has generated some powerful forces that are moving the world toward greater inter-regional and intra-regional equality, and have already rendered obsolete, in many respects, the old categories of global configuration based on distinguishing North/South, First World/Third World, and West/non-West. What best expresses the main geopolitical hierarchy in this early phase of the era of globalization is some application of the non-geographically bound categorization based on center, semi-periphery, and periphery.[28] What has undermined the claims of the periphery on global public goods in this period has been the ideological consensus (on neo-liberalism) and the geopolitical reconciliation (the end of the Cold War) at the center.[29]

Globalization is not necessarily detrimental to environmental protection even as guided by neo-liberalism. For instance, there are various market incentives to evolve environmental benign technologies and products, and to disseminate them in a manner that challenges environmentally detrimental activities. Furthermore, the prospect of an end to the epoch of hydrocarbons is stimulating market mechanisms to push for more research and development on alternate sources of energy that are less damaging to the environment.

28. For interpretation and recent formulation by social scientists who have been most creative in their reliance on such a taxonomy, see SAMIR AMIN, RE-READING THE POSTWAR PERIOD: AN INTELLECTUAL ITINERARY (1994), and IMMANUEL WALLERSTEIN, AFTER LIBERALISM (1995).

29. In the Cold War period, the political destiny of disadvantaged countries provided major stakes in the East/West rivalry, with the two superpowers using resources to subsidize, or intervene, on behalf of ideological surrogates; without the Cold War calculus, these outcomes in peripheral countries are matters of geopolitical indifference.

It is also true that the governance capacities that have been fashioned to promote trade and investment could, in an altered ideological climate or given a different kind of accountancy on costs and benefits, easily incorporate environmental concerns. In a sense, under altered conditions the market could begin sending more of the right signals, and earlier. And finally, given the social inequalities that exist, economic pressures for a more level playing field on wages do discourage the most environmentally irresponsible behavior. The leveling-up phenomenon, while having mixed impacts by increasing both environmentally damaging consumerism and citizen demands for a cleaner and healthier environment, can help to reinvigorate support for environmental regulation at a regional and global level.

Nevertheless, it is my basic contention that economic globalization is environmentally harmful in its cumulative effects as currently operating within the broad parameters of neo-liberal ideology. The broadness of these parameters takes account of the quite illiberal, mercantilist approach of several Asian countries that rely on a far more active role for the state in planning investment and trade policy.[30]

Against this general background, there are, in my view, several adaptive responses to globalization that give some promise of diminishing, but of altogether eliminating, such harmful effects.

## 1. The Path of Trust and Reliance on the Enlightened Self-Interest of the Private Sector

Maurice Stong gave this approach great prominence at the UNCED at Rio in 1992. He invited the Swiss industrialist, Stephan Schmidheiny, to be his advisor and encouraged him to form the Business Council for Sustainable Development that inserted an active voice of business into the debate at the Earth Summit about how "sustainable development," as the agreed goal, could be best achieved. The basic message of the Business Council was to endorse the goals of sustainable development, to solicit public trust, to affirm

30. Also, there are misleading and contradictory features of the application of neo-liberalism. *See* Stephen Gill, *Globalisation, Market Civilisation, and Disciplinary Neoliberalism*, 24 Millennium 399 (1995); Gill writes that "[t]he current phase of economic globalisation has come to be characterized increasingly not by free competition as idealised in neoclassical theory, but by *oligopolistic neoliberalism:* oligopoly and protection for the strong and a socialisation of their tasks, market discipline for the weak." *Id.* at 405.

its own faith in the market and the neo-liberal outlook, to rely exclusively on growth for human betterment, and to propose some modest adjustments to encourage the market to send better signals on cost and price, especially in relation to longer term effects.[31] Although Schmidheiny insists that the Business Council for Sustainable Development "speaks not for global business but as a small group of business leaders, by definition represents a small minority," there is a definite impression that the outlook presented in their Declaration and in the book is the best that can be expected at this time, and represents a vanguard of business leaders who do view the viability of the world economy to rest on a degree of attentiveness to environmental protection.[32] Without adopting the label, the Business Council reflects a "stakeholder" approach that is supposed to offset the acknowledged reduction of the environmental protection role that had been earlier played by the state. In the language of the Declaration, "[t]he world is moving toward deregulation, price initiatives, and global markets. This requires corporations to assume more social, economic, and environmental responsibility in defining their roles. We must expand our concept of those who have a stake in our operations to include not only employees and shareholders but also suppliers, customers, neighbors, citizens' groups, and others." And further, "[p]rogress toward sustainable development makes good business sense because it can create competitive advantages and new opportunities."[33] The book contains self-proclaimed success stories that support these general sentiments and manifests the enlightened business environmentalism of such dubious multinational corporate players as Shell Oil, DuPont, and ALCOA.

Without doubting the veracity of these authors, I would still say, "if you are willing to believe in this approach, then you are inviting environmental catastrophe." There is nothing in the history of business operations to suggest that the long-term public good can be safely entrusted to those whose priority is short-term profits. To some extent, such claims could be credible only if accompanied by a realization that a profound change in business orientation is being proposed, and this is hinted at somewhat by the choice of *Changing Course* as the title. But on a deeper level, the reassurance moves in

31. This perspective is fully set forth in a book growing directly out of this experience: Stephan Schmidheiny, Changing Course: A Global Business Perspective on Development and the Enviroment (1992).

32. *Id.* at xxi; the Declaration is reproduced at xi–xiii.

33. *Id.* at xiii.

the opposite direction, insisting that the fundamental solution for human misery remains market-driven growth: ". . . we do not base our hopes for success on radical changes in human nature or on the creation of a utopia. We take humans the way we find them, the way we are all made, with all our strengths and weaknesses."[34]

The problematic character of this perspective is that if it is meaningful, then it represents an abandonment of neo-liberalism, and a back-door return to a kind of eco-social activism with agency shifted from the state to the market. As such, as with other approaches to stakeholder capitalism, it engenders a sharp backlash from the powerful gatekeepers of neo-liberalism.[35]

Both the logic of the market and the history of private sector operations suggest the implausibility of relying on the self-corrective mechanisms of the market and the wisdom of business leaders to protect the general public interest in sustainable development. Those in positions of responsibility in large institutions, whether public or private, are not trustworthy, simply because their own job security and respectability depends on delivering short-term benefits to their principal constituency, whether it be the citizenry or shareholders. In general, public institutions have the advantage over private ones because their core mandate is to protect the public, but to the extent that governmental bureaucracies endorse the neo-liberal creed, their behavior would also avoid encumbering market operations. Arguably, private institutions are more efficient and less corrupt than their public analogues, but their whole orientation is to treat public goods as a matter of public relations rather than as a cost of doing business. There are variations, of course, but the idea of a self-regulated world economy is as close to the projection of a negative utopia as the political imagination is capable of producing at this historical time.

34. *Id.* at xxii.

35. See many critiques of "stakeholder capitalism" from these perspectives, including cover story, THE ECONOMIST, Feb. 10, 1996, at 9, 23–25; typically pointed is William Safire's equating of "the stakeholder society" with what he calls "the New Socialism" in William Safire, *"New Socialism" Menaces Corporate Headquarters in America*, INT'L HERALD TRIB., Feb. 27, 1996; *see also* Editorial, *Europe fails its jobs test*, INT'L HERALD TRIB., Mar. 16, 1996 at 8; Lawrence Malkin, *Wall Street Plunges 3% On Strong Jobs Data*, INT'L HERALD TRIB.,, Mar.9–10, 1996. In relation to introducing environmental standards into trade relations, see, e.g., Reginald Dale, *"Blue-Green" Danger Signs for Trade*, INT'S HERALD TRIB., Feb. 20, 1996; Reginald Dale, *Coming Soon: Worldwide Free Trade*, INT'L HERALD TRIB., Mar. 8, 1996. On the marginalization of environmental concerns in the setting of NAFTA, see Alberto Szekely, *International Law in North America: Beyond NAFTA*, *in* GREENING INTERNATIONAL LAW 250 (Philippe Sands ed., 1994).

Without demonizing business, it is possible to point impressionistically to the results of deregulated economic activities. Consider the case of Cambodia. Desperate for development in the aftermath of a ruinous and still unresolved civil war, the Cambodian government invited foreign lumber companies into the country on a deregulated basis. Recently, King Norodom Sihanouk stated that Cambodia as a country faces "death" from two distinct sources: "Wars without end and total deforestation, it is this which would threaten the death of our homeland."[36] There are many instances of corporations forbidden to sell pesticides and drugs in the North dumping these products on the South, that is, privileging profits over a decent concern for the well-being of people in vulnerable societies. The struggles of tobacco companies to survive, and to promote smoking in ways that divert attention from adverse health effects is also a well-known scandal, but more broadly illustrative of corporate priorities. It is important to realize that, with the mobility of operations, most business undertakings are driven by profit-maximization in the short-run and the move to alternate markets and sources of supply and technologies in the middle-term.

Even without the lure of profits, even absent corruption, there is ample reason to be skeptical about all positions on the environment that rely basically on a structure of trust. Respected governments in countries with long records of constitutionalism have exposed their own citizens to horrifying risks so as to serve bureaucratic purposes. One thinks of American military personnel exposed to Agent Orange in the Vietnam War or of workers in nuclear facilities, or more morbidly of tainted blood distributed without informing the users about known risks as occurred in France and Japan.[37] The bottom line is the need for checks and balances within whatever institutional arrangement is relied upon to protect the public good. When states are deeply involved in building confidence in the effectiveness of international arrangements, the demands for verifying compliance are very exacting, as in arms control agreements; and in the absence of such agreements, the operative basis of security rests on the premise of distrust, as with respect to nuclear deterrence. And certainly

36. INT'L HERALD TRIB.,Feb. 20, 1996.

37. See report of the resignation of Kiyoo Mogi, head of Japan's earthquake prediction program because of the failure of the Japanese government to warn the citizenry of earthquakes unless the prediction was of the order that could be taken as proof. Because warnings would be disruptive, even if prudent, the bureaucratic disposition is to await the disaster and then react. *See Ignored, Japan's Earthquake Predictor Quits,* Mar. 20, 1996.

strong checks are required whenever institutional policy goals seem to be in frequent tension with public policy goals, as is the case with environmental protection entrusted to the private sector. In this regard, the Business Council initiative is rather meaningless, or worse, a source of false reassurance, unless it is woven into a reliable framework of regulatory authority with a strong institutional base at the global level. Nothing that has occurred in the last several years suggests any reason to alter this skeptical view of what can be expected to result from self-regulating approaches by businesses in relation to sustainable development.

As Peter Haas and Ernst Haas have written, "[i]n the absence of a dominant state willing to lead, a strong, shared universal vision, or a world government, collective responses to the global problematique depend on international institutional mechanisms."[38]

The conclusion, then, is that, in an atmosphere dominated by the neo-liberal consensus, it would be foolish to expect very much by way of profit-making adjustments on the part of global market forces for the sake of sustainable development. Only in a more supportive atmosphere of environmental governance could such initiatives as those depicted in *Changing Course* have much prospect of exerting a strong constructive impact. It is evident that business and finance realizes this need for governance as it promotes congenial institutional initiatives at a regional and global level, epitomized at this time by support for a neo-liberal identity for the World Trade Organization.

Closely related to the "trust us" line of argumentation is the more academically oriented "leave it to the market" attitude endorsed by most influential economists. In fact, their actual position is "leave it mainly to the market," or "presume that the market will signal environmental requirements in timely fashion." In the background of this view is the historically conditioned belief that the market has been responsible for a large and continuing improvement in the life circumstances of the present generation and all prior generations. Richard Cooper, a widely respected and influential economist, expresses this standard economistic view in the course of defending the reluctance of the United States to accept more environmentally stringent constraints on its growth prospects:

38. Peter M. Haas and Ernst B. Haas, *Learning to Learn: Improving International Governance*, GLOBAL GOVERNANCE I 255, 256 (1995).

> To put it bluntly, those [market-based] arrangements have directed an all-but-universal personal vice, greed, into socially constructive channels. Pursuit of personal gain under approximately competitive conditions in a stable social and political system receptive to new technologies has over the decades greatly increased the material well-being, reduced the drudgery of labour, increased leisure, lengthened life, increased tolerance of diversity, and created more possibilities for realization of human potential than any other arrangements known. Given that broad record of success, a heavy burden of proof must be met by proposals for radical alterations.[39]

Lawrence Summers uses a similarly economistic perspective to justify a cost-benefit approach to upholding the obligations of present policy to future generations, concluding that the best present return on investment will yield, automatically, a positive result for the future. As Summers contends:

> [s]urely it is ethically relevant that our grandchildren will in all likelihood be better off than we are. While nobody can accurately predict long-term growth rates, remember that standards of living are three times higher than 60 years ago in the United States, seven times higher in Germany, and almost ten times higher in Japan. Should my American grandparents have reduced their standard of living, when life was considerably more nasty, brutish and short than now, to leave raw materials in the ground for my benefit?[40]

Summers makes the implicit leap of faith that the future can be reproduced in a manner that resembles what has transpired in the relatively recent past. No account is taken of serious doubts about the carrying capacity of the earth, the growth of world population and living standards, and the various ecological warning signs such as increasing holes in the ozone shield, data on global warming, and depleted fish stocks.

There is a kind of ahistorical commonsensical view of economic growth and its benefits that tends to be cavalier about environmental

39. Richard N. Cooper, *United States Policy Toward the Global Environment, in* The International Politics of the Environment 290, 290–91 (Andrew Hurrell and Benedict Kingsbury eds., 1992); *see also* Grossman & Krueger, *supra* note 11.

40. Lawrence Summers, Letter, The Economist, May 30, 1992, at 65 *as reprinted in* International Environmental Law 268–71 (Lakshunan D. Guruswamy, Sir Geoffrey Palmer and Burns H. Weston eds., 1994). *Compare* Edith Brown Weiss, In Fairness to Future Generations 5–15 (1989).

harm, taking added comfort from the exaggerated warnings of the 1970s about dire results that have never materialized and underpinned by a kind of faith that technology will find the cure should the market fail to signal its own warnings. Globalization reinforces these viewpoints because they correspond with the discipline of global capital and the marketization of economic activity. As indicated earlier, such reliance provides no rationale for diverting resources for the sake of added environmental protection. As such, economism is not truly an adaptive strategy, despite its central message of "relax!" as it overlooks the serious disabling of the state as an actor capable of challenging as necessary environmentally destructive aspects of a more integrated global economy.

## 2. The Politics of Populist Backlash as a Reaction to Globalization

The rise of a new rightist politics as typified by Patrick J. Buchanan and Le Pen, and the recent labor unrest in France, Belgium, and elsewhere, are expressive of one type of backlash against the negative territorial impacts of globalization on vulnerable sectors of the domestic workforce.[41] Other negative reactions against globalization feed into the rise of religious and identity politics, the revival of traditional cultural values, and essentially anti-modern conservatism that is evident in many settings. Unlike the rightist populism that is drawing support from disadvantaged working people, the more culturally oriented backlashes are concerned with the alleged cultural decadence of the West.

These reactive movements that are arising to challenge the globalizing momentum are not at all conducive to environmental protection as their locus of understanding seems to be either mainly economic or principally cultural. Neither critique of globalization offers much aid and comfort to environmentalists or to any meaningful commitment to sustainable development, and, because of its priorities, might actually exert additional pressure upon environmental stability.

41. For assessment of a growing constituency for such political extremism, see Klaus Schwab and Claude Smadja, *Start Taking the Backlash Against Globalization Seriously*, INT'L HERALD TRIB., Feb. 1, 1996; *James Bennet, Buchanan Targets Free-Trade Policy*, INT'S HERALD TRIB., Mar. 22, 1996.

## 3. A Resurgence and Strengthening of Globalization-From-Below

Environmentalism from its outset has depended strongly on transnational and grassroots initiatives.[42] As suggested, the Earth Summit in 1992 was a mobilizing occasion for transnational efforts, bringing together an extraordinary range of activists from all parts of the world. Since Rio there has been a loss of focus for environmental efforts, and an overall preoccupation in civil society with social, economic, and occasionally cultural, issues. The environment, with some exceptions, seems again relegated to "low politics," the back burner of human concerns. There remains a powerful latent transnational environmental capability as was evident in the success of the 1994 Greenpeace campaign to reverse the Shell Oil decision, approved by the British government, to sink an oil rig, the Brent Spar, in the North Sea. Controversy persists as to whether the Greenpeace opposition was justified with respect to the likelihood of serious environmental harm, but what remains beyond doubt is that the tactics of a threatened boycott of Shell's network of service stations in Europe and public pressure was effective in reversing a policy of a major transnational corporation. In the public press Greenpeace was criticized for its tactics and the media lamented its status as "an environmental superpower," but such action and reaction does support the view that one way to neutralize globalization-from-above in relation to marketized priorities is to support the moves of actors associated with globalization-from-below. The widely organized protest against French nuclear testing in 1995 again suggested the capacity to put sensitive state policy on the political agenda, but in this instance the tactics of confrontation and boycott failed to alter French policy, although arguably it imposed a high reputational and economic cost on France that is likely to influence its future approach to nuclear testing and weapons policy more generally.

At this stage, the transnational monitoring and protest roles are definitely of adaptive importance in two critical respects: first, by identifying serious specific issues of environmental harm or danger resulting from the acts of transnational corporations, environmental resistance operates in resistance and deterrent modes; second, by monitoring environmental trends in a reliable way, as is done by

42. For assessment, see RICHARD FALK, EXPLORATIONS AT THE EDGE OF TIME: PROSPECTS FOR WORLD ORDER (1992); and RICHARD FALK, ON HUMANE GOVERNANCE: TOWARD A NEW GLOBAL POLITICS (1995).

Worldwatch Institute and other groups, there is created an information base that challenges to various degrees the complacency of purely economistic appraisals of environmental danger. There is also the possibility of a reawakened grassroots and transnational militancy, possibly associated with some dramatic evidence of health impacts arising from a worsening of critical dimensions of environmental stability. There has been, since the late 1960s, a kind of cyclical attitude toward environmental protection, with a decade of heightened concern and activity alternating with decades of reduced interest and support. Whether the current down phase of the cycle will be followed by a new upswing is difficult to predict, but if the worsening environmental data result in harmful impacts that are so interpreted, then it is quite likely that new forms of environmental militancy of a transnational character are likely to emerge, in effect reinvigorating globalization-from-below, and possibly moving toward the construction of a global civil society that strikes a world-order bargain on social and environmental issues that effectively counters deregulation and other dangerous aspects of economic globalization.[43]

More broadly, Robert Cox has suggested that those who are adversely affected by globalization create the basis, at least, for a new dialectical surge of countervailing forces. The environmentalist constituency has definitely regarded globalizing tendencies to complicate the challenge of environmental protection, and would likely join in whatever politics resulted from countervailing perspectives, provided their essence was not of a purely negative, backlash character, as discussed above.[44]

## 4. Institutional Reformism That Achieves Global Environmental Governance Comparable to Global Economic Governance

It seems evident that there is an insufficient institutional basis for effective environmental regulation at this time. The United Nations Environmental Program (UNEP) is caught up in the downsizing momentum within the United Nations system generally. As such, despite

43. See the related argument to the effect that globalization has disturbed the historic domestic social contract that achieved economic stability in exchange for social protection of the workforce in John Gerard Ruggie, *At Home Abroad, Abroad at Home: International Liberalisation and Domestic Stability in the New World Economy*, 24 MILLENNIUM 507–26 (1995).

44. *See* Cox, *supra* note 3; Cox, *supra* note 10.

various sorts of reformist recommendations to strengthen the U.N. regulatory capacity with respect to the environment associated with various fiftieth anniversary proposals, none was politically resonant and nothing tangible was forthcoming, nor is it likely to be, given the current mood in world opinion on such matters.[45]

What is also worth pondering is whether the relatively impressive European achievement in reconciling market, social, and environmental goals at a regional basis can be reproduced in other regions, and whether the developments in Europe can withstand competitiveness pressures without regressing into various forms of protectionism. It may be possible that a historic compromise at the regional level can be negotiated within various regional settings that take account of uneven global circumstances.

As matters now stand, it will be only an argumentative point to mention the gross disparity between the institutional attention that is given to economic policy of global scope and that accorded to environmental issues. This reality can be underscored by the willingness of the heads of state of leading industrial countries, the Group of Seven, or G-7, to attend annual economic summits, and the absence of any disposition to accord high profile attention to environmental challenges. Even the Earth Summit was viewed more as a ritual occasion for heads of state to manifest concern than as a serious process for ensuring sustainable development. The main push was an effort by way of the Global Environmental Facility to subordinate environmental efforts to the administrative control of the Bretton Woods part of the world economy, that is, the institutional aspects that embody most fully neo-liberal precepts.[46]

## 5. Environmental Conditionality as a Strategy for Leveling the North/South Playing Field

To recover or retain market shares in the face of lower cost production in the South, there has been pressure around human rights

45. For a characteristic proposal to build up the U.N. institutional capacity in relation to environmental issues, see proposal to convert the U.N. Trusteeship Council into a body entrusted with managing and protecting the global commons set forth in OUR GLOBAL NEIGHBOURHOOD, *supra* note 14, at 251–53.

46. For a scathing indictment of the regressive attitude of the World Bank on environmental matters, see BRUCE RICH, MORTGAGING THE EARTH: THE WORLD BANK ENVIRONMENTAL IMPOVERISHMENT AND THE CRISIS OF DEVELOPMENT (1994). There is some indication of a more environmentally sensitive approach by the bank in the very recent past; for more sympathetic accounts, see Jacob B. Werksman, *Greening Bretton Woods*, in THE GREENING OF INTERNATIONAL LAW, *supra*

and environmental quality. The claim is that countries in the Asian-Pacific region, especially, have taken advantage of low wages, poor working conditions, and the absence of environmental regulation to achieve a competitive edge that is taking employment away from workers in the North. In effect, environmental conditionality would help level the playing field. Of course, there are many ironies present, as it was the South that for decades sought its own version of a level playing field, with its most concerted effort being the push in the mid-1970s to promote a New International Economic Order.[47]

## D. CONCLUSION

There are several main conclusions:

- it is important to consider the environmental impacts of a more globalized world economy, especially in relation to policy formulation by and orientation of governments;

- it appears that the main relevant impact of globalization has been to weaken political support for the use of public funds for the sake of environmental goals, especially of a predominantly global character;

- it seems that it will be difficult to challenge these adverse dimensions of globalization unless an alternative to neo-liberalism emerges at the level of national politics; and

- it may be that either anti-globalization backlashes of various kinds and regionalizing tendencies provide the most encouraging short-term prospect for giving credibility to a rhetorical commitment to sustainable development.

note 23, at 50–64; and Kenneth Paddington, *The Role of the World Bank*, in THE INTERNATIONAL POLITICS OF ENVIRONMENT, *supra* note 24, at 212–27.

47. See texts of the Declaration on the Establishment of a New Economic Order and its related Prorgram of Action in BASIC DOCUMENTS IN INTERNATIONAL LAW AND WORLD ORDER 550–67 (Burns H. Weston, Richard A. Falk and Anthony D'Amato eds., 2d ed. 1990).

# CHAPTER VI

# A PEACEFUL FUTURE FOR THE OCEANS?

It is both a privilege and a challenge to participate in a Pacem in Maribus conference, given the reputation that has accumulated over the years for leadership of the International Ocean Institute in forging a beneficial future for the oceans. Participation has an added personal dimension for me, as I have known and been a friend of Elisabeth Mann Borgese ever since she first began articulating her vision of the future of the oceans while she was still attached to the Center for Democratic Institutions in Santa Barbara. My attempt in this chapter is to consider somewhat critically the status of military activities on the oceans as it bears on the prospects for a peaceful future. I am drawn to this inquiry partly because so much of the literature seems, by its neglect, to regard virtually unregulated military activities on the oceans as either an unshakable fact of international life or as a non-problem. My own point of departure is to question both of these alternative lines of explanation.

First of all, let me indicate my approach to this topic. It would be quite sensible to conceive of "peace" in broad terms that encompass sustainable and equitable development, in keeping with the attractive view that a peaceful world implies something more than the absence of war, and that the something more involves establishing the conditions for human dignity without reliance on force. Despite the importance of such an argument for a broader conception of peace, my emphasis will be on peace more narrowly and traditionally understood as relating to those military activities associated with the use of the oceans, and the related quest for global security.

There have been several notable international controversies with significant military implications for the oceans in recent years: one thinks immediately of the Gulf War, with its massing of an armada of naval vessels; of the implementation of U.N. sanctions against Iraq and former Yugoslavia partly by way of an embargo on shipping; of

French testing of nuclear devices at underwater Pacific atoll sites; of the multi-state conflicts relating to sovereignty over the Spratley and Paracell Islands in the South China Sea; of the Canadian-Spanish conflict that moved close to war with respect to fishing rights in the North Atlantic; and of the conflict between Turkey and Greece concerning an Aegean islet. And yet, despite these diverse and repeated challenges to world order and others that could be mentioned, the subject matter of military activity in the oceans has been generally neglected in recent years. For instance, in Secretary-General Boutros Boutros-Ghali's *Agenda for Peace,* there is not a single reference to the oceans, or their possible relevance to the peacekeeping roles of the United Nations. At first glance, this seems to be such a gross oversight as to be impossible to explain, yet more carefully considered, this oversight is quite revealing of the deeper challenge posed by the effort to ensure a peaceful future for the oceans.[1] *Our Global Neighbourhood,* the report of the Commission on Global Governance, also exhibits this same failure to include the oceans in its comprehensive assessment of a world order agenda for the future, except to discuss ecological concerns in relation to upholding the global commons, and then only most scantily by reference in a single phrase that takes note of "the depletion of ocean fisheries."[2]

Let us consider some of the obvious reasons for this astonishing neglect of these obvious threats to a peaceful future for the oceans. To begin with, recent conflicts have been resolved or stalemated by diplomatic means, or seem to be over the horizon of present concerns as is the case with respect to a possible role for Chinese naval forces in support of their claims to Taiwan and in the Spratley Islands. Further, with the exception of China, the major maritime powers do not seem to have any strongly antagonistic interests and, more significantly, associate a strong sense of benefit with respect to existing permissive patterns of regulation relative to military activities on the oceans. More to the point, these powers are exceedingly sensitive about the expression of any doubts about the persisting viability of the traditional ocean security regime premised upon the "freedom"

1. This oversight is effectively commented upon in ELISABETH MANN BORGESE, OCEAN GOVERNANCE AND THE UNITED NATIONS 175–92 (1995).

2. COMMISSION ON GLOBAL GOVERNANCE, OUR GLOBAL NEIGHBOURHOOD 215 (1995). Perhaps most surprising is the failure to even mention the oceans in the course of an extended discussion of "demilitarizing international security" or elsewhere in a report of several hundred pages that claims to provide an overall picture of "global governance"; with oceans covering 70% of the Earth's surface, such an oversight cries out for explanation.

to make virtually unrestricted military use of all ocean waters lying beyond territorial waters. Non-maritime countries, in contrast, generally avoid these issues, presumably because of their sense of futility and impotence when it comes to questioning the military prerogatives of powerful states. But I believe we have reached a stage in world order experience where such unquestioning deference no longer continues to serve global security interests as we near the end of the millennium, and seems inconsistent with the fundamental effort of contemporary international law to confine the role of military force to strictly defensive roles.

With respect to public concern and scholarly attitudes, the neglect of military activities in the oceans can be explained somewhat differently. That portion of the public that considers such matters at all appears to believe that the sweep and extensiveness of the 1982 Convention on the Law of the Seas somehow establishes a framework that applies to all activities on the oceans, including those of a military character, and that these latter are sufficiently regulated by an overall imperative, as enunciated in the Convention's Preamble, to ". . . promote the peaceful uses of the seas and oceans," a general sentiment that is repeated several times in the body of the treaty, (e.g., in articles 88, 141, and 301), but each time without any implication of an operational interference with the traditional prerogatives of regional and global navies whose range of activities does not seem "peaceful" as that word is most generally understood.[3] In fact, the 1982 Convention does not attempt to regulate directly military activities as such beyond the bare minimum that has been accomplished over time by customary international law and by a few specialized treaties that have imposed several insignificant restrictions on maritime freedoms. In essence, the 1982 Convention gives global maritime powers an exemption from scrutiny with respect to their military activities, and as a practical and legal matter these maritime powers retain their full discretion to carry out whatever naval and related air activities their leaders deem relevant to national security and foreign policy goals even if such behavior generates widespread protest and controversy and is best understood as non-defensive. This failure to challenge traditional international naval prerogatives is forthrightly

3. These provisions affirm the abstract commitment under international law to act peacefully and in accordance with the U.N. Charter prohibition directed at all nondefensive uses of force, but specify no restraints of a more particular kind that might define such general obligations in the setting of naval activities.

expressed in President Clinton's Letter of Transmittal to the U.S. Senate to encourage ratification of the 1982 Convention. The American president asserts clearly that the treaty makes no inroads on traditional maritime freedoms on the oceans, and is helpful as it confirms these rights under contemporary conditions: "The Convention advances the interests of the United States as a maritime power. It preserves the right of the U. S. military to use the world's oceans to meet national security requirements . . ."[4] The one partial exception, which again lacks operational guidelines, is the generalized duty to exercise this freedom in a manner that does not interfere with other uses of the oceans. On this basis nuclear testing has always been controversial because the alleged security justifications pose manifest and serious environmental dangers for other legitimate ocean uses, and because, during and after the tests, navigational uses are precluded.

There is a further explanation for the failure to give attention to the military dimensions of ocean use. The most preoccupying types of conflict in the immediate past, that is, during the years since the end of the Cold War, have involved ethnic, nationalist, and religious/secular tensions within existing sovereign states. It is true that efforts to intervene in such conflicts have had an oceanic dimension arising from the imposition of sanctions and embargoes under U.N. auspices, but these activities have been protected from any serious critical scrutiny because they have generally enjoyed the imprimatur of the United Nations.

Perhaps, in the end, the most significant explanation of all for this disregard of conditions for peace on the oceans in the future is the continued prevalence of the realist mindset within the maritime countries. A realist consensus dominates the political imagination of scholars, media, and bureaucrats, particularly in the domain of security planning. We can notice here the contrast between the statist structure of international society with respect to peaceful activities on and in the oceans, and the geopolitical structure pertaining to security issues that results in unequal control and unilateral prerogatives for those few states with naval and air capabilities that extend beyond the local imperatives of territorial defense. In this respect, the geopolitical attachment of leading maritime powers to their freedom of action on the oceans is so firmly entrenched as to have the aura of being beyond

4. President William J. Clinton, Letter dated Oct. 7, 1994, 6 U.S. State Dep't Dispatch Supp. 1 (Feb. 1995).

the pale of responsible challenge, and as such should be accepted without question as a given, a part of the reality within which international political life unfolds. In my view, such a blinkering of inquiry is not healthy, because it implies that only when some awful breakdown of maritime order occurs in the future will proper attention be given to arguments for international reform. It is useful to recall that the most dramatic encounter of the Cold War, replete with apocalyptic implications for the entire world, was played out by the contending superpowers on the high seas in the course of the Cuban Missile Crisis in 1962. We will never know what might have happened if the Soviet Union had not backed down, despite their rather traditional statist claim of a right to supply weaponry to a friendly government (Cuba) that was under threat of attack. But we do know that the superpower leaders, once the crisis atmosphere cleared, realized how close they had come to catastrophe, and did take several prudential steps to avoid the repetition of such an incident. Yet this entire process of adjustment was a matter of discretion, as international law supplied no constraining guidelines even with respect to the deployment of nuclear weapons on naval vessels.[5]

It is helpful to recall that, prior to World War I in Europe, the grounding of "peace" in the balance-of-power mechanism was similarly taken for granted by all "responsible" opinion, and thus effectively sheltered from criticism. Are we then doomed to await oceanic catastrophes before we are allowed even to discuss the need and desirability of far stricter standards governing distant naval activities? Can we continue to believe that this unrestricted use of the oceans to project a given country's military power at great distances from national territory is consistent with the international law and Charter effort to restrict uses of force to exercises of self-defense or in furtherance of United Nations undertakings? Of course, the legal and political argument can become complicated if power projection on the oceans is linked to the security roles of defensive alliances and deterrence, as well as with anti-piracy and anti-terrorist activities that depend heavily upon the capabilities of these same few maritime powers. Part of the complexity arises because of the failure of the United Nations system to ensure the security of vulnerable states around the world, thereby often leaving the latter with the choice

5. To avoid an unwanted naval arms race on the ocean floor, several nuclear powers negotiated in 1971 a Treaty Prohibiting Emplacement of Nuclear Weapons on the Seabed and Ocean Floor. For convenient text, see BASIC DOCUMENTS IN INTERNATIONAL LAW AND WORLD ORDER 207–08 (Burns H. Weston, Richard A. Falk and Anthony D'Amato eds., 2d ed. 1990).

between seeking protection from a distant power or seeking to augment its own military capability in a manner that interferes with national priorities associated with the pursuit of development goals. But even conceding these functions for global navies, the difficulty remains that, under the current mandate to exercise freedom on the high seas, no distinction is drawn between constructive world order activities and traditional interventionary diplomacy which, it should be noted, even after the end of colonialism, moves predominantly from North to South. In this era of increasing globalization, there is also a strong, yet questionable, link between the dominant priorities of the world economy and the custodial role of military power as protector of the interests of global capital. Such a link was evident in the Gulf War, although it does not by itself explain the strong response fashioned to reverse Saddam Hussein's aggressive move in 1990 against Kuwait.

Stepping back momentarily from our concern with military activity, it seems useful to reflect briefly upon the contemporary impulse to bring law to bear more ambitiously on other aspects of ocean use. The main cumulative explanation for this development has been the intensifying pressures exerted by the increased quantity and the changing character of peaceful uses. These pressures have fundamentally altered the circumstances of ocean use from one of abundance to one of scarcity. Under conditions of abundance, the capacity to accommodate use and to reconcile diverse use far exceeds the total volume of use and places no great strain on the laissez-faire character of the system. Under such conditions, no very precise set of regulatory standards is needed. As a condition of scarcity emerges, however, various ocean uses encroach upon capacity, causing damage and threatening various dimensions of sustainability; the overlap of uses increasingly accentuates incompatibilities, as when ocean dumping of wastes endangers fishing. Under these conditions, restraints on certain forms of use are needed, and a careful delineation of the relationship among uses and of the allocation of responsibility for harmful effects becomes imperative. The evolution of the law of the seas, culminating in UNCLOS III, has responded impressively to this change of circumstances even if the pattern of adjustment has disappointed some of the more idealistic hopes that this occasion of momentous legal reform would encourage the negotiators to adopt a more community-oriented approach to sharing those benefits of ocean use that remained largely untapped, especially the prospect of seabed mineral wealth.

In my view, the objective change in conditions that pertains to military uses is even greater in its actual and potential impact than is the case with regard to civilian use. Long-range missile technology and nuclear weaponry put all countries permanently at severe risk from military activities on the oceans, and make them vulnerable to catastrophic accidents or to long-term problems that might arise from ocean dumping, nuclear weapons testing, naval missiles, and damage done to reefs and continental shelves. The original rationale for the extension of territorial sovereignty over a coastal band of waters was based on the range of shore artillery; that is, there was a sense that all states should be protected defensively to a degree from offshore military harassment by naval powers. Despite enlarging the band of territorial waters from three to twelve miles, there is now no longer any protection accorded to non-naval powers that are subjected to coercive diplomacy mounted from the seas. The case, in other words, for greater regulation of military activities on the oceans in response to these technological changes seems overwhelming, especially the need for a new balance both between the freedoms of maritime powers and the defensive security and sovereign rights of other states and between the freedoms of maritime powers and the well-being of the global community as a whole.

My preliminary conclusion, then, is that, despite comparable changes in conditions, military activities on the oceans have not been regulated in a manner remotely comparable to the restrictions imposed on non-military uses of the oceans over the course of the last several decades, and that maritime powers continue to insist on retaining their "freedom" to use the oceans in any manner that accords with their national security and hegemonic conception of national interests. In effect, the broad maritime claim is to use the oceans in much the same manner that territory under sovereign control has been used, and this has traditionally included the freedom to send navies to the four corners of the globe on missions of contemporary gunboat diplomacy. Representatives of the military in these leading naval powers are quite unabashed in their assertion of these expectations.[6] As one respected commentator, Guilo Pontecorvo, expresses this feature of the regulatory framework in the context of the

6. "From the standpoint of national defense strategy, the LOS Convention provides the legal underpinning to naval forward presence, which, in turn, supports our ability to maintain our security alliances, to respond to regional contingencies, and to keep pace with potential shifts in the threat to peace and security." *Cf.* William L. Schachte, Jr., *The Value of the 1982 UN Convention on the Law of the Sea—Preserving our Freedoms and Protecting the*

long negotiations that finally led to the 1982 Convention: "The military interests of the U.S. and [Soviet Union] set limits on what the Conference could decide . . . The superpowers just would not accept any limitation on what they regarded as their military necessities."[7] The strength of this military expectation is evident in the maintenance of "freedoms" for naval operations in relation to Exclusive Economic Zones (EEZ) and to transit of warships through international straights; the small concessions to constraining military activities that arise from widening the width of territorial waters to twelve miles and the retention of the requirement that submarines in transit through territorial waters travel on the surface of the water are not seriously inhibiting. This freedom of maritime powers to operate in the EEZ means, among other things, the right to emplace structures and electronic devices on the continental shelf of foreign countries without obtaining their permission. This military ethos is so strong in relation to the oceans that two respected specialists on the law of the oceans, R.R. Churchill and A.V. Lowe, express a conviction that legal inhibitions are not likely to stand up against military pressures: "The only thing that can be said with confidence is that it is most unlikely that major naval powers will cease from the use of the seas for military exercises and the deployment of such (sonar surveillance) systems, no matter what the Convention might say."[8]

One further aspect of this defining reality is the extent to which the non-treaty portion of the law of the seas is evolved by state practice that is effectively asserted. That is, a powerful state posits its right to engage in contested naval activity and, despite interference with the freedoms of others or the potential harm to the environment, there is a tendency to base future rights on the previous assertion of effective claims or, as Michael Reisman has put it, on "incidents" in the past that qualify as "precedents" or as "state practice." One of the few partial exceptions has been the legal challenges recently directed at nuclear testing, most recently involving the 1995 French test series, but even here, in the face of undivided regional opposition and widespread condemnation, the French claims have been tacitly or openly endorsed by the other major maritime powers, maintaining

*Environment, in* THE MARINE ENVIRONMENT AND SUSTAINABLE DEVELOPMENT: LAW, POLICY, AND SCIENCE 93, 95 (Alastair Cooper and Edgar Gold eds., 1993).

7. THE NEW ORDER OF THE OCEANS 60, 60–61 (Guilo Pontecorvo ed., 1986).

8. R.R. CHURCHILL AND A.V. LOWE, THE LAW OF THE SEA 311 (rev. ed. 1988); *see also* Submittal Letter from the Secretary of State to the U.S. President, dated Sept. 23, 1994, 6 U.S. STATE DEP'T DISPATCH SUPP. 2, 16–17 (Feb. 1995).

a solid front on military prerogatives as remaining beyond effective legal or political challenge.

There are several dimensions of concern that arise from this continuing discretion claimed by leading states to use the oceans to serve their national security policies. First of all, there is an alarmingly high level of militarization that includes the use of the oceans for purposes of nuclear weapons deployment. As of 1991, there were 9,100 strategic nuclear warheads associated with naval activities, the majority of which were deployed on 106 missile-carrying submarines belonging to the five declared nuclear states; many nuclear warheads were also carried on surface ships that entered the ports of many countries in all parts of the world. Although not officially disclosed, there are indications that most, if not all, strategic nuclear warheads have been removed from surface ships in recent years. In addition, there are, or have been, many "tactical" nuclear weapons carried on surface ships, including cruise missiles with relatively short ranges. Although these numbers have been reduced by agreements and unilateral downsizing since the end of the Cold War, there remains a permanent nuclear weapons presence in the oceans, the extent of which is shrouded in secrecy as are rules of engagement that disclose the intended patterns of use in circumstances of conflict and crisis.

This presence would pose severe dangers even if the weapons are never to be used. Joshua Handler writes that "[f]ive nuclear-powered submarines with seven nuclear reactors and some thirty-eight nuclear warheads have sunk to in Atlantic because of accidents."[9] Further, Handler reports that as many as sixteen nuclear-powered reactors have been deliberately dumped in the oceans (fifteen by the former Soviet Union), and that many accident-prone nuclear-powered military vessels roam the oceans subject only to the regulatory authority of their own government, although they pose various dangers to the community as a whole as well as to the living resources of the oceans and its environmental quality. These dangers are aggravated by the veil of secrecy that covers naval activities, including mishaps and the discretion to deploy inadequately tested high-risk technologies.

Some treaty initiatives have attempted to diminish certain widely acknowledged specific risks. Perhaps the most consequential effort has been to restrict, and soon to prohibit, any type of nuclear weapons testing in the oceans. The Limited Test Ban Treaty of 1963 was,

9. Joshua Handler, *Denuclearizing and Demilitarizing the Seas*, *in* FREEDOM FOR THE SEAS IN THE 21ST CENTURY 420, 431 (Jon M. Van Dyke, Durwood Zaelke and Grant Hewison eds., 1993).

at the time, a partial breakthrough in that it prohibited testing in the atmosphere, in outer space, and under water; the benefit of the treaty was diminished because France and China refused to become parties or to respect the constraints imposed. The 1971 Treaty on the Prohibition of the Emplacement of Nuclear Weapons and Other Weapons of Mass Destruction on the Seabed and the Ocean Floor and in the Subsoil Thereof imposes one set of important outer limits on the nuclearization of the oceans, although again without the participation of France and China. Additionally, during the Cold War, bilateral agreements between the two superpowers sought to improve communications during crises and to contain incidents that occurred on or above the high seas. Another type of attempt by non-nuclear countries has been to establish nuclear-free zones on a regional basis through the Treaty of Tlatelolco (1967) in Latin America that commits parties to prohibit testing, deployment, and use within the region, and the Treaty of Raratonga (1985) that prohibits testing and stationing of nuclear weapons within a wide expanse of the Pacific, and leaves it up to the parties as to whether to follow the lead of New Zealand in restricting port visits of naval vessels that will not confirm the absence of nuclear warheads on board. Whether nuclear powers will respect these zones is doubtful, especially with respect to the movements and deployment of their nuclear submarines and, given the range of strategic missiles, it almost doesn't matter.

Is this general situation a cause for concern? I think it is in relation to current conflict situations and, with respect to the future of peaceful governance of the oceans. Whether much can be done to alter these realities in the near future is another matter. A first step, however, is to acknowledge the problematic character of the prevailing complacent view that a peaceful future for the oceans can be assured by universal adherence to the 1982 Convention or as a result of concrete valuable steps such as adherence to a Comprehensive Test Ban by all nuclear weapons states, an outcome that had been anticipated to occur by the end of 1996, but has been put on indefinite hold as a result of the nuclear weapons tests conducted by India and Pakistan in 1998. There are a number of serious difficulties that cast a dark shadow across the prospect for peaceful uses of the oceans:

- Secrecy with respect to national security operations on the oceans, including those involving nuclear weaponry;

- Absence of safety and accident prevention regulations pertaining to virtually all naval operations, which enjoy comprehensive immunities retained by UNCLOS in articles 30–32;

- Primacy accorded to national security imperatives when in opposition to other political, moral, and legal duties;

- Absence of regulation of military deployments, exclusionary zones, and arms transfers through and over the oceans;

- An international law of war framework that is badly outdated in relation to the oceans; even this anachronistic framework consists of very old authoritative written instruments, and these are only in the form of very general guidelines for a limited number of circumstances, in the comparatively archaic circumstances of 1907; as of 1998, the 1907 law of naval warfare seems primitive and fragmentary, and the failure to attempt even periodic updates expresses the reluctance of naval powers to subject their freedoms to restraints based on wider community concerns or their own practical considerations;

- A supplemental reliance on customary international law and evolving patterns of state practice that is shaped very much by the dominant maritime states that resist any substantive limitations on their "freedoms" to use the seas for purposes of national security; and

- A condition of increasing scarcity pertaining to the capacities of the oceans, perhaps most dramatically in relation to the living resources of the oceans; such conditions have already generated several serious conflicts, and have led to efforts by transnational social forces to protect the ocean environment in the face of commercial pressures reinforced by military protection.[10]

What, then, in light of these factors, should be done to improve the prospect for peaceful oceans in the future? I think that at least five directions of effort are worthwhile, although it must be realized that the realist sources of resistance in the naval states make it quite unlikely that there will be any immediate progress.

The most obvious place to begin is by encouraging academic and civic groups to demystify the existing state of play relative to the oceans, and to depict the problematic character of leaving naval

10. *Cf. generally,* Thomas F. Homer-Dixon, *Environmental Scarcities and Violent Conflict,* 19 INT'L SECURITY 5 (Summer 1994).

activity regulated according to guidelines formulated in 1907 when war itself was treated as matter of sovereign discretion and as beyond the scope of international law.

Second, in a manner already proposed by Elisabeth Mann Borgese, extend the peacekeeping categories set forth in *An Agenda for Peace,* including especially "preventive diplomacy," to the range of conflict situations posed by contradictory claims involving the use of the oceans or the resources thereof.[11]

Third, extend efforts to achieve denuclearization of the oceans by building on the series of ad hoc arrangements that have so far been agreed upon and going beyond the prospective Comprehensive Test Ban Treaty. The 1996 Advisory Opinion of the World Court on the legality of nuclear weaponry provide one wedge to enable raising broader questions.

Fourth, explore prohibiting the use of the oceans for military actions, as well as contemporary forms of gunboat diplomacy against so-called "rogue states," that cannot be justified before the Security Council as instances of self-defense or reasonable instances of international law enforcement (e. g., anti-piracy or anti-terrorist actions).

Fifth, and finally, follow through with the proposed convening, in 1999 or 2007, of a new peace conference on the Hague model at the end of the last century to draft a new law for naval warfare, and more generally, a regulatory framework relevant to naval activities on the oceans. Given the revolutionary changes in all aspects of military technology and tactics, a continued reliance on a legal framework that is a century old seems quite absurd; the mere process of attempting this modernizing of the normative architecture, undertaken with significant success with respect to International Humanitarian Law in Geneva in 1949, and further extended in 1977, would have some beneficial effects in identifying the concerns relating to present regulatory arrangements governing military activities for the oceans. It should be noted that, before the extensive 1982 revision of the law of the seas, more modest attempts were made in 1958 and 1960. Can military activities relating to the oceans continue to be treated as a sacred cow beyond the reach of regulation as we approach the threshold of the twenty-first century?

11. *See* Borgese, *supra* note 1, at 175–93.

# CHAPTER VII

# NUCLEAR WEAPONS, INTERNATIONAL LAW, AND THE WORLD COURT: A HISTORIC ENCOUNTER

## A. INTRODUCTION

The International Court of Justice has issued an advisory opinion of great weight on the legality of nuclear weaponry.[1] It is the first time ever that an international tribunal has directly addressed this gravest, unresolved threat to the future of humanity. The case divided the judges jurisprudentially and doctrinally in fundamental ways, with a narrow majority (that depended on a second casting vote by the President of the Court, Judge Mohammed Bedjaoui of Algeria)[2] forging a consensus that lends strong, yet partial and somewhat ambiguous, support to the view that nuclear weapons are of dubious legality.

In an important sense the narrowness of the majority is misleading, as three of the six dissenting judges refused to support the decision because it failed to find that existing international law supported a categorical prohibition on the threat or use of nuclear weapons. In another sense, the absence of a clear majority reflects the Court's failure to resolve fully the legal status of nuclear weapons. In fact, those judges who favored a stronger legal condemnation of nuclear weaponry appear to have regarded the majority decision as, if anything, a step backward, undermining the claims of scholars and others who had previously maintained that any threat or use of nuclear weaponry was illegal *as such,* without any consideration of context. What does seem definite, however, is that a fair reading of the decision represents a serious setback for the legal rationale relied upon by the nuclear weapons states and their academic supporters.

1. Legality of the Threat or Use of Nuclear Weapons, Gen. List No. 95 (advisory opinion of July 8, 1996)[hereinafter Nuclear Weapons].

2. *See* I.C.J. Statute, art. 55(2).

The most crucial aspect of the *dispositif* on the core issue of legality reached a result that surprised those who had anticipated an either/or outcome, The Court created some new doctrinal terrain by deciding that the threat or use of nuclear weapons is prohibited by international law, subject to a *possible* exception for legal reliance on such weapons, in extreme circumstances of self-defense in which the survival of a state is at stake.

It seems helpful to distinguish the common ground that united the Court as a whole from the narrowly crafted majority that (arguably) accentuates the uncertainty surrounding the applicability of international law and from the various minority positions that gave rise to a series of dissenting opinions. An impression of the dispersion of views, as well as the importance attached to the case by the Court's members, is confirmed by the fact that all fourteen participating judges saw fit to write an opinion or statement of some kind that set forth their individual views.

## B. COMMON GROUND

Most obviously, the common ground is established by those elements of the *dispositif* that enjoyed the unanimous or near-unanimous support of the fourteen participating judges. Thus, the advisory opinion concludes unanimously that "neither customary nor conventional international law" contains "any specific authorization of the threat or use of nuclear weapons."[3] In somewhat more contested fashion, the judges voted eleven to three that "neither customary nor conventional international law" contains "any comprehensive and universal prohibition of the threat or use of nuclear weapons as such."[4]

A second unanimous conclusion is that any use of nuclear weapons contrary to article 2(4) of the United Nations Charter, and not vindicated by article 51, is "unlawful."[5] It was agreed by all the judges as well that a threat or use of nuclear weapons is governed by "the international law applicable in armed conflict, particularly those of the principles and rules of international humanitarian law, as well as [by] specific obligations" arising from treaties and other

3. Nuclear Weapons, *supra* note 1, at para. 105(2)(A).
4. *Id.* at para. 105(2)(B).
5. *Id.* at para. 105(2)(C).

undertakings that "expressly deal with nuclear weapons."[6] None of this is very startling, nor was it challenged by any nuclear weapons states in their pleadings.[7]

More significant, undoubtedly, especially if read in conjunction with the reasoning in the text of the decision,[8] is paragraph 2F of the *dispositif*, which unanimously calls upon states to uphold their "obligation to pursue in good faith and bring to a conclusion negotiations leading to nuclear disarmament in all its aspects."[9] This emphasis in the advisory opinion on the obligatory character of article VI of the Non-Proliferation Treaty (NPT) appears to represent common legal ground between nuclear and non-nuclear weapons states. It is a tacit acknowledgment of the deep split among the judges and in international society generally as to the legal status of nuclear weapons. This split makes it unlikely that regimes of prohibition of the sort negotiated for biological and chemical weapons could be achieved for nuclear weapons. The constructive alternative is to give weight to the legal commitment by the nuclear weapons states to pursue disarmament as a serious policy goal. Although the decision refrains from criticizing the current behavior and practice of particular states, it seems rather evident that the most important nuclear weapons states have for several decades preferred, and even insisted upon, an arms control approach based on minimizing the risks of possessing nuclear weapons. In diplomatic practice, this reliance on arms control has led to a repudiation of general and complete disarmament as a policy goal, and an unwillingness to submit or consider nuclear disarmament proposals as a basis for international negotiations.[10] The unanimity of the Court as to the disarmament obligation

6. *Id.* at para. 105(2)(D).

7. The Court's conclusion here does seem to support strongly the view that the authority of article 2(4) persists, despite a great deal of contrary state practice. Given the importance of the issues, much scholarly attention has been devoted to this tension between Charter norms and the claims of states to use force. *See* Thomas M. Franck, *Who Killed Article2(4)? or: Changing Norms Governing the Use of Force by States,* 64 AM. J. INT'L L. 809 (1970); Louis Henkin, *The Reports of the Death of Article 2(4) Are Greatly Exaggerated,* 65 AM. J. INT'L L. 544 (1971); Oscar Schachter, *In Defense of International Rules on the Use of Force,* 53 U. CHI. L. REV. 113 (1986); MYRES S. MCDOUGAL AND FLORENTINE P. FELICIANO, LAW AND MINIMUM WORLD PUBLIC ORDER (1961); ANTHONY CLARK AREND AND ROBERT J. BECK, INTERNATIONAL LAW AND THE USE OF FORCE (1993).

8. Nuclear Weapons, *supra* note 1, at paras. 98–103.

9. *Id.* at para. 105(2)(F).

10. This posture can be contrasted with the proclaimed disarmament goals of the nuclear superpowers that held up through the mid-1960s. The official framework for disarmament policy was set forth in the famous McCloy-Zorin Agreed Principles on Disarmament Negotiations, Sept. 20, 1961. For a skeptical interpretation of this alleged pursuit of disarmament goals, see RICHARD J. BARNET, WHO WANTS DISARMAMENT? (1960). A momentary glimmer of commitment

thus goes against the prevailing outlook of the declared nuclear weapons states, especially that of the United States and the United Kingdom, and could become *substantively* important at some subsequent time. Indeed, it gives indirect encouragement to peace groups around the world that have been calling for nuclear disarmament ever since the first atomic explosions in 1945. This legal endorsement of disarmament also amounts, even if unwittingly, to a sharp criticism of the nuclear weapons states for their abandonment of any serious pursuit of disarmament goals in recent decades.

In addition, there is a broad consensus among the judges on a positivist assessment of international law obligations, resting on evidence that states have directly or indirectly consented to the applicability of given rules and standards. None of the judges rested their legal analysis on naturalist or Marxist canons of jurisprudence, although the three dissenters who favored an unconditional prohibition, especially Judge Christopher G. Weeramantry, arguably blended a positivist conclusion with some natural law reasoning. Judge Rosalyn Higgins seems somewhat enigmatically to reflect the value-oriented contextualism of the New Haven School in the final, decisive sentence of her dissent: "It is not clear to me that either a pronouncement of illegality in all circumstances of the use of nuclear weapons or the answers formulated by the Court in paragraph 2E best serve to protect mankind against the unimaginable suffering that we all fear."[11] Implicit here is the view that if the normative end of avoiding nuclear catastrophe could be reliably discerned, then international law would be construed to prohibit it. In effect, the Court exhibits acceptance of a "soft *Lotus*" approach, namely, the view that limitations on a state's freedom of action cannot be presumed or deduced from world order values, but must rest on the consent of the state or the application of legal rules and principles to the context of actual use. The majority did not favor the "hard *Lotus*" view, namely, that whatever is not explicitly forbidden to a state is permitted.[12]

Also of great importance is the near-unanimity of the Court on the matter of complying with the request of the General Assembly for an advisory opinion on the legality of a threat or use of nuclear

to nuclear disarmament occurred at the minisummit of November 1986, when General Secretary Gorbachev and President Reagan met in Reykjavik, Iceland.

11. Nuclear Weapons, *supra* note 1 (dissenting opinion of Judge Higgins at para. 41).

12. This reading is strongly supported by Nuclear Weapons, *supra* note 1 (declaration of Judge Bedjaoui at paras. 12–16).

weapons. The judges voted thirteen to one in favor, with only Judge Shigeru Oda opposed, not on jurisdictional grounds but through reliance on the discretionary power of the Court to decline to respond.[13] The majority opinion convincingly explains the importance of responding to questions properly put to it by U.N. organs, as provided for by articles 96(1) and (2) of the Charter, and disregards the strongly argued objections of several states, including the United States, that the question was too vague and abstract, too fraught with political baggage, and too obstructive of other, more appropriate diplomatic efforts to control the dangers posed by the existence of nuclear weapons. The approach of the Court to the delimitation of its advisory role gains in clarity because of the reasoned refusal to respond in the companion case arising out of a request by the World Health Organization (WHO) for an advisory opinion on the legality of using nuclear weapons, which was treated by an eleven-to-three majority as an inappropriate question, given the proper scope of WHO concerns.[14]

The acceptance of the General Assembly's request in this instance is also important as an expression of judicial independence by the Court. After all, such an outcome was strongly opposed by all of the permanent members of the Security Council except China, both in the debates on the General Assembly resolution and in the written and oral pleadings before the Court. Not only did all but one of the judges support jurisdiction and refuse to use their discretion to refrain from issuing a response, but the Court as a whole substantively affirmed the applicability of international law to the status of nuclear weapons.[15] Part of the common ground among the judges, then, is a broad duty to respond to appropriate requests for advisory opinions, despite the objections of leading states and the political difficulties

13. The considerable irony here is that Japan has suffered more directly than any other country from the contested weaponry, and it was Japanese society more than any other that exhibited grassroots support for recourse to the International Court of Justice.

14. Legality of the Use by a State of Nuclear Weapons in Armed Conflict, Gen. List No. 93 (advisory opinon of July 8, 1996).

15. This outcome helps to neutralize the impression of the Lockerbie decision that a majority of the Court is subservient to geopolitical pressures, especially in light of the repudiation of the authority of its earlier decision in the Nicaragua case (Military and Paramilitary Activities (Nicar. v. U.S.), Merits, 1986 I.C.J. 14 (June 27)). *See* Questions of Interpretation and Application of the 1971 Montreal Convention arising from the Aerial Incident at Lockerbie (Libya v. U.K.; Libya v. U.S.), Provisional Measures, 1992 I.C.J. 3, 114 (orders of Apr. 14). For an important jurisprudential interpretation of the outcome in the Nicaragua case, arguing that the decision was diplomatically effective in shaping a peace process despite the rejection of the authority of the Court by the U.S. government, see JOAQUIN TACSAN, THE DYNAMICS OF INTERNATIONAL LAW IN CONFLICT RESOLUTION (1992).

arising from the poor prospects that the advice proffered will be accepted, or even treated by affected governments with seriousness and respect.

## C. THE DECISION

The official response to the most crucial aspect of the question put by the General Assembly is contained in paragraph 2E of the *dispositif* and was supported by seven of the fourteen judges, with the majority needed for the decision depending on the casting, second vote of President Bedjaoui. Does this suggest a 50/50 split with respect to legality? Not really. If the decision is read as in important respects constraining the discretion of states to threaten or use nuclear weapons, the three dissenting judges who believe that nuclear weapons are categorically illegal can be counted as part of the majority, creating a ten-to-four vote. Furthermore, the arguments of the seven judges who dissented (counting Judge Gilbert Guillaume's "individual opinion" as a dissent) lack any internal coherence, and only Judges Stephen Schwebel, Higgins, and Guillaume gave support to the claim of the nuclear weapons states that, although international law applies, it does so only in the context of an actual threat or use of nuclear weapons. However, it must be acknowledged that important supporters of the General Assembly resolution among the U.N. membership did not give much prominence to their request for an advisory opinion, and seemed to opt for a low-profile approach in the setting of written and oral pleadings, quite possibly reflecting the partial effectiveness of U.S. diplomacy, which tried hard to discourage any recourse to the Court on these matters.

The substantive issue that the judges agreed was at the core of the General Assembly's question is addressed in paragraph 2E of the *dispositif*. It is here that the Court breaks new ground that will invite controversy about the correct interpretation of international law, generating criticism and commentary from the two main camps: those who believe that nuclear weapons are a legitimate weapon unless used in a manner otherwise violative of international law and those who are convinced that nuclear weapons are inherently illegal. In this crucial respect, the decision will disappoint both those who endorse the approach of the nuclear weapons states and those who attack reliance on any threat or use of nuclear weaponry as automatically a violation of international law, but it will not disappoint them equally; its overall reasoning is far more supportive of the latter than the former outlook.

Paragraph 2E contains only two sentences. The first part, resting on the earlier aspects of the *dispositif,* states a general conclusion: "It follows from the above-mentioned requirements that the threat or use of nuclear weapons would generally be contrary to the rules of international law applicable in armed conflict, and in particular the principles and rules of humanitarian law."[16] The innovative orientation toward the issue of legality arises from the insertion of the word "generally," which gives a conditional character to the language of prohibition. The second sentence of 2E reduces somewhat the ambit of ambiguity:

> However, in view of the current state of international law, and of the elements of fact at its disposal, the Court cannot conclude definitely whether the threat or use of nuclear weapons would be lawful or unlawful in an extreme circumstance of self-defence, in which the survival of the State would be at stake.[17]

Note, especially, that the Court is clearly not validating a threat or use of nuclear weapons in "an extreme circumstance of self-defence," but asserting that it "cannot conclude definitely" one way or the other with respect to the legality of such a claim even in that situation. This acknowledged inability to describe the legal character of a threat or use of nuclear weapons in extreme self-defense introduces the issue of *non liquet* centrally into the legal debate among the judges on the Court, and will undoubtedly divide the scholarly community in an analogous fashion.

In a somewhat unusual move, but one that deserves serious notice, the decision precedes the *dispositif* with a call to comprehend and interpret the conclusions it contains by referring back to the reasoning in the body of the opinion:

> [T]he Court emphasizes that its reply to the question put to it by the General Assembly rests on the totality of the legal grounds set forth by the Court above (paragraphs 20 to 103), each of which is to be read in light of the others. Some of these grounds are not such as to form the object of formal conclusions in the final paragraph of the Opinion; they nevertheless retain, in the view of the Court, all their importance.[18]

16. Nuclear Weapons, *supra* note 1, at para. 105(2)(E).
17. *Id.*
18. *Id.* at para. 104.

Such a mandate to interpreters underscores the sensitivity and nuanced character of the vital issues being addressed, suggesting immersion in the overall decision, and to some extent merges the holdings or conclusions reached and the legal reasoning relied upon.

The most problematic character of the majority decision is its failure to clarify its understanding of the restrictions to be placed upon a potential self-defense argument on behalf of a particular threat or use of nuclear weaponry. It does seem clear that a claimant state can legally threaten or use nuclear weapons only in a situation of self-defense, and then only in extreme circumstances where survival is at stake. What is confusing, however, is the extent of this possible loophole. The *dispositif* declares that a self-defense claim could be legally valid in situations in which the survival of "a State" is sufficiently threatened, apparently opening the door to claims of collective self-defense. However, a narrower construction of the conceivable legal right to threaten or use nuclear weapons in self-defense does seem implied by the language in the decision that limits such a right to "an extreme circumstance of self-defence, in which its very survival would be at stake."[19] This view is reinforced by the observation in the separate opinion of Judge Carl-August Fleischhauer that "[t]he margin that exists for considering that a particular threat or use of nuclear weapons could be lawful is therefore extremely narrow."[20] It is unfortunate that the majority did not resolve this internal tension between the language of the *dispositif* and the legal reasoning of paragraph 97. But it should be emphasized that the Court is not confirming the legality of such a self-defense exception but arguing that at present international law does not definitely rule out such an exception.

On a related matter, the decision unfortunately also does not address the status of self-defense claims in circumstances where no nuclear weapons are threatened, used, or even possessed by an aggressor state that has put the survival of its adversary at risk. It thus undermines, by implication, the argument of those who contend that, by practice and formal action, the nuclear weapons states have already substantially renounced first-use options against non-nuclear adversaries, at least where the claim is one of collective, rather than individual, self-defense.[21]

19. *Id.* at para. 97 (emphasis added).

20. *Id.* (separate opinion of Judge Fleischhauer, para. 6, as reinforced by declaration of President Bejaoui, *supra* note 12, at paras. 11, 15.)

21. For a forceful argument along this line, see Jeremy J. Stone, *Less than meets the eye*, BULL. ATOM. SCIENTISTS, Sept./Oct. 1996, at 43–45.

The Court never gives concrete instances to clarify what is specifically entailed by its doctrinal statement on self-defense, possibly for reasons of discreetness, possibly as a tacit acknowledgment of the limits to its competence to address strategic questions with any authority. But it would appear, at the very least, that the atomic attacks on Hiroshima and Nagasaki, given the imminent defeat of Japan in August 1945, should be regarded as violative of international law, and quite independently of whether in the context of use there were parallel violations of rules and principles of international humanitarian law pertaining to discriminateness, avoidance of unnecessary suffering, and proportionality.[22] In effect, the Court has endorsed a partial prohibition on the threat or use of nuclear weapons as embodied in *existing* international law that would forbid any future threat or use even if the claim of extreme self-defense had been available at the start of the war and the main American justification of "saving lives" that had been relied upon in relation to the atomic attacks at the end of World War II was treated as persuasive on the facts. Nuclear weaponry would also seemingly not be available to punish or deter a state that resorted to illegal tactics in the course of armed conflict, as Iraq did to some extent in the Persian Gulf War.[23] Nor would threats to use nuclear weaponry to deter a so-called rogue state that possessed a limited nuclear (or chemical or biological) capability be compatible with the broad outlines set forth, especially the impression conveyed that threats and uses of nuclear weapons are only legally available, if at all, under the pressure of extreme necessity, that is, in the absence of alternatives when aggression threatens the survival of the state.

What would the scope of legality be? In the first instance, it would be a plausible claim of self-defense in a situation where the survival of the state was credibly at stake. Possibly, on the basis of such reasoning, an Israeli threat or use during the opening days of the 1973 Arab-Israeli War would qualify. But would a Soviet attack on Florida during the Cuban missile crisis give the United States a legal right to respond with nuclear weapons? What about a Soviet military

22. It was on such contextual grounds that a Japanese domestic court legally condemned the atomic attacks in the only formal judicial appraisal of these events. For commentary, see Richard A. Falk, *The Shimoda Case: A Legal Appraisal of the Atomic Attacks upon Hiroshima and Nagasaki*, 59 AM. J. INT'L L. 759 (1965).

23. See Judge Schwebel's dissent for an argument as to the contextual legality of nuclear weapons, but without consideration of claims that run counter to U.S. foreign policy, for example, if China threatens to reincorporate Taiwan.

challenge to the viability of West Berlin at the height of the Cold War? The formal answer provided by the Court is that, in accordance with article 51, the legality of any use of nuclear weapons in circumstances of a claimed right of self-defense would in the first instance be made by the claimant state or its ally but subject to the procedural requirements of immediately reporting to the Security Council for a final determination as to lawfulness.[24]The most obviously controversial aspect of the decision is the central conclusion that *existing* international law embodies a position situated somewhere between those who argue the "hard *Lotus*" view that any weapon not expressly forbidden is permitted, provided it conforms in actual use to the law of armed conflict, and those who contend that the various prohibitions of customary international law, reinforced by application of the Martens Clause, make illegal any and every threat or use of nuclear weapons. The scholarly literature did not anticipate the result reached by the Court, but tends to divide between the contextualists (legal if used in accordance with rules and principles of the law of war) and the prohibitionists (illegal under all circumstances).[25]

In support of the Court's position is the view that its conclusion most accurately reflects the complex and contradictory mixture of normative elements, including the tension between the logic of prohibiting all weaponry of mass destruction and the logic of self-defense, as well as the cumulative impact of anti-nuclear efforts in global civil society and the U.N. General Assembly to delegitimize reliance upon, and even the retention of, nuclear weaponry. As the Court expresses its own sense of this evolution by reviewing various treaties and assurances associated with limiting the domain of nuclear weapons, concluding that this trend "certainly point[s] to an increasing concern in the international community with these weapons; the Court concludes from this that these treaties could therefore be seen

24. Nuclear Weapons, *supra* note 1, at para. 44.

25. The academic treatment of these issues that most closely resembles the approach and substantive conclusions of the World Court is that of Burns H. Weston, *Nuclear Weapons versus International Law: A Contextual Reassessment*, 28 McGILL L.J. 542 (1983). The main difference is that the majority in the advisory opinion stresses legal uncertainties arising from claims of self-defense in extreme circumstances, whereas Professor Weston focuses on comparable uncertainties associated with first and second defensive uses, that is, differentiating between introducing nuclear weapons into a conflict (first use) and responding to a prior reliance by the aggressor on nuclear weaponry (second use). Because Weston qualifies both uses as "defensive," his distinction is an alternative to the Court's way of identifying extreme occasions of self-defense where recourse to nuclear weapons might be legal. Weston's approach would meet the objection to the advisory opinion that it potentially authorizes a defensive first use. *See* note 21 *supra*.

as foreshadowing a future general prohibition of the use of such weapons."[26] To similar effect, the Court finds "a growing awareness of the need to liberate the community of States and the international public from the dangers resulting from the existence of nuclear weapons," but not so much as to establish "a comprehensive and universal conventional prohibition on the use, or the threat of use, of those weapons as such."[27]

The Court also gives certain normative weight to the resolutions of the General Assembly over the years that have disclosed "the desire of a very large section of the international community to take, by a specific and express prohibition of the use of nuclear weapons, a significant step forward along the road to complete nuclear disarmament."[28] While the Court notes a deep concern about legality in international society, it concludes that it is not yet of such a character as to satisfy the requirements of *opinio juris* associated with the emergence of a customary rule of unconditional prohibition specifically associated with nuclear weapons. The Court uses an intriguing formulation to express its perception of current legal status of nuclear weaponry, discerning "the continuing tensions between the nascent *opinio juris* on the one hand, and the still strong adherence to the practice of deterrence on the other."[29] It explicitly avoids making any legal assessment of deterrence in theory and practice.[30] At the same time, the decision does circumscribe the legal right to threaten or use nuclear weaponry in a manner that seems inconsistent with the practice of deterrence in most of its forms, other than possibly so-called minimum deterrence. A problematic character of the decision arises from this failure to address more directly the current doctrines and practice of nuclear weapons states, which leaves in doubt the policy implications of the legal advice being given. Admittedly, the Court was confronted by a dilemma: had it attempted to remove doubt as to the legality of current practice by making detailed commentary on strategic doctrines in various settings, it might have manifested a degree of technical incompetence that would likely have considerably damaged its reputation as a responsible judicial body.

Judge Higgins based her dissent in relation to paragraph 2E mainly on a critique of the inconclusiveness of the outcome, considering it

26. Nuclear Weapons, *supra* note 1, at para. 62.
27. *Id.* at para. 63.
28. *Id.* at para. 73.
29. *Id.*
30. *Id.* at para 67.

a decision that reaches a formally unacceptable result of *non liquet* tantamount to acknowledging the incompleteness of international law as a legal system.[31] The Russian judge, Vladlen S. Vereshchetin, in a helpful declaration, offered a response to Judge Higgins, arguing that, if the Court is to avoid "the burden of law-creation," it must refuse to fill in the gaps and acknowledge the inconclusiveness that it finds. This view is particularly persuasive, according to Judge Vereshchetin, in the setting of the Court's "advisory procedure" where there is no need "to resolve an actual dispute between actual Parties," but where the appropriate role of the Court is "to state the law as it finds it at the present stage of its development."[32]

The attack on the majority decision made by the three dissenting judges, who argued in separate opinions that the threat or use of nuclear weapons is invariably illegal, is based on the view that the inherent characteristics of the weaponry, as well as its use in World War II and contemplated use ever since, are radically inconsistent with the existing obligations of international humanitarian law. To reach this conclusion, these judges rejected the view that there is a need for a *specific* customary or treaty norm of prohibition (as exists in the instance of other prohibited categories of weaponry). Their opinions accord priority to human survival and the unconditional nature of the restrictions of international humanitarian law even in the context of extreme self-defense, and they reject the inconsistent legal claims and practice of the important nuclear weapons states. In effect, these dissenters interpret this practice as a pattern of unlawful conduct that was commenced with the atomic attacks at the end of World War II. They regard the Court's decision in some respects as a setback, giving states a potential legal option to use nuclear weaponry that allows them to invoke claims of self-defense to reconcile such a posture with the decision.[33]

31. Compare the interesting paragraph on "the question of lacunae" in ROSALYN HIGGINS, PROBLEMS AND PROCESS: INTERNATIONAL LAW AND HOW WE USE IT 10 (1994).

32. Nuclear Weapons, *supra* note 1 (declaration of Judge Vereshchetin at 1). To similar effect is the separate opinion of Judge Fleischhauer, *supra* note 20, which contains the following important sentence in paragraph 6: "The present state of international law does not permit a more precise drawing of the border-line between unlawfulness and lawfulness of recourse to nuclear weapons." This line of interpretation is forcefully elaborated upon in President Bedjaoui's declarations, *supra* note 12, at para. 7, where he insists that the essence of judicial responsibility is to apply law as it exists, and neither "denigrate nor embellish" it. *See generally, id.* at paras. 6–10.

33. This assessment is made explicit near the beginning of the dissenting opinion of Judge Shahabuddeen, at 1–2.

The fact that the three judges chose to dissent may deprive the decision of a higher degree of authoritativeness than might have resulted if they had decided to write separate opinions. Instead, the combination of the three anti-nuclear dissents and the four other dissents fosters a misimpression of a deep and essentially equal division on the core issue of legality. It is misleading because the majority judges share with the dissenters a considerable area of overlap when it comes to doubts about the legality of threats or use of nuclear weaponry. At the same time, deciding to dissent was undoubtedly a carefully considered choice and expresses deeply felt matters of jurisprudential integrity, as well as concerns about the effectiveness of international law that do relate to the *non liquet* controversy, whose technical character obscures its practical relationship to varying approaches to strengthening the role of international law among states.[34]

Only the Vice-President of the Court, the American Judge Schwebel, fully argued the case for responding to the question put by the General Assembly in a generally affirmative manner, taking the view that, in the absence of an explicit rule of prohibition, the legality of using nuclear weapons must be assessed in the same manner as using any other weapon that has not been banned by treaty. Judge Schwebel believes that "[t]he essence of the problem" facing the application of international law is the difficulty of reconciling the legitimating impact of "[f]ifty years of the practice of States" that "does not debar, and to that extent supports, the legality of the threat or use of nuclear weapons in certain circumstances" with the antecedent principles of international humanitarian law.[35] For Judge Schwebel, the practice of the nuclear weapons states is deserving of particular respect because they are leading members of international society, as is partly evidenced by their permanent membership on the Security Council. Unlike the majority, Judge Schwebel does not balance the practice of the nuclear weapons states against the anti-nuclear sentiments of the international community as a whole, ignoring the legal relevance of the latter. This selectivity as to sources

34. It is not possible here to discuss in an adequate manner the various positions argued by the dissenters, each of whom contributed a comprehensive and important assessment of the main question as to legality. Judge Weeramantry's 85-page dissent is likely to be widely studied, commented upon, and quoted, especially by transnational social groupings that over the years since 1945 have been mainly responsible for mounting a challenge to those governments relying on nuclear weaponry and by scholars attentive to the legal debate likely to be generated by the advisory opinion.

35. Nuclear Weapons, *supra* note 1 (dissenting opinion of Judge Schwebel at 1).

facilitates the clarity of Judge Schwebel's main conclusion, but it gives his dissent a rather one-sided tone, especially as he approvingly relies exclusively on the recent practice of his own government.

Judge Schwebel bolsters his contextual approach to legality with a rather detailed presentation of what he believes to have been the constructive role played by uncertainty about whether the United States might use nuclear weapons in the Gulf War. His broader contention is that the Court, given the status of nuclear weapons under international law, cannot prejudge by abstract pronouncement the appropriateness of reliance on threats or uses of nuclear weaponry, and that on the basis of experience since 1945, it is preferable as a matter of policy that this authority be left in the hands of political leaders in the nuclear weapons states who have demonstrated their prudence and competence.

It is not possible to do critical justice to the full gamut of argument set forth by Vice-President Schwebel in support of his conclusions, but it is worth noting his rousing attack on the formulation by the majority of the self-defense exception in the second part of paragraph 2E. He finds it to be "an astounding conclusion" because of its confession of inconclusiveness, and stresses the utter unacceptability of what he conceives to be a *non liquet* on such a vital question.[36] In this jurisprudential concern about an indefinite outcome, the various dissenters, despite their contradictory substantive positions, are far closer to one another than to the majority.

## D. ASSESSMENT

It is not possible to do more than consider a few highlights from various interrelated points of view: development of international law, reputation of the World Court, political impact, and pedagogical significance.

### 1. Development of International Law

In my view the majority reaches *a* plausible, but not the only plausible, conclusion, given the contradictory elements associated with the status of nuclear weapons under existing international law;

36. *Id.* at 8.

and it does so in a manner that impressively comes to grips with the complexity of the issues. Significantly, it attaches legal weight to the anti-nuclear consensus among the U.N. membership and trends in global civil society without overlooking the contrary practice and legal views of the nuclear weapons states and some of their allies.[37] To do this, however, results in an element of inconclusiveness about the legal result, which introduces learned discussion of whether a *non liquet* had been declared, and if so, whether this itself is contrary to international law in the setting of an advisory opinion.

It is important to appreciate that legal uncertainty pertains to only one aspect of the main conclusion of the majority: that the threat or use of nuclear weapons is unlawful except possibly in extreme circumstances of self-defense where survival of a state is at stake. As suggested above, aside from these circumstances, any threat or use of nuclear weapons would seem contrary to international law. What constitutes a threat, however, is not clarified in relation to deterrence, and this leaves considerable discretionary scope to the nuclear weapons states. This discretion can be viewed as itself somewhat contingent, if the legal duty to pursue nuclear disarmament is diligently pursued in good faith.

Would the majority have made a larger contribution to the development of international law if it had definitely concluded that the threat or use of nuclear weapons was illegal except in circumstances of extreme self-defense understood as involving the survival of the claimant state? Such clarity would have undercut the objections by various dissenters to the inconclusiveness of the central legal holding, but in its place it would have raised the more dangerous contention of judicial legislation. There was no way for the majority to avoid this dilemma in view of its assessment of the incoherent interplay of rules, principles, and practice that constitutes existing international law. In this regard, careful students of international law will appreciate the challenge confronting the Court and give respect to its response to the General Assembly, even if they disagree to varying extents with the legal assessments made. Whether international law will develop in accordance with the advice given, namely, in the direction of nuclear disarmament, depends on the reception of the decision in various arenas of influence, including those within government, the United Nations system, civil society, academia, and the

37. For support of such an approach, see Richard A. Falk, *The World Order between Inter-State Law and the Law of Humanity: The Role of Civil Society Institutions, in* Cosmopolitan Democracy 163–79 (Daniele Archibugi and David Held eds., 1995).

media. Also relevant, of course, are views among policymakers as to the viability of nuclear disarmament, given current world conditions.

## 2. Reputation of the World Court

It is difficult to tell at this point whether the decision will be treated as sufficiently significant to affect the Court's reputation one way or the other as a judicial organ. It appears, in the very short run, that the impact of the decision will be marginalized. The nuclear weapons states have an obvious interest in minimizing the attention accorded to it, and are not so centrally challenged in their current policy postures as to induce frontal attacks on the Court (of the sort made by the United States government after losing out in the context of its anti-Sandinista policies in Nicaragua).[38] In the longer run, I believe, the decision will enhance the reputation of the Court, first of all, by its strong consensus in favor of taking on such a politically sensitive and geopolitically risky request from the General Assembly, especially in light of the mood in the United Nations at this time. Further, I think the decision will receive a significant response from civic groups around the world concerned with nuclear issues, including professional lawyers' associations that had been so active in encouraging recourse to the Court by the World Health Organization and the General Assembly.[39]

## 3. Political Impact

In one central regard, it is necessary to be skeptical. States are habitually resistant to legal challenges directed at their national security policies, and powerful states are especially so. There is little likelihood in the near future that the decision will have any discernible impact on the behavior of nuclear weapons states, either with respect to the roles assigned to nuclear weapons or with regard to the duty to seek nuclear disarmament. This prospect is reinforced by the reluctance of most non-nuclear states to take a confrontational stance toward the nuclear weapons states at this time, and by the overall current weakness of the General Assembly as an organ of decision

38. *See* citations and discussion in note 15 *supra*.

39. I have in mind particularly the International Association of Lawyers Against Nuclear Arms and the U.S. Lawyers' Committee on Nuclear Policy.

and influence. This set of conditions is likely to be intensified if nuclear testing is stopped, either by treaty or otherwise, as much of the grassroots anti-nuclear pressure of recent decades has been associated with continued testing, rather than with the existence of the weapons.

However, it would be a mistake to confine inquiry to short-term intergovernmental impact. The decision is likely to have a consciousness-raising effect on informed public opinion around the world, which might at some point result in renewed and intensified anti-nuclear pressures, especially if there are any new catastrophic events, even if not of a strictly military character (e.g., Chernobyl). Such pressures could be made more effective if there is a heightened belief in governmental circles that present security requirements can be satisfied without any reliance on nuclear weapons, including in their deterrent mode. Also important would be the resolution of festering regional conflicts, especially in the Middle East and East Asia, and the emergence of visionary individuals as political leaders of one or more of the nuclear weapons states. The language and reasoning of the decision of the Court provides strong encouragement to anti-nuclear social and political forces to push for abolition, with respect to both existing security policy and nuclear disarmament.[40] It also provides a legal grounding for the advocacy of anti-nuclear positions *within* government, and strengthens the bargaining positions of non-nuclear states in relation to the nonproliferation agenda, especially with respect to the article VI obligation of the NPT.

## 4. Pedagogical Significance

There is little doubt that the decision will have a major impact on study and reflection associated with the legal status of nuclear weapons. The decision, read in conjunction with various of the dissents, is a unique and invaluable pedagogic tool for addressing the question put by the General Assembly to the World Court and, beyond this, for considering the relationship between law and politics in international relations and the function of the World Court, especially its advisory role within the U.N. system. I anticipate a surge of

40. This encouragement is also strongly promoted by the issuance of REPORT BY THE CANBERRA COMMISSION ON THE ELIMINATION OF NUCLEAR WEAPONS (Aug. 14, 1996). The Canberra Commission is an independent body, consisting of 17 eminent persons, appointed by the Australian government in November 1995.

scholarly attention to the legal status of nuclear weapons in light of the decision, as well as to the legal scope of the right of self-defense, which in turn will stimulate greater academic and public interest.

## E. CONCLUSION

The Court lived up to its historic challenge by responsibly addressing the momentous question posed by the General Assembly about the legal status of a threat or use of nuclear weapons. As suggested, alternative readings of international law were plausible, but the conclusions reached by the Court represent a large step forward with respect to doctrinal clarification. As the majority itself suggests, there remains significant work to be done, through either a specific prohibition of nuclear weapons or nuclear disarmament, but the direction of effort is clear, and of great encouragement to all those who have struggled since 1945 for the legal prohibition and physical elimination of nuclear weapons. As with other normative projects, such as the abolition of slavery and the repudiation of apartheid, perseverance, struggle, and historical circumstance will shape the future with respect to nuclear weaponry, but this process has been pushed forward in a mainly beneficial direction by this milestone decision of the World Court.

# CHAPTER VIII

# THE NUCLEAR WEAPONS ADVISORY OPINION AND THE NEW JURISPRUDENCE OF GLOBAL CIVIL SOCIETY

## A. THE JURISPRUDENTIAL RELEVANCE OF GLOBAL CIVIL SOCIETY

Despite the notable attention given by international law scholars to the normative status of trends toward democratization in state/society relations, remarkably little notice has been paid to the jurisprudential significance of the emergence of transnational democratic tendencies as a feature of the international legal order at the end of the twentieth century.[1] In a manner that appears ethnocentric, and lacking in normative authority, liberal North American scholars have been, in effect, proclaiming the universal applicability of the American political and legal system, its commitment to constitutionalism, electoral politics, and civil and political rights.[2]

There are also deeper questions about the interplay between democratic politics, as expressed through electoral processes and representative institutions, and world order in the setting of a deformed or regressive political culture. Consider in this regard East European countries; the Israeli election in 1996 of a hardline Likud leader as President, dooming the peace process in the Middle East; the support

1. *See* Thomas M. Franck, *The Emerging Right to Democratic Governance,* 86 AM. J. INT'L L. 46 (1992), which has attracted major support in a variety of settings; *see also* W. Michael Reisman, *Sovereignty and Human Rights in Contemporary International Law,* 84 AM. J. INT'L L. 866 (1990).

2. *Compare* John Rawls, The Rights of Peoples, and Richard Rorty, Human Rights, Rationality, and Sentimentality in Oxford (Amnesty Lectures), *with* their acceptance of nonliberal societies provided that human rights are upheld *in* ON HUMAN RIGHTS 41–82, 111–34 (Stephen Shute and Susan Hurley eds., 1993). Are we to say that because Singapore is less "democratic" it is hence less "legitimate" than would be an inept democracy in the Western sense?

among the American electorate for military initiatives in foreign policy, the refusal of the U.S. Congress to approve of plans for the repayment of arrears in U.S. financial obligations to the United Nations, and the apparent reluctance to support a world order bargain on the reduction on the emission of greenhouse gasses as negotiated in Kyoto (1997).[3]

There are also serious empirical and conceptual questions as to whether this style of Western liberalism can be encoded in international law without violating the right of self-determination, which is definitely, although not in a form that is doctrinally established, part of contemporary international law.[4] Also, in the background is the more overtly ideological efforts to associate legitimate government with "market-oriented constitutionalism," as enunciated by the annual summit of the Group of Seven.[5]

Such a problematizing of democracy as a political form is not meant to question seriously whether it is appropriate to regard political democracy at the level of the sovereign state as a norm of public international law at this stage of international history, but the issue is raised at the outset to set the stage for a related, but quite different, less frequently pursued line of inquiry. What is being pursued here relates to the jurisprudential relevance of *transnational* democratic initiatives to the processes of international lawmaking at this stage of history, and to the failure of even the most ardent democratic theorists in the conventional sense to give any sympathetic attention to this set of moves "beyond Westphalia."[6] What does seem to be beyond

3. *See* Richard Falk, The Quest for Normative Democracy in an Era of Neo-Liberal Globalization, (unpublished Hesburgh Lectures, University of Notre Dame, Feb. 19–20, 1997).

4. *See* Richard Falk, *The Right of Self-Determination Under International Law: The Coherence of Doctrine Versus the Incoherence of Experience, in* SELF-DETERMINATION AND SELF-ADMINISTRATION: A SOURCEBOOK 47–63 (W. Danspeckgruber ed., 1997).

5. See the numerous writings of the "democratic peace" theorists, including triumphalist versions such as FRANCIS FUKUYAMA, THE END OF HISTORY AND THE LAST MAN (1992); the most persuasive works in this line are Michael W. Doyle, *Kant, Liberal Legacies and Foreign Affairs,* 12 PHIL. & PUB. AFF. 203–34, 323–53, and MICHAEL W. DOYLE, WAYS OF WAR AND PEACE 205–311 (1997); *see also* BRUCE RUSSETT, CONTROLLING THE SWORD (1990). *Cp* Huntington's assertions that "democracy" is part of Western civilization, but not of its non-Western rivals, SAMUEL P. HUNTINGTON, THE CLASH OF CIVILIZATIONS AND THE REMAKING OF WORLD ORDER 192–98 (1996).

6. See BEYOND WESTPHALIA? STATE SOVEREIGNTY AND INTERNATIONAL INTERVENTION (Gene M. Lyons and Michael Mastanduno eds., 1995) for a useful, yet somewhat misdirected, inquiry into the broader issue of world order that focuses on the specific issue of whether a transfer of discretion over interventionary diplomacy to the U.N. can be said to have taken place. Such a specific concern is misdirected because the U.N. is itself an extension of statism, and thus not the most effective way to demonstrate the extent to which the state is being diminished in its capabilities by globalizing developments.

statism in a manner that is relevant to the future of world order and the overall situation of law as a regulative mechanism, is the emergence of what is being widely characterized as "globalization," a consequence of the rise of global market forces that is rapidly eroding the statist character of world order in a manner that is far more consequential than the rise and fall of the United Nations in the peace and security domain.[7] I have drawn a distinction between globalization-from-above and globalization-from-below to identify two interrelated tendencies: the restructuring of the world economy on a regional and global scale through the agency of the transnational corporation and financial markets from above, and the rise of transnational social forces concerned with environmental protection, human rights, peace, and human security from below.[8] The cumulative effects of globalization-from-below is the emergence of a recent social construction of international reality that is being identified as "global civil society."[9]

What is being proposed here is that these developments are of a revolutionary significance for our understanding of the growth and character of international law, especially with regard to the process by which norms are given the force of law, and the dynamics by which these norms are implemented or not. In some respects, this wider conception of international law has important antecedents. Public pressures have long exerted an influence on the behavior of democratically elected governments with respect to their international legal obligations, either in encouraging compliance or disregard, as well as in relation to norm-creation. It is well-known, for instance, that the Genocide Convention was brought into being shortly after World War II largely through the heroic exertions of a single private citizen, Raphael Lemkin, and over the years it has been private sector activism of various sorts that has been responsible for

7. There is a vast globalization literature. Among the various lines of interpretation, see IAN CLARK, GLOBALIZATION AND FRAGMENTATION: INTERNATIONAL RELATIONS IN THE TWENTIETH CENTURY (1997); ANKIE HOOGVELT, GLOBALIZATION AND THE POSTCOLONIAL WORLD: THE NEW POLITICAL ECONOMY OF DEVELOPMENT (1997); WILLIAM GRIEDER, ONE WORLD, READY OR NOT: THE MANIAC LOGIC OF GLOBAL CAPITALISM (1997); PAUL HIRST AND GRAHAME THOMPSON, GLOBALIZATION IN QUESTION (1996).

8. *See* Ronnie Lipschutz, *Restructuring World Politics*, 21 MILLENNIUM (1992); PAUL WAPNER, ENVIRONMENTAL ACTIVISM AND WORLD CIVIC POLITICS (1996); THE STATE AND SOCIAL POWER IN GLOBAL ENVIRONMENTAL POLITICS (Ronnie Lipschutz and Ken Conca eds., 1993); on globalization-from-below, see Richard Falk, *The Making of Global Citizenship*, *in* GLOBAL VISIONS: BEYOND THE NEW WORLD ORDER 39–50 (Jeremy Brecher, John Brown Childs and Jill Cutler eds., 1993).

9. Richard Falk, *Global Civil Society: Perspectives, Initiatives, Movements*, *in* 26 OXFORD DEV. STUD. 99–110 (1998).

mounting pressures on governments that increased prospects for the implementation of international law in relation to such central normative concerns as the promotion of human rights and the protection of the global commons. And it seems obvious, at least from 1972 onwards, that the growth of international legal protection for the environment has been mainly a consequence of civic initiatives within countries and across boundaries. In the 1980s, the rise in Europe of green political parties changed mainstream policy agendas so that the populist surge of environmentalist activism could be contained and adherents coopted. What also transpired into the 1990s was the increasing use of the global arenas provided by U.N.-sponsored conferences to promote lawmaking goals on such issues as environment, human rights, status of women, and social and economic policy.

Indeed, these intrusions of globalization-from-below on the normal intergovernmental activities of the United Nations have turned out to be so effective (and threatening to the supremacy of Westphalian ideas about world order) as to produce a statist backlash that is currently closing off these arenas of participation by transnational political forces. There is evident a deliberate reaction against cosmopolitan extensions of democracy beyond traditional state/society relations.[10] It seems, at least from the perspective of the late 1990s, that the resistance to these extensions of democracy is also mixed with ideological perceptions that globalization-from-below seeks to moderate market forces and takes issue with the laissez-faire tenets of neo-liberalism.

States, when reinforced by globalization-from-above, have been quite prepared to take initiatives that involve substantial restructuring of world order in a manner that erodes the Westphalian framework. This has been the case in relation to the creation of the World Trade Organization, and even more so with regard to the radical economic initiatives associated with the European Union in the 1990s; in these instances, it is the leading governments that are most inclined to support supernationalizing transfers of sovereignty over economic policy-making. To offset these globalizing steps, adversely affected segments of the citizenry invoke the territorial community and its priorities as the basis of human well-being, indicting government

10. David Held, Democracy and the Global Order: From the Modern State to Cosmopolitan Governance 267–86 (1995); for a range of views, see Cosmopolitan Democracy: Beyond the New World Order (Daniele Archibugi and David Held eds., 1995).

from both a chauvinist perspective on the right and a pro-labor perspective on the left.

The United States has been the most vocal champion of democratization at the level of the state, although this posture has not been consistently maintained, giving way on occasion to more opportunistic concerns.[11] Despite its sponsorship of "democracy," the U.S. government has been generally antagonistic to the rise of global civil society and its efforts to extend democracy beyond the level of the state in the spirit of globalization-from-below. Globalization-from-below needs to be understood, in part, as a reaction to the sterility of "choiceless democracy" in the face of the discipline of global capital. As such, it expresses a sense of dissatisfaction and frustration with electoral politics in relation to coping with the challenges of globalization-from-above and with regard to embodying an ethos of solidarity that underlies transnational concerns about violations of human rights. This "democracy fatigue" can create dangerous openings for authoritarian politics, as occurred in Germany during the Weimar Republic when the ineptitudes of government were widely blamed on politicians and the empty talk of the parliamentary process.

International law has generally attempted to confine jurisprudential debate within fairly conventional statist limits being subject to one or another versions of legal positivism that roots obligations in sources of law that rest upon some formal expression of the consent of the state. The New Haven approach to international law represents an ambitious and significant jurisprudential undertaking to overcome many of these limitations. Its conception of law encourages a far wider understanding of legal process, including an accommodation of participants from civil society.[12] Nevertheless, its impact and stature has been diminished because many of its prominent scholarly applications have appeared to devote attention only to the role of authoritative and effective decision-makers in shaping the contours of law. Its concerns about the value implications of public order systems, while phrased in a universalistic language, have seemed

11. Among these contradictions acquiescence in a takeover by the military in Algeria to reverse the outcome of the FIS victory in the 1992 elections; the support of Yeltsin despite turning Russian guns on the Parliament; a pattern of response that seems to regard a pro-market orientation as far more important than adherence to democratic procedures.

12. For the most influential early examples of this New Haven approach, see MYRES S. MCDOUGAL AND ASSOCIATES, STUDIES IN WORLD PUBLIC ORDER (1960)[hereinafter STUDIES].

deeply committed to Western Enlightenment traditions. The occasional attempts to identify convergent perspectives in other civilizational traditions seem superficial and unconvincing.[13] There is very little critical thought directed at the West or even in relation to the geopolitical practices of the United States; the basic work was done under the shadow of the Cold War.[14] It is this tendency to fuse policy analysis under the impact of the New Haven approach with an endorsement of the most controversial aspects of American foreign policy that has done the most to lend force to contentions that this policy-oriented jurisprudence is little more than an exercise in geopolitical apologetics.[15] What does not come clearly across is the fundamental shift in authority and value structures that is being brought about by economic globalization, within the context of neo-liberal ideology and a consumerist ethos, and the civic responses in the form of transnational political and legal initiatives, as well as the emergent multi-civilizational dialogue, which casts doubts on the universalistic claims previously assumed as inhering in the international legal order.[16]

What is being suggested is the need for a jurisprudence of international law that encompasses globalization in both its main expressions: from above and from below.[17] This dualism is itself a simplification of a far more complex reality that must also address the relevance of regional frames of reference that are very uneven with respect to the juridical character. One aspect of this call for a jurisprudential renewal of international law is to acknowledge the vital, innovative lawmaking and law-implementing roles played by agents of global civil society. A vivid illustration of this new dynamic is provided by attention given to the background and reception of the World Court Advisory Opinion, "Legality of the Threat or Use of

13. *See* Myres S. McDougal and Harold D. Lasswell, Jurisprudence for a Free Society 725–86 (Vol. II 1992); see also McDougal's and Lasswell's own persuasive critique of Jenks' false universalism in Studies, *supra* note 12, at 3–41.

14. *See, e.g.*, Studies, *supra* note 12.

15. *See* important book, Martti Koskenniemi, From Apology to Utopia: The Structure of International Legal Argument (1989)(if not apologetic, then certainly utopian).

16. Such doubts are less substantive than reflective of exclusions in relation to participation. Richard Falk, *False Universalism and the Geopolitics of Exclusion: The Case of Islam*, 18 Third World Q. 7–23 (1997).

17. Also important, but not considered here, is the accommodation of plural civilizational perspectives.

Nuclear Weapons."[18] Such scrutiny can be compared with conventional discussions of the international legal process that completely ignore the nongovernmental or grassroots origins of the legal process in civil initiatives and overlooks as juridically irrelevant, the impact of the judicial outcome on the status of nuclear weaponry within global civil society, as well as the relevance of transnational social forces to prospects for implementation. In these regards, the Advisory Opinion is a major contribution to the substantive discussion of the important questions to which it is addressed, but also manifests these new tendencies in international law for which even the most anti-positivist styles of juridical thinking have not been prepared to acknowledge to any significant extent.[19]

## B. GLOBALIZATION-FROM-BELOW AND THE JURISPRUDENCE OF RECOURSE

The legal challenges that have been directed toward the threat or use of nuclear weaponry have increasingly been associated with transnational civic initiatives organized under the aegis of peace-oriented NGOs. It was not always this way, or at least it did not appear to be the case. Early in the nuclear age, in the aftermath of the atomic bombings at the close of World War II, prominent leaders of states, including Winston Churchill and Harry Truman, spoke insistently about the importance of achieving total nuclear disarmament under international supervision to make sure that such weaponry was not developed further, much less used. What emerged from these efforts, with public opinion certainly playing a role, was a much heralded plan for nuclear disarmament, known at the time as either "the Baruch Plan" or "the Baruch/Acheson/Lilienthal Plan" after the main author(s) of the proposal. This proposal was rejected by the Soviet Union, allegedly on the grounds that the disarming process put on the table was structured in such a way as to freeze the technological advantages of the West and, in the event of a new arms race in the future, would give the United States and its allies a decisive edge. Soviet counter-proposals were rejected by the West supposedly because of their unwillingness to include in their framework adequate

18. Legality of the Threat or Use of Nuclear Weapons, Gen. List No. 95 (advisory opinion of July 8, 1996)[hereinafter Nuclear Weapons].

19. See references notes 8 and 9.

provision for inspection and enforcement. Arguably, neither superpower was genuinely interested in finding an approach that could compromise these differences. Later in the 1960s, partly in response to peace movement activities, both the Soviet Union and the United States tabled plans for general and complete disarmament that included the phased elimination of nuclear weaponry, but again there were strong reasons to doubt the sincerity of the effort.[20] It should be appreciated that the advocacy of nuclear disarmament, as such, does not by itself cast doubt upon the legal status of the weaponry, although the push to achieve elimination often merges with the view that weaponry of mass destruction cannot be reconciled with international humanitarian law. In a sense, disarmament is a way of acknowledging illegality, and its stress reflects the view in some quarters that a legal prohibition standing alone provides little improvement upon the current situation and elsewhere that it is easier to find a consensus in favor of mutual nuclear disarmament than to lend support to a rule of prohibition.

To the extent that the notion of "illegality" was seen as a step in the direction of delegitimizing past, present, and possible future uses of nuclear weaponry, the main impetus in the West came from peace movements in Europe and North America. The Soviet bloc, probably acting mainly on the basis of strategic considerations relating to their advantages in geopolitical position on the Eurasian landmass and with respect to conventional weaponry, pushed hard over the years to oppose nuclear weaponry, and gave to their worldwide propaganda machine the difficult assignment of spreading the view that nuclear weapons, and doctrines pertaining to their possible use, were immoral and illegal, even criminal. The most dramatic expression of this Soviet propaganda drive was undoubtedly the support given to the Stockholm Appeal in the early 1950s that clouded the issue by making it appear that being anti-nuclear somehow blended into being pro-Soviet. The U.S. government adopted the opposite stance, also probably reflecting strategic factors, to the effect that calls for nuclear disarmament were undesirable to the extent that they complicated overall security, either by adding to costs or by undermining deterrence.

20. For standard account, see McGeorge Bundy, Danger and Survival 130–234 (1988); for a more skeptical view, see Richard J. Barnet, Who Wants Disarmament? (1960); *see also* Robert J. Lifton and Richard Falk, Indefensible Weapons: The Political and Psychological Case Against Nuclearism (rev. ed. 1991); Marcus Raskin, Abolishing the War System (1992).

Despite these geopolitical overlays, the ebbs and flows of concern in society, corresponding to the crises that arose periodically in the context of the Cold War, generated an effort to push forward the view that nuclear weapons were illegal. This view gradually gained support and momentum within the Western peace movement. Three initiatives exhibit different dimensions of this process: first, the proceedings of the London Nuclear Warfare Tribunal in 1985 brought together many witnesses on all aspects of the weaponry, and the panel of four judges (three of whom had been Nobel laureates), concluded without any qualifications and in the heat of the Cold War, that nuclear weaponry was unconditionally illegal and that any threat or use would amount to a crime against humanity.[21] Second, the pledge to work for a formal legal prohibition on threat or use was circulated by the International Peace Bureau (in Geneva), endorsed by thousands of lawyers from all over the world, and championed with great zeal by Sean MacBride, a prominent international figure in the 1970s and 1980s who had been Foreign Minister of Ireland and was serving as President of IPB. Third were the heroic efforts, starting in 1987, of Harold Evans, a retired lower court judge from Christchurch, New Zealand, in a series of well-argued letters (later reinforced by an impressive "legal memorandum" on the case against legality) to government leaders in the Pacific, especially in New Zealand and Australia, urging them to seek an Advisory Opinion from the International Court of Justice on the issue of legality.[22] This was a period of time when there was a heightened awareness in the Pacific about the health and environmental hazards associated with French nuclear testing in the region.

This third initiative in particular generated a process that led to the establishment of what came to be known as the World Court Project, sponsored by the International Peace Bureau, the International Physicians for Social Responsibility, and most important, by a newly constituted transnational network of legal professionals called the International Association of Lawyers Against Nuclear Arms (IALANA).

21. Proceedings, London Tribunal on Nuclear Weapons.

22. *See* Harold James Evans, Case for the World Court, an open letter to Members of the New Zealand Section of the International Commission of Jurists, Sept. 4, 1987; Evans, Supplement to Open Letter of 4 September 1987, Nov. 21–22, 1987; for narrative of civic process, see Katie Boanes-Dewes, *Participatory Democracy in Peace and Security Decision Making,* 5 INTERDISCIPLINARY PEACE RESEARCH 80–108 (1993); Robert Green and Kate Dewes, *The World Court Project: How a Citizen Network Can Influence the United Nations,* 15 SOC. ALTERNATIVES 35–37 (1996). For an account of how the World Court Project pursued its goals, see JOHN BURROUGHS, THE (IL)LEGALITY OF THREAT OR USE OF NUCLEAR WEAPONS 9–11 (1997).

This Project raised the level of political awareness about the international law argument, it followed upon and emulated the very successful campaign by doctors against atmospheric nuclear testing, and, from the beginning, set its sites on achieving an authoritative rendering from the World Court on the legal status of the weaponry.

By persuading both the WHO and the General Assembly to pose fundamental questions about the legality of nuclear weaponry to the Court, the World Court Project succeeded in its initial objective. Underneath this process was a confidence by the lawyers who took part in the Project that the Court, if once faced with the issues as to legality, would cast legal doubts upon existing claims that nuclear weapons were not prohibited by international law. Such recourse to the Court was, to a large extent, a result of the effective mobilization of global civil society, but it depended very much on an ad hoc dynamic that managed to achieve a coalition of more than 700 voluntary associations in the course of its campaign. To ensure a more systematic representation of global civil society within the U.N. system and elsewhere, there have been several recent proposals of a Global Peoples Assembly.[23]

What seems evident is that the stimulus for lawmaking originated in global civil society with respect to nuclear weaponry, and that it would not have resulted in formal calls to the World Court without the pressures mounted by the World Court Project. Further, this lawmaking role is concealed by existing scholarly approaches that emphasize only authorized arenas with an explicit mandate. Of course, it is reasonable to ask whether all forms of pressure and influence should be given lawmaking stature. For instance, given the strength of global market forces, there are many settings where their lawmaking leverage is felt. The argument put forward here is part of a larger claim that the global village dimensions of international society need to be democratized so that the peoples of the world will be protected against dangerous, unregulated forms of extraterritorial behavior. Nuclear weaponry, with its global implications, raises questions of legality that affect not just the citizenry of the nuclear weapons states, but the entire world, thereby dangerously eroding the legitimacy of world order arrangements.[24] To resolve such questions by way of the rule

23. *See* Andrew Strauss and Richard Falk, *For a Global Peoples Assembly,* INT'L HERALD TRIB., Nov. 14, 1997; *see also* Jeffrey J. Segall, *A First Step for Peaceful Cosmopolitan Democracy,* 9 Peace Review 337–44 (1997).

24. The argument here is, first, that the legitimacy of Westphalian world order depends upon the will and capacity of states to address the problems of global society through their

of law provides some measure of assurance that globalization-from-above, together with statism, will not subject the peoples of the world to unacceptable risks.[25]

This dual set of requests from the WHO and the U.N. General Assembly thus confronted the Court with an opportunity and a dilemma. The opportunity was to be both constitutionally rigorous in relation to the WHO request, construing "health" fairly narrowly, while being forthcoming with respect to the General Assembly request. In this respect, the great majority of the judges managed to find a bright line between the two requests, but even here within the Court itself there were three strong dissents appended to the majority view that the WHO Assembly lacked the constitutional capacity to put forward a question that dealt with weaponry and not health.[26]

The dilemma was presented by the subject matter of nuclear weaponry and the expressed opposition by the leading nuclear weapons states to the General Assembly initiative in seeking legal guidance. Although not so formulated, the radical element in this request was to transfer the question of nuclear weapons policy from the domain of geopolitics, where it had remained since the first attacks on Hiroshima and Nagasaki, to the domain of international law.[27] Thus, even putting the issue of legality on the global agenda was alarming to the nuclear weapons states, almost regardless of the substantive result. It is an obvious conjecture that one likely source of concern was associated with the agitation of civil society and public anti-nuclear pressures that could be expected to result from any increased visibility for the question of legality, even in the unlikely event that existing policies toward nuclear weaponry were to be legally endorsed by the Court. It should be remembered, in this connection, that the most conservative judgment in the ICJ rendered by a divided

unilateral undertakings; and second, that nuclear weapons together with long-range delivery and the management of the global commons have eroded the legitimacy of a territorially based system of world order. *See* RICHARD FALK, ON HUMANE GOVERNANCE: TOWARD A NEW GLOBAL POLITICS (1995).

25. It is only a hesitant initial step, as global civil society is only seeking access to a judicial body that is selected and operated by reference to Westphalian criteria; there is no democratic participation in the formal proceedings of such an inter-governmental institution.

26. For companion case, see Legality of the Use by a State of Nuclear Weapons in Armed Conflict., Gen. List No. 93, 1996 I.C.J. (July 8).

27. The *Shimoda* case, decided by the Tokyo District Court in 1963 in response to claims brought by survivors, can be understood as the lone exception, and important as such, but still of only marginal relevance to the general sort of issue raised by the questions submitted to the Court. For the text of *Shimoda, see* Shimoda v. The Japanese State, JAP. ANN. INT'L L. 212–52 (1963).

Court in the South-West Africa Cases back in 1966 led paradoxically to an acceleration of extra-judicial anti-apartheid pressures on South Africa both in civil society and even within the United Nations system.[28]

Another fear of the governments in the nuclear weapons states must have been associated with their expectations that it was quite likely that the Court would issue a majority opinion that would challenge directly the legality of nuclear weaponry, thereby strengthening both governmental and civic anti-nuclear pressures. At the very least, strong legal objections to nuclear weaponry were likely to be voiced in separate and dissenting opinions by individual judges. For this combination of reasons, it was not surprising that a major effort was made to discourage recourse and, in the Court, to argue against responding to the requests.

It can also be assumed that most members of the Court must have realized that, unless its majority opinion generally approved of the existing approaches being taken by nuclear weapons states on the legal status of threats and uses of nuclear weaponry, its pronouncements would be in all probability evaded, if not rejected, by the relevant governments. Under these circumstances, the temptation to stand aside must have been great, allowing the Court as a creature of the state system (including its geopolitical orientation toward peace and security) to go quietly along with a set of security policies that had prevailed for half a century and were wildly applauded in some circles as having made positive contributions to peace.[29]

Judge Shigeru Oda's approach to this dilemma is particularly interesting, especially if one takes account of his Japanese nationality. Of all countries Japan had the most mobilized grassroots support for recourse to the Court; it submitted a petition with well over one million—and possibly as many as three million—signatures. Japan was also a society still suffering from "the nuclear allergy," which was clearly a consequence of having been the only country ever to

28. For overview, see THE SOUTH WEST AFRICA/NAMIBIA DISPUTE: DOCUMENTS ON THE SCHOLARLY CONTROVERSY BETWEEN SOUTH AFRICA AND UNITED NATIONS (J. Dugard ed., 1973); *see also* G.A. Res. 2145(XXI); the political reaction included efforts to shape the outlook of the Court to accord with views prevalent in international society, with one result being a request for an advisory opinion, which resulted in a decision that effectively reversed the conclusions of the 1966 judgment. Legal Consequences for States of the Continued Presence of South Africa in Namibia Notwithstanding Security Council Resolution 276 (1970), 1971 I.C.J. 16 (1971).

29. In this regard, the dissenting opinion of the American judge, Stephen M. Schwebel, who is now president of the Court, is a notable example.

experience the lethality of the nuclear age, even if only in a preliminary form.[30] Toward the very end of his dissent, Judge Oda labels paragraph 54 as "*My personal appeal,*" and goes out of his way to say there that, "I would emphasize that I am among the first to hope that nuclear weapons can be totally eliminated from the world," but insists that such a result "is a function of *political* negotiations among states in Geneva or New York and is not one which concerns our judicial institution here at The Hague. . . ." In concluding, for various reasons, that the Court should reject the request of the General Assembly, Judge Oda alone points his finger directly and by name at the role of the NGOs as confirming his impression that this whole process of invoking the Court is a political matter that needs to be entrusted to states. Note that the thirteen other judges are united in opposing this view of judicial function. In their view, it is not appropriate to inquire into the background or motivation of the General Assembly request, but rather to respond to it if the question posed raises an issue of international law that falls within the competence of the organ.

But Oda's point is deeper, and he drives it home by pointing to the "equivocations" of the majority that are present in the crucial paragraph of the *dispositif* relating to illegality: "The equivocations of sub-paragraph E prove my point that it would have been prudent for the Court to decline from the outset to give any opinion at all in the present case."[31] In contrast, the majority is careful to steer clear of any reference to the influence of outside pressures, determining its jurisdictional competence by reference to positivistic factors such as the scope of competence of the WHO Assembly in the one request and of the General Assembly in the other. As to alleged "political" aspects of the issue, the Court seizes the high ground of juridical autonomy, observing that "[w]hatever its political aspects, the Court cannot refuse to admit the legal character of a question which invites it to discharge an essentially judicial task, namely, an assessment of the legality of the possible conduct of States with regard to the obligations imposed upon them by international law."[32]

The response of the majority here is to contend that in an Advisory Opinion it is not necessary to resolve all doubts as to legal status,

30. For more details on the numbers of signatures received and their significance, see Nuclear Weapons, *supra* note 18 (dissenting opinion of Judge Weeramantry at 4–5); he notes that these signatures are "evidence [of] a groundswell of global public opinion which is not without legal relevance. . . ". *Id.*

31. Nuclear Weapons, *supra* note 18 (dissenting opinion of Judge Oda at para. 55, p. 37).

32. *Id.* at para. 13, p. 9 (*citing* several earlier ICJ advisory opinions).

but to convey the best professional understanding of the law as it currently exists. Such a view disappoints the anti-nuclear judges on the Court and infuriates those who are unprepared to go as far as does the majority in declaring any threat or use of nuclear weaponry to be generally contrary to international law. All of these judicial perspectives on the Court are formulated without reference to the outlook of civil society, or the past and future roles of civil society in reinforcing the anti-nuclear tenor of the outcome.

Only Judge Weeramantry in his historically important dissent roots the issue of recourse to the Court in observations relating to the importance of the issue within civil society. At the outset of his opinion, he notes that, "[t]his case has from its commencement been the subject of a wave of global interest unparalleled in the annals of this Court."[33] He goes on to acknowledge the large number of submissions to the Court, including several from NGOs, as well as the "nearly two million signatures [that] have been actually received by the Court from various organizations and individuals from around 25 countries."[34] Weeramantry also takes note of "the wide variety of groups that have exerted themselves in the anti-nuclear cause—environmentalists, professional groups of doctors, lawyers, scientists, performers and artists, parliamentarians, women's organizations, peace groups, students, and federations."[35]

Judge Weeramantry, while emphasizing this background, is also intent on putting to rest the contention that an inquiry of this sort is based on morality, not law. In his words, "[t]he anti-nuclear forces in the world are immensely influential, but that circumstance does not swerve the Court from its duty of pronouncing the use of the weapons legal if that indeed be the law"; and "[t]he Court's concern in answering this Request for an Opinion is with *lex lata* and not with *lex ferenda*."[36] All of the judges accept a "soft *Lotus*" approach, according deference to states to act if not forbidden from doing so, but not going so far as to require the rules of prohibition to be drafted with explicit reference to the behavior under consideration. In other

33. *Id.* at 4.

34. *Id.* (refers to additional signatures "so voluminous that the Court could not physically receive them. . .").

35. *Id.* at 87.

36. *Id.* at 6; *see also* the conclusion of the long dissent in which the judge reasserts his own orientation: "In this Opinion I have down my conclusions as to the law. While conscious of the magnitude of the issues, I have focused my attention on the law as it *is*. . ." *id.* at 87.

words, a prohibition on recourse to threats or uses of nuclear weapons can be derived from the general mandates of international humanitarian law without requiring a specific rule addressing nuclear weaponry. Here again it may be reasonable to note that transnational activism has probably contributed to an overall atmosphere that is extremely opposed to any reliance on nuclear weaponry, but surely this fact was in no way acknowledged by any of the judges.

For Judge Weeramantry, the equivocations of the majority in Paragraph E are to be deeply regretted because he believes them to be distortions of the law that are so serious as to lead him to define his position as one of dissent rather than that of a separate opinion that goes beyond the majority. At the same time, he does not accept the view of Judge Oda that such equivocations are an inevitable consequence of the political, and hence inappropriate, nature of the request, which casts its shadow across the response, depriving it of an acceptable level of legalist professionalism. According to Judge Weeramantry "[t]he Court needs to discharge its judicial role, declaring and clarifying the law as it is empowered and charged to do, undeterred by considerations that pertain to the political realm, which are not its concern."[37] He also confronts and rejects the argument that an Advisory Opinion on the legal status of nuclear weapons "would be devoid of practical effects," presumably because the nuclear weapons states will not take advice that challenges their fundamental security policies.[38] In an interesting aside, drawing on a comparison with the global struggle waged against apartheid, Judge Weeramantry seems to be affirming the view that the clarification of law "will assist in building up a climate of opinion in which law is respected."[39] In effect, law in this instance, as in the earlier case of apartheid, is a legitimate mobilizing basis for reformist action in global civil society. In this sense, Judge Weeramantry is indirectly enlarging our understanding of how international law becomes effective, recognizing that a range of social forces, including "the conscience of humanity," are relevant to the way in which governments conceive of their alternatives, and shows how law and politics interpenetrate properly in the fields of struggle against injustice. For these reasons, it is quite easy for Judge Weeramantry to insist on his identity as an adherent of a positivist jurisprudence in relation to the task

37. *Id.* at 85.
38. *Id.*
39. *Id.*

of ascertaining the law while relying on a sociological, and even a naturalist, jurisprudence when it comes to the post-judicial challenges of implementation. In effect, the participation of global civil society is endorsed, but not in the law library!

## C. GLOBALIZATION-FROM-BELOW AND THE ADVISORY OPINION AS LEGAL DOCTRINE

There are special difficulties associated with an assessment of the impact of global civil society upon the actual process of decision within any court of law, and, perhaps, especially in relation to the World Court.[40] Because most of the judicial activity of the World Court is a result of voluntary submissions by governments, its reputation as an institution that is protective of sovereign rights is of particular importance. In exercising its advisory roles, certain additional considerations are at work, including the role of the Court within the U.N. system, leading many judges to seem quite reluctant to respond to appeals for legal guidance received from major organs of the organization. Such factors were undoubtedly relevant in this situation, although perhaps not consciously so.

At the same time, members of the Court realize that if their views run counter to firm geopolitical commitments of important states, then prospects for compliance, or even respectful deference to its pronouncements, are quite minimal. And more than likely, attempts will be made to attack the Court as an institution.[41] If the Court reinforces a geopolitical consensus, then its pronouncements will be invoked by governments but may occasion scorn and bitterness in civil society, leading the institution to be labeled as a rubber stamp for geopolitics, the fate partly experienced by the Security Council in the

40. More than most courts, the World Court is seeking to establish its credentials as an independent judicial body that can be trusted to apply the law in a professional manner; partly, the issue of credibility reflects the precarious reputation of international law itself, but partly it also is connected with suspicions associated with all U.N. activities in which the representatives of peoples are selected by an intergovernmental process.

41. Experience with the litigation associated with the U.S. role in Nicaragua led to a furious attack upon the Court by the highest officials in the U.S. government, as well as to a direct refusal to implement the decision and a withdrawal of the conditional U.S. acceptance of compulsory jurisdiction; the actual behavior of the United States government was far more compatible with the World Court outcome than was its *rhetoric* of repudiation. As a result, a diplomacy of reconciliation proceeded along lines prefigured by the ICJ decision. For argument to this effect, including its jurisprudential implications, see JOAQUIN TACSAN, THE DYNAMICS OF INTERNATIONAL LAW IN CONFLICT RESOLUTION (1992).

aftermath of the Gulf War and, to some extent, by the Court in relation to the Lockerbie decision.[42] How then should the Court deal with a request from an organ of the U.N. system for guidance on a geopolitically hot issue? This question, then, needs to be connected with another that is equally subversive of purely statist ideas about the international legal order: suppose the geopolitically hot issue was referred to the Court because of the successful exertions of transnational democratic forces with deep roots in global civil society?[43]

I believe that these contextual factors led the Court to be doctrinally as conservative as possible, by which I mean, to operate according to a strictly positivist jurisprudence. Such a framing of judicial function was especially true for the majority, and yet the performance was subject to positivist lines of criticism from both those judges that believed the Court went too far in Paragraph E in an anti-nuclear direction and those who believed that it did not go far enough. Both groups of judges criticized the majority for its failure to provide clear guidelines as to the legal status and, despite their substantive disagreements, these dissenters agreed that the law was clear: either permitting nuclear weaponry to be used in a manner that was reasonable in context as was the case in its deterrent modes, or finding that any threat or use of nuclear weapons was prohibited by existing international law. The dissenters rejected the uncertainty of the majority on positivist grounds of disallowing the issuance of a *non-liquet,* or on "soft *Lotus*" grounds of finding existing customary norms of international humanitarian law radically inconsistent with any proposed threat or use of nuclear weaponry.[44]

Arguably, the three judges who believed that international law does not embody a general prohibition on threat or use of nuclear weapons were allowing their understanding of international customary norms to be shaped mainly by patterns of geopolitical practice that had evolved in the half-century since Hiroshima. It is probably not irrelevant to note that these judges came from the three most explicitly nuclearist states: the United States, Great Britain, and

42. *See* Richard Falk, *Reflections on the Gulf War Experience: Force and War in the U.N. System, in* THE GULF WAR AND THE NEW WORLD ORDER: INTERNATIONAL RELATIONS OF THE MIDDLE EAST 25–39 (Tareq Y. Ismael and Jacqueline S. Ismael eds., 1994).

43. *See* THOMAS J. BODIE, POLITICS AND THE EMERGENCE OF AN ACTIVIST INTERNATIONAL COURT OF JUSTICE (1995); *see also* RICHARD FALK, REVIVING THE WORLD COURT (1986).

44. *See* chapter vii; *see also* Nuclear Weapons, *supra* note 18 (opinions of Judges Higgins, Schwebel, Weeramantry, Koroma, Guilliame, Shahabuddeen).

France. On the other side, the three judges who interpreted existing international law as condemning existing practices relating to threat and possible use were guided by an apparent mixture of views associated with the properties of the weaponry and the conscience of humanity as leading inevitably to an unconditional condemnation. In both sets of dissenting responses, leaving out important nuances among the two groups of judges, the jurisprudential difficulties of equivocation or ambiguity were avoided.

The majority undoubtedly embodied a series of concealed compromises, including a search for some sort of consensus in the face of contradictory considerations. Not consciously, but operationally, the Advisory Opinion found the elusive middle ground between geopolitical deference (Lockerbie) and defiance (Nicaragua), as well as between repudiating the moral consensus of international society (as in the 1966 Judgment in the South-West Africa Cases) and translating this moral consensus into a political mandate (as in the Namibia Advisory Opinion of 1971). As such, the Advisory Opinion did not satisfy the main constituencies, but neither did it outrage them. It allowed the nuclear weapons states to interpret the outcome as compatible with their existing policies, and it permitted the anti-nuclear forces in international society to hail the outcome as a great encouragement for their efforts. Unlike the context of apartheid, the anti-nuclear majority in the General Assembly is passive and unmobilized, and whatever response ensues will depend on further exertions by the global anti-nuclear movement.

Jurisprudentially, this middle ground in the context of an Advisory Opinion was a reflection of contradictory elements in international society arising from tensions that were present in international practice: the nuclear weapons states had evolved one kind of practice based essentially on the legitimacy of deterrence, whereas the non-nuclear majority of states had generated another pattern of practice in the form of periodic expressions of the view that any and all threats or uses of nuclear weaponry were not only prohibited by international law, but that any violation of this prohibition would constitute a crime against humanity. The majority, then, in effect refused to adjudicate between these conflicting lines of interpretation, and accepted ambiguity as expressive of existing international law. For them, as was clear in some of the separate statements and declarations by judges who voted with the majority, the role of the Court, especially in its advisory functions, was to refrain from any kind of "legislative" clarification of the law in these circumstances.

What was surprising, and a third point of convergence (the other two being the acceptance of the General Assembly request and the shared adoption of a "soft *Lotus*" approach), was the unanimous call in Paragraph F of the *dispositif* for greater efforts to achieve nuclear disarmament as a matter of legal obligation. In a sense, such a call was not responsive to the question put by the General Assembly as to legal status of the weaponry, yet it did provide an opportunity for all the judges to affirm their shared sense that international society was committed to the elimination of the weaponry, which provided judges taking very different views of the legal issues at stake to express a certain solidarity with a sentiment dominant among anti-nuclear groups active in global civil society.

## D. A CONCLUDING ASSESSMENT

At this point, the undertaking of the World Court Project might appear somewhat inconsequential, even quite disappointing, reinforcing cynical views that international law is of marginal relevance with respect to the shaping of national policy in matters of peace and security, especially when the constraints of law challenge major geopolitical positions. There is no doubt that the nuclear weapons states have so far managed successfully to turn a blind eye to the Advisory Opinion without as yet experiencing any sort of significant anti-nuclear backlash in either the General Assembly or even in global civil society. The equivocation in crucial Paragraph E gave the nuclear weapons states just enough crawl space to deflect the impact of the finding that "the threat or use of nuclear weapons would generally be contrary to international law."[45] But the other side of the equivocation is to give definite encouragement to the campaign that has been waged in civil society ever since Hiroshima to rid the world of nuclear weaponry, especially when combined with Paragraph F's unanimous holding imposing a legal obligation on the nuclear weapons states "to pursue in good faith and bring to a conclusion negotiations leading to nuclear disarmament in all its aspects." This latter element of the *dispositif* represents potentially more than a bland sentiment as it challenges the avoidance of such negotiations by the nuclear weapons states, despite the end of the

45. For use of this crawl space by one who argued the U.S. position before the Court, see Michael J. Matheson, *The Opinions of the International Court of Justice on the Threat or Use of Nuclear Weapons*, 91 AM. J. INT'L L. 417 (1997).

Cold War and the recommendations of such independent initiatives as the Canberra Commission on the Elimination of Nuclear Weapons.[46]

It remains too early to tell whether the Advisory Opinion will exert any important influence on the future role and status of nuclear weapons. We know that the governments of nuclear weapons states do not seem disposed to alter their policies. We know that the main anti-nuclear pressures that mounted the World Court Project in the first place are more determined than ever to persist with their efforts, possibly shifting, at least temporarily, from an emphasis on illegality to support for a nuclear disarmament process.[47] The U.S. Lawyers' Committee on Nuclear Policy has already prepared a model treaty, and has been lobbying governments at the United Nations to lend their support.[48]

Jurisprudentially, the Advisory Opinion suggests the capacity of the transnational NGO community to make use of the World Court to advance its goals, both by mounting the decisive pressure that led to the requests being forwarded by the WHO and the General Assembly, and by preventing the outcome from being altogether lost in the noise of geopolitics.[49] That is, both in relation to lawmaking

46. Report by the Canberra Commission on the Elimination of Nuclear Weapons (Aug. 14, 1996); *see also* General (Ret.) Lee Butler, *Chaining the nuclear beast*, 27 Ploughshares Monitor 17–18 (Dec. 1996).

47. *See* Phon van den Biesen, *Foreword, in* Burroughs, *supra* note 22, at ix–x, which argues strongly along these lines:

"The importance of this section of the Advisory Opinion cannot be overstated. It means that states which are at this very moment *not* involved in a negotiating process specifically focused on the goal of total nuclear disarmament, are at this very moment violating their obligations under international law. The natural outcome of such a negotiating process would be the adoption of a comprehensive Nuclear Weapons Convention creating a framework for the complete elimination of nuclear weapons."

*Id. See also* Burroughs, *supra* note 22, at 48–51 for analytic discussion of this disarmament legal duty.

48. See Lawyers' Committee on Nuclear Policy, Model Nuclear Weapons Convention (draft) (Apr. 1997).

49. Some positive impact has been discerned, including: a formal decision by the Canadian government to review its position on nuclear weapons in light of the advisory opinion; a series of formal calls by governments and international organizations to move toward a nuclear weapons convention that entails elimination of the weaponry; a coalition of more than 600 NGOs in support of the Abolition 2000 campaign to rid the world of nuclear weaponry; a spurt of responsive publications and initiatives by the Nuclear Age Peace Foundation and its energetic president, David Krieger; The Hague Appeal for Peace in 1999, emphasizing the nuclear weapons issue; new civic initiatives of resistance based on the illegality of nuclear weapons as confirmed by the advisory opinion. These and other developments are summarized in IPPNO Newsletter, Dec. 1997 at 1–2; *see also* David Krieger, Countdown to Abolition 2000, undated paper of Nuclear Age Peace Foundation.

and implementation, the role of global civil society is evident. With respect to the substantive results, the relationship is far more speculative and indefinite, accounting for some counterweight to the pressures associated with geopolitical factors, but to an extent that could not for reasons of legal professionalism be disclosed, even if present.

The endeavors of global civil society with respect to nuclear weaponry were seeking an outcome in the World Court that minimized geopolitical influences and maximized the impact of the conscience of humanity as expressed by activist anti-nuclear forces. The result embodied in the Advisory Opinion was a compromise that was politically quite adept: the legality of nuclear weapons was given an unprecedented salience by this whole process, geopolitical forces were annoyed but in the end their approach has not yet been terribly threatened, and global civil society was given encouragement, but has not responded with sufficient intensity to keep the issue on the global agenda.

Not only in relation to the legal status of nuclear weaponry, but with regard to a range of other global issues, the time has come to rely on a post-Westphalian jurisprudence to interpret the role of law with respect to the well-being of peoples. The old statist categories, while never entirely satisfactory, are now incapable of capturing the lawmaking dynamics at work in an era of globalization. The 1997 Nobel Peace Prize Committee acknowledged as much by awarding the prize to a grassroots activist, Jody Williams, and to the associated NGO campaign to ban anti-personnel land mines, a process that produced what has been aptly called "a 'people's' treaty" to ban land mines."[50] Admittedly, banning land mines is far less challenging to the geopolitical mentality than is the effort to prohibit and eliminate nuclear weaponry, but the jurisprudential point is, if anything, clearer: it is no longer satisfactory to conceive of international law on the basis of classical "sources of law" and "enforcement." A global law of peoples is emergent, and it is time for jurists to provide a suitable framework for its comprehension and assessment.

50. See Editorial, 28 PLOUGHSHARES MONITOR 1 (Dec. 1997), for comment along these lines; 122 countries have signed the treaty (although the United States, China, and Russia are notably absent); the formal name of the treaty signed in Ottawa on December 4, 1997, is "Convention on the Prohibition of the Use, Stockpiling, Production and Transfer of Anti-Personnel Mines and on their Destruction." The role of transnational activism has also been important in relation to other aspects of nuclear weapons policy, including the various efforts over the years to limit, and then stop, the testing of nuclear weaponry, and in relation to regional initiatives to establish nuclear weapons zones.

# PART III

# TOWARD HUMANE GOVERNANCE

# CHAPTER IX

# THE COMING GLOBAL CIVILIZATION: NEO-LIBERAL OR HUMANIST?

Integrative tendencies in international life, combined with the widely imagined future of a cyberworld, ensure that a global civilization *in some form* will take shape early in the twenty-first century. But this probable world is a civilization only in a technical sense of being bound together by a high rate of interaction and real time awareness, with reduced relevance attached to distance, boundaries, and the territorial features of the domains administered by sovereign states. If such a global civilization is also, as is likely, market-driven and subject to the logic of global capital, it will, as a matter of principle, related to its stress on efficiency, be indifferent to the plight of the poor and the jobless, insensitive in the face of oppression and exploitation, and irresponsible with respect to the environment and the crisis of sustainability that is likely to beset generations born in the next century.[1]

The current ideological climate, with its neo-liberal dogma of minimizing intrusions on the market and "downsizing" the role of government in relation to the provision of public goods that compose the social agenda, suggests that the sort of global civilization that is taking shape will be widely perceived, not as fulfillment of a vision of unity and harmony, but as a dysutopian result of globalism-from-above that is mainly constituted by economistic ideas and pressures.[2]

1. For a full world order argument about the consequences of a world economy that adheres to neoliberal policy guidelines, see Richard Falk, *An Inquiry into the Political Economy of World Order,* I NEW POL. ECON. 13–26 (1996); Richard Falk, ON HUMANE GOVERNANCE: TOWARDS A NEW WORLD POLITICS (1995).

2. Among the many interpretations of this dark prospect, one that is worthy of note is that of BENJAMIN R. BARBER, JIHAD VS MCWORLD (1995); for the range of negative (and positive) scenarios about the future, see Majid Tehranian and Laura Reed, *Human Security and Global Governance, in* PROSPECTUS FOR COLLECTIVE RESEARCH PROJECT 71 (Toda Institute for Global Peace and Policy Research 1996).

## A. A JURIDICAL APPROACH TO GLOBAL CIVILIZATION: COMPLETING THE ENLIGHTENMENT PROJECT

Organizing the world in accordance with the discipline of global capital is at sharp variance with the image of global civilization that Judge C. G. Weeramantry has depicted and promoted throughout the course of his notable professional life as scholar, jurist, and most lately, as judge. His conception of a global civilization is informed by a normative orientation that he believes is already embodied in the most sacred texts, traditions, and belief systems of the leading living cultures in the world. This normative content is humanistic and universalistic in character, premised on the overriding importance of achieving conditions that are conducive to human survival in social and political conditions of harmony, dignity, and tolerance, and reliant on the clarifying insight of human reason but not carried to the cultic extremes of rationalism.[3] In effect, achieving this understanding of global civilization, as the basis for reforming world order, bears some superficial resemblance to the program of the Enlightenment as it unfolded in Europe in the twilight of feudalism during the fourteenth and fifteenth centuries, but universalizes its positive cultural foundations by relying upon the wisdom and insight of non-Western civilizations.[4]

What sets Judge Weeramantry apart among international law specialists is his deep belief that these goals are not only integral to cultural identity, but have been long inscribed in the deep structures of international law, which prefigures a beneficial future for humanity, as contrasted with the Hobbesian sense of fundamental antagonism and struggle as the permanent reality of the human condition, capable of mitigation, but only through the imposition of a leviathan in the form of a law-enforcing state. From his humanistic standpoint, it follows for Weeramantry that it is the task and duty of the scholar, jurist, and judge to be responsive to this reality in relation to the concrete issues of the day whenever the occasion to do so presents itself. In this regard, for Weeramantry, the character of a global civilization is what might be described as "an embedded utopia," that

3. *See* JOHN RALSTON SAUL, VOLTAIRE'S BASTARDS: THE DICTATORSHIP OF REASON IN THE WEST (1992).

4. For a clear and comprehensive sense of Weeramantry's distinctive approach on these issues, his indictment of Western materialism and individualism, as well as his criticism of the West for its destructive impact on the Third World during the colonial era, see WEERAMANTRY, EQUALITY AND FREEDOM: SOME THIRD WORLD PERSPECTIVES (1976).

is, its contours are already present and discernible within existing worldviews and belief systems, and those with authority to interpret the law have an opportunity and responsibility to bring this utopic possibility a step closer to social and political reality. However, because the world is still run according to the geopolitical parameters of the Hobbesian worldview, this normative order is concealed from the general view and is contradicted and resisted by the daily practice of states. Of course, this utopian affirmation collides with realist worldviews and conventional wisdom. For these reasons, it can only be brought to bear on practice and behavior as a result of the conviction and courage of the jurist, an undertaking that Weeramantry has heroically sought to actualize in his career, and with particular intensity during his brief period as a judge on the International Court of Justice. He has done this, especially, in his extended dissenting opinions in *Lockerbie, East Timor,* and most significantly and enduringly, in the Advisory Opinion on *The Legality of the Threat or Use of Nuclear Weapons.*

It is important to notice that, despite this seemingly visionary defining professional commitment, Judge Weeramantry's method and jurisprudence is avowedly positivistic in the central respect that his conception of judicial function is to apply international law as it *exists,* without encroaching on legislative prerogatives by any claim of a lawmaking role for the World Court. The important challenge confronting a judge is to apply the law in this manner, but to do so without flinching in the face of geopolitical pressures and without giving the sovereign state a blank check in the form of a broad application of the *Lotus* case that has been widely understood, especially by most legal positivists, as affirming the legal capacity of the state to do whatever it wants provided only that it is not expressly prohibited by law from so doing. On the contrary, where humanistic factors are at stake, Weeramantry's approach to positivism moves dramatically in the opposite direction, especially in the context of peace and security, by giving specific prohibitory effects to very generalized legal principles of limitation, such as the Martens Clause and that often-cited provision of the Hague rules of the law of war that the means used to injure an enemy are not "unlimited." Such a jurisprudential move imports into positive international law a strong set of naturalist tendencies, and effectively nullifies a broad reading of *Lotus,* thereby enabling a powerful challenge to geopolitics and sovereign discretion to be mounted from *within* the frame of *existing* international law, and this in accord with the most commonly accepted standards of professionalism applicable to judicial behavior.

In each of the three prominent legal controversies presented to the World Court during his tenure, Weeramantry, unlike the majority of his brethren, refuses to strike what appears to be a tacit Faustian bargain with geopolitics, either in the form of a compromise that significantly defers to the practice of leading states, as in the majority opinion in the *Nuclear Weapons* case, or by outright deference to the priorities of those political actors with predominant power and wealth, as seems arguably to occur in the *Lockerbie* and *East Timor* decisions. Weeramantry's contrasting sense of law's humanistic authority is most evident, perhaps, in his long dissenting opinions in the companion *Nuclear Weapons* cases.[5]

All of these features of Weeramantry's distinctive jurisprudential signature can be vividly illustrated by a brief consideration of his approach in the *Nuclear Weapons* Advisory Opinion that responds to the General Assembly request.[6] In explaining his reasons for dissenting rather than offering a separate opinion, despite acknowledging that the Court moves significantly "in the direction of illegality," which he so fervently favors, Weeramantry contends that the most crucial parts of the decision "are both less than clear and clearly wrong," as they "state the law wrongly and incompletely."[7] What he is particularly objecting to is, first, the assertion by the Court that each and every use of nuclear weapons would be "generally" illegal rather than the stronger assertion that any use be regarded as unconditionally illegal and, second, the Court's further admission of its inability to "conclude definitively" at this time whether a use of nuclear weapons would be lawful or not in "an extreme circumstance of self-defence, in which the very survival of the state would be at stake."[8] Weeramantry believes that despite the absence in international law of an explicit prohibition directed at nuclear weaponry,

5. See also Weeramantry's notable dissent in the companion nuclear weapons case in which the World Health Organization poses the question of the legality of nuclear weapons; in this setting Weeramantry is one of only three judges who believes the Court should have responded affirmatively to the request for an advisory opinion, basing his core reasoning on a humanistic view of "health," and the corresponding mandate of the WHO.

6. My own somewhat more positive view of the majority decision is contained in Richard Falk, *Nuclear Weapons, International Law, and the World Court: A Historic Encounter,* 91 AM J. INT'L L. 64–75 (1997).

7. The texts of the Advisory Opinion are contained in a provisional publication of the International Court of Justice with the title Legality of the Threat or Use of Nuclear Weapons, Advisory Opinion, General List No. 95, 8 July 1996. The separate and dissenting opinions of individual judges are given separate page numbering, and will be referred to by name. Judge Weeramantry, 1. Subsequent footnote references to the Advisory Opinion will be identified as 'Nuclear Weapons'.

8. *Nuclear Weapons,* Weeramantry, 2–3.

these weapons are categorically illegal under existing international law, and that thus the Court is technically wrong to mention even the possibility, however circumscribed, that a threat or use of nuclear weapons could conceivably be legal, a conclusion that he believes to be both a misstatement of the law and a dangerously unwelcome opening of a Pandora's Box.[9]

More revealing than the substantive issue itself is the reasoning relied upon by Weeramantry to arrive at this reading of international law, namely the view that every use of nuclear weapons, whatever the allegedly justifying circumstances, "contradicts the fundamental principle of the dignity and worth of the human person on which all law depends." And further, that all uses must be prohibited because nuclear weaponry "endangers the human environment in a manner that threatens the entirety of life on the planet." Weeramantry gives many additional reasons for reaching such a categorical conclusion, including his view that all the great cultures of the world are opposed at their core to any actions that violate "elementary considerations of humanity."[10] He also relies on the conclusions reached by the U.N. General Assembly in several resolutions that call for the "complete elimination" of nuclear weapons, and that are in his view an authoritative expression of "the international community's attitude" to the effect that the weaponry poses "a danger to civilization and must be eliminated."[11] Beyond this, Weeramantry interprets the general principles and directives of international humanitarian law as supportive of the conclusion that nuclear weaponry is inherently illegal. The main point here is not the legal rationale underpinning Weeramantry's views on nuclear weaponry, but the way such a rationale illustrates his more general view that the jurist is guided by an inner universalism and humanism that is already present and authoritative, embodied in the foundational principles of international law. Quite obviously, the threat to the survival of the human species, and even to life itself, that has always been associated with the prospect of large-scale reliance on nuclear weaponry, is inherently universal. Its implications are, accordingly, transcivilizational, and cannot be fully comprehended from the perspective of any particular civilization. As a result, the humanist aspects of Weeramantry's jurisprudence are

9. For accord, *see* Richard Falk, Elliott L. Meyrowitz, and Jack Sanderson, *Nuclear Weapons and International Law,* 20 INDIAN J. INT'L L. 541 (1980); C.G. WEERAMANTRY, NUCLEAR WEAPONS AND SCIENTIFIC RESPONSIBILITY (1987); ELLIOTT L. MEYROWITZ, PROHIBITION OF NUCLEAR WEAPONS: THE RELEVANCE OF INTERNATIONAL LAW (1990).

10. *Nuclear Weapons,* Weeramantry, 32–33.

11. *Nuclear Weapons,* Weeramantry, 71.

accentuated and the civilizational aspects are somewhat subordinated, although far from absent. Also, as will be discussed, Weeramantry seeks to underpin his ethical posture with a credible professionalism that is sensitive to the limits of judicial discretion, that is, a judge does not legislate, but applies the law that exists with divergencies among judges presumably explained by varying lines of interpretation adopted with reference to a complex array of pertinent sources.

In the conclusion of his lengthy dissent, Weeramantry notes that there are two divergent possible ways to think about the role of international law. First, there is the power-oriented approach classically formulated by Thomas Hobbes that accepts "the dependence of international law on terror" and then there is "the international rule of law as visualized by Grotius." Weeramantry's view is that, between these "widely divergent world views. . . . international law has clearly a commitment to the Grotian vision," and that the Court, in this case, missed its historic opportunity to make manifest the character of this commitment with respect to an issue of transcendent importance.[12] Weeramantry directly confronts the argument that a decision that flies in the face of geopolitics, here in the form of the almost certain unwillingness of the political leadership in the nuclear weapons states to defer to the Court's conclusion as to illegality, and argues that the essence of the judicial function is to "assert the law as it is" regardless of political consequences, and that the integrity of such an avowal will have "its own inherent authority" that is likely over time to alter seemingly rigid and opposed current assessments of feasibility. He bolsters this abstract assessment of how law eventually prevails by noting that the Court's repudiation of apartheid in its advisory opinion on Namibia (1971) seemed at the time to fly in the face of political reality, but that its conclusion of illegality became itself a factor in altering power relationships in support of political and social forces working to dismantle apartheid, and eventually remade historical reality. In Weeramantry's eloquent words, "[t]he Court needs to discharge its judicial role, declaring and clarifying the law as it is empowered and charged to do, undeterred by considerations that pertain to the political realm, which are not its concern."[13] It is evident that Weeramantry believes that a judge has no business making political calculations about the effectiveness of a particular

12. 923 I.L.M. 86.
13. 922 I.L.M. 85.

line of decision, but should limit her role to the strictly legal challenge of discerning and applying the law.[14]

## B. QUESTIONING THE POSTULATE OF NORMATIVE UNIVERSALISM

Weeramantry is profoundly convinced that the fundamental normative reality embodied in international law, at least as it pertains to survival threats, is the convergence of values and beliefs at the root of all civilizational identities. As such, he is at odds with the many recent developments associated with the assertion of distinct civilizational orientations toward values and beliefs. Such a sense of civilizational diversity need not, of course, proceed down the Huntington road of "the West against the rest" or even the view of a looming "clash of civilizations" that is in the process of superseding the rivalry of states with the new Hobbesian order made up of warring civilizations.[15] In its more moderate formulation, a pluralist view of civilizational identity argues that there are notable divergencies on matters of values and beliefs, as well as with respect to historical experience, that subverts, or at the very least, qualifies claims of a universal normative order. Further, a salient feature of the contemporary world scene is the assertion of these differences, which is more evident than ever, since the end of the Cold War and its more transitory preoccupation with ideological differences between Marxism and market-oriented constitutionalism that were internal to the Western projects of modernization and global hegemony, as were the two so-called "world" wars earlier in the century.[16] Until decolonization had run its course by the mid-1960s, it was arguable, at least, to

14. Note that in a different setting two very conservative judges gave the same jurisprudential rationale for ignoring the political consensus in a controversial case. South West Africa case (2nd Phase) I.C.J. Rep. (1966) 3, which was later effectively reversed by a subsequent advisory opinion, Legal Consequences of the Continued Presence of South Africa in Namibia (South West Africa) Notwithstanding Security Council Resolution 276, Namibia Case, I.C.J. Rep. (1971) 16.

15. For the full expression of this perspective, see SAMUEL P. HUNTINGTON, THE CLASH OF CIVILIZATIONS AND THE REMAKING OF WORLD ORDER (1996).

16. For an influential and important stress on the normative significance of these Cold War differences in relation to the international legal order, and a refutation of C. Wilfred Jenks' universalism (as expressed in A COMMON LAW OF MANKIND (1958)) as well as an implicit refutation of F.S.C. Northrop (THE MEETING OF EAST AND WEST (1946)), see Myres S. McDougal and Harold D. Lasswell, *The Identification and Appraisal of Diverse Systems of Public Order, in* STUDIES IN WORLD PUBLIC ORDER 3–41 (Myres S. McDougal and Associates eds., 1960)

conflate the Western experience with the totality of world history.[17]

In my view, there is a mainly creative tension currently at work between universalism and the particular outlook of a given civilization that needs to become the dialectical basis for intercivilizational dialogue. The non-Western world is definitely invoking civilizational identities as a means to avoid the homogenizing effects of economic globalization, and even more insistently, as a means to overcome the memories and persisting realities of Western domination. Such a tendency has been especially evident in recent Islamic and Asian efforts to assert a range of differences, and to mount a critique of Western manipulation and domination of the world economy, of the dynamics of global security, and even of the operations of such supposedly global endeavors as are mandated or performed by the United Nations.[18] This line of normative interpretation seeks, as well, to emphasize the importance of intercivilizational equity and participation as part of the ongoing process of constructing a legitimate world order.[19]

It seems evident, for instance, that the exclusion of indigenous peoples from participation in the processes of creating, and later developing, an international law of human rights resulted in an unsatisfactory outcome. The outcome was, from the perspectives of indigenous peoples, which are themselves diverse, a generally illegitimate framework. Indigenous peoples, through their own initiative, have been doing their best to rectify the deficiencies of this framework, not by invoking a clarifying set of universal normative directives, but by positing their own distinctive perspectives articulated in relation to their rendering of the master-norm of the right of self-determination. This is indeed borrowed from the univeralist framework but then adapted to the particular claims and conditions of indigenous peoples as seeking, above all, to safeguard a way of life, and to ensure control over their own destiny by reemerging in history as a series of *subjects,* as contrasted to their modernist experience within sovereign, secular states of extreme oppression and assimilative deprivation through

17. *Compare* William H. McNeill, The Rise of the West (1963), *with* Arnold Toynbee, A Study of History (1954).

18. For representative writing, see Ahmet Davutoglu, Civilizational Transformation and the Muslim World (1994); Chandra Muzaffar, Human Rights and the New World Order (1993); Chandra Muzaffar, Dominance of the West Over the Rest (1995).

19. For an elaboration of this line of argument, see Richard Falk, *The Geopolitics of Exclusion: The Case of Islam,* 18 Third World Q. 7 (1997).

their treatment as *objects*, with either an overtly exploitative or paternalistic rationale.[20] The struggle of indigenous peoples to rely upon international law is related to the earlier discussion of the legality of nuclear weapons as it also poses, in its most fundamental form, a question of survival, not of the species, but of a given civilization, or more accurately, a group of civilizations that share a traditional or pre-modern world picture. In this instance, the relevance of international law seems to be the protection of civilizational identity and diversity rather than the preservation of the human species as such.

Of course, civilizational identities are also being used by oppressive non-Western regimes as a way of justifying their refusal to uphold minimum human rights standards or to overcome cruel cultural practices, and shielding prevailing governmental policies from certain lines of internal and external criticism. By acknowledging this double reality of civilizational pluralism, its positive and negative aspects, the foundations are firmly laid for inter- and intracivilizational dialogic approaches to normative order.

In this regard, Weeramantry's universalism needs to be comprehended on the basis of his full range of writings, and not just on the basis of his pronouncement as World Court judge. Without that fuller understanding of his outlook, Weeramantry's approach may be understood as somewhat incomplete, and not sufficiently responsive to the historical reality of intercivilizational assertiveness and its related resistance to Western hegemonic threats and structures.[21] It remains a matter of controversy, however, whether at this stage of international society that normative universalism can provide the basis for a generally accepted jurisprudential point of departure. Instead, what is here being urged, in contrast to my understanding of Weeramantry's *judicial* approach, is an incorporation of civilizational perspectives into a jurisprudential framework that also seeks to establish effective transcivilizational standards and procedures of universal applicability and

20. *See* S. James Anaya, *Canada's Fiduciary Obligation Toward Indigenous Peoples in Quebec Under International Law in General, in* Canada's Fiduciary Obligation to Aboriginal Peoples in the Context of Accession to Sovereignty by Quebec 9–40 (Royal Commission on Aboriginal Peoples Report)(Aug. 1995). The word "subject" is ambiguous. Here it is used in contrast to "object," but often it is used in quite the opposite manner: in contrast to "citizen." In the latter instance, the subject is passive and conceived in relation to a king or royal personage, while in the former case, the subject is active, an autonomous agent of destiny and not a manipulated object of hegemonic forces.

21. *See especially*, Weeramantry, Equality and Freedom: Some Third World Perspectives, *supra* note 4, for fuller sense.

legitimacy, but only gradually, and through participation in a multi-civilizational dialogic process.[22] The interrogation of Weeramantry's approach is twofold: first, on attentiveness to the *process* of law creation and the inclusion and exclusion of civilizations at various stages; and second, in the degree of acknowledgment that international law, as it exists, loses authoritativeness in certain of its aspects, because it was titled in support of distinctly Western interests and values.

## C. INTERNATIONAL LAW AND GEOPOLITICS: SUSTAINING A BAD MARRIAGE

Judge Weeramantry has opted strongly for a view of judicial function and jurisprudential posture that is predicated on the necessity of divorcing the application of law from the governing structures of geopolitics, with their Hobbesian lineage and their subordination of international law to the dynamics of power relationships and priorities. It is his further belief that the autonomy of international law provides the basis for ensuring that progressive and humanistic tendencies will eventually prevail in international life, and culminate in the full flowering of a global civilization based on reason and justice, and governed with a vigilant eye toward human survival.[23]

In polar opposition to this outlook is the ultra-realist sense that international law, and its institutions of interpretation and adjudication, are creatures of an international society that is shaped by reference to the workings of great power politics, and that a particular judge or scholar is inevitably aligned to particular actors within an existing world order, either by an accident of birth and national identity or as an expression of genuine ideological or ethical allegiance.

22. Weeramantry seems favorably disposed to mediating universalism through the specificities of cultural tradition, but primarily, as I understand his outlook, to discover and develop in the most meaningful way the shared universal normative roots that unite certain commonalities of civilizational perspectives without abolishing or denigrating civilizational particularities, especially in non-Western settings where it is important to resist the Western juggernaut. In this regard, Weeramantry's orientation has certain characteristics in common with that of Jenks and Northrop (as cited *supra* note 16), but also with Arnold Toynbee, to whom Weeramantry approvingly refers on several occasions in his scholarly writings. *See, e.g.*, WEERAMANTRY, EQUALITY AND FREEDOM: SOME THIRD WORLD PERSPECTIVES, *supra* note 4, at 142, 186.

23. For a strong argument along these lines that jurisprudentially has much in common with Weeramantry, see FRANCIS ANTHONY BOYLE, WORLD POLITICS AND INTERNATIONAL LAW (1985); and FRANCIS ANTHONY BOYLE, THE FUTURE OF INTERNATIONAL LAW AND AMERICAN FOREIGN POLICY (1989).

For obvious reasons, such a marrying of jurisprudential standpoint and geopolitics is vigorously denied by mainstream international law scholars, and even by government officials and appointees, unless the approach of their ideological adversaries is under scrutiny. The West scornfully dismissed Marxist jurists from Soviet bloc countries, while the Communist establishment did the same for their Western counterparts.[24]

In the West, the linkage between law and policy is disguised or suppressed in arenas of decision to avoid undermining respect for legal analysis, which depends on maintaining an aura of objectivity. To acknowledge openly that legal outcomes reflect the fortuities or affinities of geopolitcal circumstances would undermine any respect for international law, as well as violate the most basic and widely shared canons of legal method. This jurisprudential orientation has been most conceptually endorsed by The New Haven School, associated with Myres McDougal, that links authoritativeness directly with effectiveness, and thus deliberately alerts a judge or other decision-maker to the need to have some reasonable prospect that a particular line of interpretation will be implemented in practice. This approach also believes that the application of international law necessarily involves ongoing international conflict, and that it is either necessary for practical reasons of effectiveness to defer to the unwillingness of leading states to accept certain restraints on their conduct or it is appropriate to support the legal expression of geopolitical claims, because the claimant is perceived as an agent for the promotion of a beneficial world order and its opponents and rivals are regarded as agents of destruction and oppression.[25] In effect, these tensions

24. My point here is not to suggest a kind of symmetry. The Soviet bloc ideological discipline was far more systematic and coercive, and arguably less effective than the Western liberal approach, which was far more subtle in its reliance on ideological monitoring devices, but not much more tolerant of deviance. *See* Edward S. Herman and Noam Chomsky, Manufacturing Consent: The Political Economy of the Mass Media (1988); *see also* Noam Chomsky, The Chomsky Reader 83–136 (1987).

25. The normative claims for linking law and geopolitics were particularly prominent during the Cold War era, and were especially evident in the work of the New Haven School: Myres S. McDougal and Associates, Studies in World Public Order (1960); John Norton Moore, The Secret War in Central America: Sandinista Assault on World Order (1987). For other works by distinguished international law scholars along these lines, but written in a positivistic vein, see Thomas M. Franck, Nation against Nation: What Became of the United Nations Dream and What the U.S. Can Do About It (1985); Thomas M. Franck, Judging the World Court 35–76 (1986); Julius Stone, Aggression and World Order: A Critique of United Nations Theories of Aggression (1958). It should be noted that many jurists of postivist or naturalist persuasion are less explicit or aware about their rationale, but are equally sensitive to the relevance of power to the interpretation of legal obligation in international society. Arguably, as well, the tilting

between the geopolitics *of our side* and international law are vigorously denied, converting international law in settings of robust political concern into what most neutral observers would regard as a legalistic species of rationalization or propaganda. It is possible, of course, that a persuasive case can be made that world order values are at stake in a manner that happens to coincide with the geopolitical situation of the jurist but, if such a convergence is alleged by an idelogical adversary, it will be quickly dismissed as mere propaganda. In my view, this jurisprudential deference to geopolitics, which often functions as an unconscious determinant of juridical analysis, erodes the role of international law in promoting a preferred world order in the form of humane governance for the planet.

Nevertheless, I favor a jurisprudential orientation toward the relations between international law and geopolitics that is closer to that adopted by the majority in the *Nuclear Weapons* Advisory Opinion than to the Weeramantry position.[26] It seeks to mediate between the normative imperatives of international law and morality and the political constraints associated with effective power and the authoritative practice of leading states, especially in the context of peace and security. In my view, the unmediated analysis of applicable legal principles assumes an unrealistic autonomy for the domain of law and an implausible objectivity of interpretation on the part of the policy-maker or judicial official. Besides, international law as a particular type of law flourishing within a societal order that lacks evolved institutions of governance, has always relied on a subtle interplay between rule and practice to introduce elements of effectiveness and adaptability into the operational reality of the international legal order, as well as to acknowledge a dialogic dimension to the implementation of controversial legal standards. Such a complex pattern of interplay has been particularly evident with respect to the development of the law of the seas, although such continuous processes

of legal results in the direction of wealth, influence, and status is also a feature of law in even well-ordered domestic societies.

26. I realize that such a view is somewhat at odds with my earlier writings on these themes. *See* Richard Falk, Elliott L. Meyrowitz, and Jack Sanderson, *Nuclear Weapons and International Law, supra* note 9, and Richard Falk, *Toward a Legal Regime for Nuclear Weapons*, 28 McGill L.J. 519 (1983). I would now partly discount my previous clarity on the legal status of nuclear weapons as an expression of heightened concern about the imminent dangers of nuclear war in the context of the Cold War; adopting now a somewhat more detached perspective, I am convinced that an effective regime of prohibition or abolition, which I continue to favor, can only be usefully achieved on the basis of an agreement that is endorsed by the nuclear weapons states.

of law creation have been somewhat diminished in impact by the implementation of the 1982 United Nations Convention on the Law of the Seas.[27]

The U.N. Charter, in its efforts to discourage war as an option, appears to preclude recourse to self-defense *prior* to an armed attack across an international boundary but, if such a legalistic rendering were the entire story, then a state that reasonably perceived the imminence of an annihilating onslaught would have to avoid any kind of armed anticipatory action. Such a legalist pattern of observance would seem naive and self-destructive, given the realities of force in the relations among hostile states. In fact, despite the generalized unpopularity of Israel in international circles in the 1960s, its initiating recourse to war in 1967, although apparently incompatible with U.N. Charter textual language in Articles 2(4) and 51, was not seriously criticized from a legal perspective in international society. This could be explained by reference to the context: given the mobilization for war of hostile Arab forces at the time and considering their avowed intention of destroying the state of Israel, and given the vulnerability of the tiny Israeli territorial domain to military attack, the Israeli response was widely perceived to be *reasonable*. In addition, the evident inability and unwillingness of the United Nations to protect victims of aggression through the mechanisms of collective security reinforced the reasonableness of Israeli self-help.[28] In other words, in resolving the tension between legalism and geopolitics, there is insinuated the quasi-legal conception of contextual reasonableness, which cannot be applied consistently because of the low degree of institutionalization in international life, but yet provides the path most likely to produce a second-order effectiveness for international law that is often all that is possible in the absence of impartial interpretative authority and reliable enforcement capabilities. There is also present here the difficulty of connecting the general rule to the particular situation in a complex world, resulting in a wide range of interpretative authority being retained by sovereign states, even in a

27. These processes have been admirably depicted by MYRES S. MCDOUGAL AND WILLIAM T. BURKE, THE PUBLIC ORDER OF THE OCEANS (1962), but this interplay exists across the entire spectrum of international activity, as well brought out in INTERNATIONAL INCIDENTS: THE LAW THAT COUNTS IN WORLD POLITICS (W. Michael Reisman and Andrew R. Willard eds., 1988).

28. Note that while Israel's recourse to force in 1967 was generally viewed as "defensive" and within the ambit of legality, this was decidedly not the case with respect to its seizure and retention of additional territories, which has been widely condemned as illegal and opposed by most governments at the United Nations and elsewhere for more than three decades. For a comprehensive development of this perspective, see ANTHONY CLARK AREND AND ROBERT J. BECK, INTERNATIONAL LAW AND THE USE OF FORCE (1993).

setting where the apparent intention was to minimize discretion. Such residual sovereignty is particularly relevant in the setting of peace and security, which confronts governments with circumstances of crisis that are perceived as relevant to political independence and territorial integrity, and possibly even to survival. In such circumstances, the law is bent and twisted to address felt security needs, and if this dynamic seems reasonable in context to most other governments, then it will not be censured and will indeed form a precedent for others similarly situated. If the interpretative claim is perceived as widely unreasonable, and if an effective response is organized, then some lines of interpretative freedom are disallowed and the core meaning of the general rule is upheld. This latter pattern seems to describe the response to Iraq's claims against Kuwait that led to their repudiation in the Gulf War of 1991.

Returning to the majority view in the *Nuclear Weapons* Advisory Opinion, the judges were trying to take account of the inconsistencies between a legalistic application of the principles of international humanitarian law and the extent to which the nuclear weapons states exhibited over a long period of time a claimed right to use this weaponry, at least in deterrent or retaliatory modes, and were supported in these claims by many academic specialists, including by those who explored the normative implications of the weaponry.[29] To ignore such confirmed geopolitical practice altogether, especially in light of the absence of sustained, formal opposition, would seem to invite contempt for the Court as an institution with its head in the clouds. However, to ignore the defiance of apparent legal rules and of catastrophic dangers associated with these practices by leading states would be to put the judicial arm of the United Nations at odds with both the cumulative consensus among governments to the effect that threats or uses of nuclear weaponry are unlawful, and even more so, with the sentiments of the transnational anti-nuclear movement, as well as the apparent views of international public opinion. Unlike other types of claims that went beyond explicit legal boundaries, those relating to nuclear weapons were always of the deepest concern to important sectors of international society and engendered a strong grassroots movement that has ebbed and flowed over the decades since 1945 when atomic bombs were used against Japanese cities in the closing days of World War II.

29. *See, e.g.*, Joseph S. Nye, Jr., Nuclear Ethics (1986), and Michael Walzer, Just and Unjust Wars 269–83 (1977).

Faced with this situation, and without the benefit of an explicit prohibitory regime addressed to nuclear weaponry, the Court took a giant step toward declaring this weaponry illegal under international law. Yet it also created a geopolitical loophole of uncertain dimensions that angered nuclearist and anti-nuclearist judges alike; the former felt that the *Lotus* principle meant that it was possible only to assess legality *after the fact,* whereas the latter, which of course included Weeramantry, were convinced by their reading of the law that the weapons were *already* prohibited in unconditional terms and that any retreat from such legal clarity would only encourage and tacitly legitimate the evasion of legal standards. The Court's assessment that simply declaring a prohibitory regime that was opposed by all five permanent members of the Security Council would amount to a juridical absurdity seems accurate, as does their surprising, yet most welcome, strong support for implementing the long dormant obligation to pursue seriously the option of nuclear disarmament, a legal duty that is itself given positivist status by forming the core obligation of Article VI of the Treaty on the Nonproliferation of Nuclear Weapons (1968).

When the legal rules and principles point in one direction and the geopolitics in another direction, then some effort at reconciliation is needed in the interest of effectiveness, including respect for the processes relied upon to resolve controversies relating to such subject matter. One approach to reconciliation is to acknowledge uncertainty as to legal requirements in that domain where law and geopolitics appear to be in contradiction, as when a state facing an extreme threat to its survival, as did Israel early in the war in 1973, readies its nuclear warheads for missile launch either to deter ultimate provocations or as a means of desperate last hour defense. The Court, in fact, combined its admission of uncertainty as to the law in this limit situation, with an insistent call for nuclear disarmament, not as a policy option, but as an imperative matter of legal duty which, if heeded, would overcome the awkwardness of concluding that international law neither forbids nor authorizes nuclear weaponry in such a limit situation of extreme self-defense. In effect, but without so naming and situating its approach, the Court is delineating reasonableness in context as it pertains to nuclear weaponry.[30]

Make no mistake, even with such sensitivity to political constraints, it is doubtful that an adverse legal assessment of current

30. Compare the approach taken in Burns H. Weston, *Nuclear Weapons versus International Law: A Contextual Reassessment,* 28 McGill L.J. 542 (1983).

policies of the nuclear weapons states will have much of a direct and immediate impact on their behavior. The primacy of geopolitics means that governments of leading states do not regard themselves as legally accountable to international society on matters of national security, a view more widely reinforced by the continuing vitality of sovereignty as a political doctrine that encourages governments to subordinate international legal obligations to national interests whenever vital interests are at issue. Such a disregard of legal challenges directed at prevailing geopolitical policies is reinforced by the leadership style of the U.S. government that refuses such accountability and helps validate the refusal of others. As will be discussed, the significance of calling these policies pertaining to nuclear weapons into legal account is mainly due to its support for and encouragement of efforts long underway within the framework of the United Nations, especially the General Assembly, and in the transnational initiatives of global civil society that has long accorded priority to the elimination of nuclear weaponry.

## D. THE EMERGENT GLOBAL CIVILIZATION, HUMANE GOVERNANCE FOR THE PLANET, AND THE ROLE OF INTERNATIONAL LAW

The integrative tendencies in international life support the view that some sort of global civilization is emergent, superseding a world picture based upon the interplay of distinct sovereign territorial states. But the ascendancy of neo-liberal, market-driven policy perspectives, especially among the most influential states in the North, suggests two forms of dysutopian global civilization:

- first, a consumer-oriented materialist world order, a global shopping mall, with the market and the internet providing the main self-organizing mechanisms of geogovernance, with no ethical sense of human solidarity or ecological commitment to safeguarding nature;

- second, a civilizationally restructured world order in which conflict intensifies in the relations of the West to the main non-Western civilizations, with the globalizing dimension consisting of a transcivilizational world economy, thereby maintaining human solidarity at the level of civilization, but repudiating all

> universalizing pretensions as being merely expressions of a concealed project of global hegemony undertaken by one or another civilization at the expense of the others.

Judge Weeramantry's vision of global civilization rejects both of these influential interpretations of globalizing tendencies, and embodies a commitment to an image of global civilization based on the universal premises of reason, human solidarity, and a shared planetary destiny driven by a species commitment to survival. International law is regarded as embodying this telos of what is desirable for the future of international society, and although a judicial official is bound by a jurisprudential duty to adjudicate, and not legislate, the essence of the interpretative task is to give appropriate expression to the embodied values of such an incipient global civilization, including its incorporation of the distinct, yet overlapping, characteristics associated with the great world religions and their civilizational expression.

There are two problematic features with this receptivity to a humanistic version of an emergent global civilization: it seems highly unlikely as a plausible scenario, given the dominance of market-driven logic and the constraining discipline of global capital on policy-makers at all levels of governance; and its mandate in the context of the application and implementation of international law creates an immediate, unbridgeable gap between geopolitical priorities and humanistic imperatives, which is particularly evident in the setting of peace and security, and became manifest in the various approaches taken by the judges on the World Court to the matter of the legality of nuclear weaponry.

For these reasons, I believe that it is more constructive at this stage to adopt an agnostic view of the coming global civilization in relation to the role of international law. In this regard, it seems more helpful to portray the emergent global civilization as taking shape in the face of a tension between the market-driven forms of globalization and the people-driven modes of resistance as exhibited by transnational movements to protect the environment, to promote human rights, and to challenge the oppression of women and the destruction of indigenous peoples. Such developments might be described as evidences of the tension between globalization-from-above, with its reliance on transnational corporations and financial markets, and globalization-from-below, with its reliance on transnational social forces and activist networks.

With respect to geopolitics, especially in the setting of formal institutions comprising the United Nations system, it seems more jurisprudentially appropriate to give weight to the authoritative practice of leading states in specifying legal obligations. Giving weight does not mean according deference, but it does imply an acknowledgment that the assessments of legal prerogative made by leading states needs to be evaluated in the interpretative process of judicial institutions, and that decontextualized readings of international law by primary reference to the postulates of universal humanism are not satisfactory. In this respect, the majority decision in the *Nuclear Weapons* Advisory Opinion challenged the legality of the policies being relied upon by the nuclear weapons states, but it did so in a manner that recognized the realities of embodied power and the widely shared consensus that an ultimate right to threaten or use such weaponry in a situation where the survival of a state was at issue *might* be legal. I think that such an outcome has the large advantage of creating the possibility of a dialogue; it encourages anti-nuclear forces but also appreciates that the force of law cannot by itself override long-term, fundamental policies of leading states. Dialogue here is not just words, but the foundation of communicative action that is the essence of democratic practice.[31]

Nevertheless, is this rejection of a humanistic standpoint merely a pragmatic reading of how to make the role of international law more credible? Does it, in other words, abandon the higher commitment of the jurist to truth, and the duty to apply the law however much it may run counter to political pressures? I think not. Given the structure of international society, and its continuing adherence to a strong doctrinal view supportive of sovereign rights, the most appropriate role for the jurist is to avoid the temptations of apologetics or of utopianism, neither relinquishing juridical autonomy to the political domain nor setting forth legalistic positions that are dismissed as pathetic fantasy by those entrusted with the responsibilities of political leadership.[32] In my view, international law and lawyers can best contribute to the prospects of fashioning a more humane type of global civilization by self-confidently entering the dialogic space between entrenched political power and transnational social forces, acknowledging the relevance of both, but subordinating their

31. *See* Jurgen Habermas, The Theory of Communicative Action (2 vols. 1984, 1989).

32. Martti Koskenniemi attempts to articulate such an intermediate view in Martti Koskenniemi, From Apology to Utopia: The Structure of International Legal Argument (1989).

autonomy to neither. To this extent, I differ from Judge Weeramantry in his heroic and invaluable efforts to rely on international law to challenge some of the most dangerous and objectionable features of the existing world order.

# CHAPTER X

# THE QUEST FOR HUMANE GOVERNANCE IN AN ERA OF GLOBALIZATION

## A. TAKING ACCOUNT OF GLOBALIZATION: POSITIVE AND NEGATIVE EFFECTS

The quest for global governance during the long period of the Cold War focused on peace and security issues, especially the avoidance of general war between the two nuclear superpowers. Other important developments were, of course, occurring, including the collapse of colonialism and the regional integration of Western Europe. But the dominant world picture consisted of two asymmetrically arranged hierarchical blocs of countries repeatedly confronting one another, generating varying degrees of tension. This encounter established the pattern of geopolitics for the interval between 1945 and 1989.

The idea of humane governance in such a setting emphasized the virtues of nonalignment, and generally supported the efforts of countries in the South to proceed with development along the lines dictated by the dynamics of self-determination. From these perspectives, intervention from the North, by either side in the Cold War, was perceived as highly destructive of prospects for humane governance on the level of the state. Such perceptions were epitomized by the worldwide reactions against the U.S. interventionary war in Vietnam and the later Soviet invasion of Afghanistan.

In a fundamental ordering sense, an initial objective of progressive world order thinking during the Cold War was to curtail the impact of geopolitics on the development of societies within recognized international boundaries to the extent possible. In this sense, the Westphalian model of autonomous sovereign states became both a defining feature of the post-colonial system and a remote aspiration;

the fiction of "nation-state" was unanimously endorsed in decolonizing settings, including Africa, to avoid divisive ethnically based conflict that would arise in the event colonial boundaries, however artificial, were allowed to be challenged. Yet at the same time, the suppression of "nations" within such states, as well as the division of Europe—including even the prior (and subsequently) unified state of Germany—into hegemonic zones, placed a heavy burden on substantive sovereignty that was reinforced by the retention in Europe of Soviet and U.S. troops since World War II. In a different sense, the imposition of a state upon the post-colonial reality of Africa has often resulted in non-viable entities in various forms.[1] Such arrangements both conformed to Westphalian expectations by respecting the formal independence of existing states, and deformed these expectations by its geopolitical denial of the substantive reality of sovereignty for many states and the entrapment of many nations in hostile state environments (as, for instance, within the borders of the Soviet Union).

The idea of humane governance responded to these realities additionally by reference to the authority and normative claims of the United Nations Charter, which had the dual advantage of treaty status and active participation by both blocs in the Cold War. This participation was again asymmetrically in favor of the West, yet it still provided a semblance of common normative ground by affirming the same constitutional document, along with a welcome framing of the world order agenda in the non-realist political language of peace, justice, development, and human rights. The Charter was important in this respect as it imposed major legal restrictions on the rights of states to use force as an instrument of policy, thereby openly challenging earlier Westphalian ideas that had left recourse to force in international law essentially at the discretion of states because it was treated as an element of sovereignty. The Charter also seemed to provide an alternative to the self-help character of the pre-World War II phase of the Westphalian system by offering the prospect of collective action in support of states under attack. Much of the thinking about humane governance during this period, in effect, if not literally, sought to convert these Charter expectations into real norms of behavior by invoking the authority of international law, and by encouraging governments to engage in serious disarming and demilitarizing negotiations.

1. Robert H. Jackson, Quasi-States: Sovreignty, International Relations, and the Third World (1991).

It is also true that more ambitious conceptions of humane governance, such as those advanced by the World Order Models Project, were insisting during this period upon a more encompassing view of the adjustments that would be beneficial and necessary from the perspective of a set of world order values.[2] These values were specified as follows: minimizing violence, promoting economic well-being, realizing social justice, and maximizing environmental protection. Such a normative agenda encouraged a critical posture toward mainstream reformist thinking that favored incremental adjustments and managerial approaches to international conflict, typified by an emphasis on arms control (and rejection of disarmament) and support for functional expansion of U.N. activities by way of the specialized agencies. This more radical stream of thought was rooted in utopian traditions of reflections about human potential, as well as on integrative interpretations of history that regarded the unification of humanity as a natural fulfillment of an animating ethos of solidarity, exhibiting a human identity that supplemented and transcended specific identities based on race, ethnicity, gender, class, nationality, and ideology with an overarching identity to humanity as a whole.

The end of the Cold War has shifted the debate on humane governance in rather profound ways. The role of the United States as sole superpower in a global setting without a credible strategic conflict creates an ambiguous geopolitical climate, especially given the prominence of global market forces. Associating this prominence with a preoccupation about "globalization" generates a tension between what might be described as the old geopolitics related to such doctrines as the balance of power, deterrence, and containment, and the new geopolitics related to currently dominating ideas about market share, free trade, and competitiveness, and to a lesser extent, issues of human rights, international crime, terrorism, and environmental protection. The United States has confusingly positioned itself at the interface between the new and the old, sometimes associated with the interpretation of modernist and postmodernist attitudes and arrangements,[3] thereby helping to spread a sense of uncertainty about the character of world order in this early phase of the era of globalization.

2. ON THE CREATION OF A JUST WORLD ORDER (Saul H. Mendlovitz ed., 1975); RICHARD FALK, A STUDY OF FUTURE WORLDS (1975).

3. For relevant discussion, see RESTRUCTURING FOR WORLD PEACE: ON THE THRESHOLD OF THE 21ST CENTURY (Katharine Tehranian and Majid Tehranian eds., 1992); *see also* ALBERT BORGMANN, CROSSING THE POSTMODERN DIVIDE (1992).

The old geopolitics continues to be expressed by efforts to contain "rogue states" by a reliance on coercive diplomacy, including sanctions, and through pressure on third countries to withhold critical technology and even resources. In contrast, the subordination of ideological differences, normative objections and balance of power considerations in favor of trade and investment opportunities, as in relation to China, expresses the new geopolitics. The realities of globalization, together with this unresolved tension between the old and new geopolitics, underscores the importance of rethinking humane governance, and extending its relevance to current world order challenges.

To interpret this interplay from the perspective of promoting humane governance requires some initial specification of the impact of globalization upon world order. A summary organized by reference to detrimental and beneficial impacts is presented below.

## 1. The Negative Effects

There is a widening gap between winners and losers. According to the HUMAN DEVELOPMENT REPORT 1997, "[t]he share of the poorest 20% of the world's people in global income now stands at a miserable 1.1%, down from 1.4% in 1991 and 2.3% in 1960. It continues to shrink. And the ratio of the income of the top 20% to that of the poorest 20% rose from 30 to 1 in 1960, to 61 to 1 in 1991—and to a startling new high of 78 to 1 in 1994."[4] These widening gaps are also evident in the relations among regions and in the internal relations between rich and poor segments of society. They seem to undermine the sense of political community upon which societal cohesion depends at the level of the state, as well as produce an alienating effect upon individuals. These developments give rise to various chauvinistic and xenophobic outlooks and movements.[5]

In addition, there is a new orthodoxy and harshness that constrains the role of government in relation to the losers, by emphasizing considerations of competitiveness and fiscal austerity as necessary priorities, given the logic of global markets. Such a pattern of thinking

4. UNITED NATIONS DEVELOPMENT PROGRAM, HUMAN DEVELOPMENT REPORT 1997 (1997) at 7.

5. For a full-fledged rationale for such a posture on the part of the West, see the book-length, somewhat modified, formulation of Huntington's famous "clash thesis." SAMUEL P. HUNTINGTON, THE CLASH OF CIVILIZATIONS AND THE REMAKING OF WORLD ORDER (1996).

and acting is left largely unchallenged, which partly reflects the decline of organized labor as a relatively coherent social force that could be counted on to advance a people-oriented perspective on the role of the state. The effect is to diminish the disposition and capacity of the state to take initiatives, thereby tolerating widespread long-term homelessness and acute urban decay in the midst of glittery affluence or, alternatively, regarding chronically high unemployment as the necessary price that must be paid if wage levels are to be kept high and inflation low, as in most of Europe. Such "principled indifference" has also undercut support for economic assistance to sub-Saharan Africa, where the political outcomes that mattered during the Cold War are no longer of strategic consequence, and hence not worth an investment that had been previously justified according to the rules of the old geopolitics.

The ideology associated with contemporary globalization has encouraged comprehensive privatization. This tendency has been reinforced by the current widespread societal dislike of government and bureaucracy, and further emboldened by the glorification of supposedly self-organizing systems, especially the market and Internet, and by the abject failures in economic and social performance of centrally planned economies of the Soviet type. The policy effect of such a shift in attitude about collective social responsibilities has been to exert strong downward pressures on support for most public goods, and especially for global public goods, such as the funding of the United Nations and action taken to sustain the global commons in the face of disturbing trends in ocean pollution and climate change. This diminished support for public goods is especially pronounced in the United States, which has given the strongest neo-liberal spin to the economic imperatives of globalization by choosing, in late 1997, to approach even the reduction of the emission of greenhouse gases by way of market devices such as tax incentives and pollution vouchers. Europe and Japan have so far exhibited a stronger capacity to strike compromises between pressures associated with the discipline of global capital and the ethos of social democracy. Despite this diversity of adaptations to pressures associated with the global market, the American leadership role has interfered with efforts in the 1990s to achieve needed levels of global governance. For instance, mainly as a result of governmental action by the United States it was possible to nullify widespread citizen activity around the world in support of major proposals to strengthen the U.N. that had been mounted in relation to the fiftieth anniversary of the organization a few years ago. Instead, the organization has been treated like a sick corporation that needs restructuring by way of downsizing to make it again seem viable.

The demobilization of progressive alternatives, combined with a tendency to establish the political agenda by the imperatives of the externally situated global (and regional) marketplace, has diminished the effectiveness of traditional modes of political participation through such means as parties, elections, and legislative institutions. The synergistic effect of these trends is to raise serious doubts about whether the virtues of "democracy" can be any longer adequately achieved within the conventional frameworks of constitutional democracy. One important dimension of the disillusionment of the young in much of the world seems related to this subtle and inconclusive type of disempowerment of the citizenry to achieve change. An opposite effect is to revitalize right-wing fringe politics that seek to conserve a purist sense of "the nation" in the face of Westernizing consumerism and ethnic challenges of greater human mobility. Religious extremism has also emerged, in part, to protect traditionalist identities at risk in a globalized world that seems in the process of being thoroughly secularized.

## 2. The Positive Effects

The economistic focus associated with globalization diminishes traditional incentives to wage war associated with the acquisition of resources and territory; oil is a partial, and probably temporary, exception to this trend, playing, as it does, such a vital role in the world economy, and the Gulf War is illustrative of the type of warfare that can be generated despite, and in some senses because of, globalization. Similarly, it is possible, although unlikely, that the energy riches of the South China Seas could generate warfare in a future struggle among claimant countries for control of these possibly major resources. Despite these examples, the overall influence of globalization seems to be making major war, at least, into an anachronism. This tendency, which is far from a certainty, is reinforced by the growing reluctance of the United States, and other countries in the North, to pursue interventionary diplomacy in view of its often inconclusive and long-deferred results, its unpredictably high costs in human life and resources, and the difficulty of mobilizing and sustaining citizen support. The risks for political leaders associated with intervention have been increasing over the course of the last several decades, commencing in the reactions to the Vietnam War, but growing over the years and reflecting, also, the reluctance to engage in high-risk commitments unless national security is credibly threatened. Especially, in the individualist atmosphere of neo-liberalism, altruistic and humanistic grounds of intervention are difficult to sell to the public.

The mobility of capital, the global application of the principles of comparative advantage and economies of scale, as well as the accompanying spread of technological innovation have enabled some of the poorest and most populous countries to achieve high rates of economic growth over significant periods of time. The effect has been to rescue hundreds of millions from acute poverty, especially in the Asia/Pacific region, and to make non-Western countries more important global participants, bringing other considerations to bear on global issues. It remains too early to tell whether this encouraging pattern can be revived in view of the world economic crisis of the last two years.

Perhaps most encouraging of all is the extent to which it now appears feasible and generally beneficial to address problems of acute poverty of the sort that continues to afflict between 1.2 and 1.3 billion people. The basic cost of eradicating poverty for the countries in the South is estimated to be about $40 billion per year for ten years, or less than 1% of global income, and only 2–3% of national income in all but the very poorest countries.[6] Furthermore, it can be argued that unless poverty is substantially reduced, it is likely that the richer countries will experience the effects, both by environmental disaster and through the spread of infectious disease, as well as by an intensification of destabilizing backlash politics that include the formation of cults composed of "successful" citizens (for instance, Aum, Heaven's Gate) and militias with paranoid conspiracy images. Already it is reported that tainted foods sent from South to North are spreading disease resulting from reliance on polluted water in the exporting country. Globalization is itself implicated in this instance, to the extent by way of the World Trade Organization, that it disallows stricter inspection of imported food than domestic food. What is also true is that the awareness of the interrelation creates a self-interest in the richer countries to facilitate pro-poor styles of economic growth in the South.

6. Human Development Report 1997, *supra* note 4, at 97, 112.

The activation of civil society, both in relation to the deepening of democracy in response to the perceived and actual reduction in the extent of political space available to government and mainstream opposition, and in relation to a transnational agenda involving human rights, environmental protection, nuclear testing and disarmament, feminism, and social and economic justice is a further benefit. This latter phenomenon, which I have described elsewhere as globalization-from-below, is motivated by a people-oriented sense of politics, and is thus opposed to the detrimental social and environmental impacts attributed to globalization-from-above, that is, driven by market forces in coalition with most governments.[7] The related effort of these civic initiatives, often inarticulate, is to find more meaningful forms of political participation than are provided by the familiar constitutional forms of representative democracy. Such democratizing projects involve expanding the idea of what qualifies as "a political arena" to include workplace, neighborhood, family, shopping mall, and corporate facilities. It also has involved the launching of a project to establish democracy on a global scale, an undertaking sometimes referred to as transnational democracy or cosmopolitan democracy.[8]

The power of global market forces has led many political elites to seek new institutional forms that would reconcile the logic of capital with the retention of cultural and social autonomy. The main expression of this development has been the emergence of various forms of regionalism, most dramatically evolved in Europe. Undoubtedly, the European initiative was originally mainly based on creating a security community strong enough to avoid any further intra-European wars, as well as united enough to protect Europe against the perceived Soviet threat. But as time passed, the economic dimensions of European regionalism, typified by the bureaucracy in Brussels, became the focus of attention. Since the Maastricht Treaty of 1992, European regionalism has been increasingly interpreted as a means for Europe to cope with the competitive challenges emanating from Asia/Pacific and North America, as well as a way to retain discretion

7. For this formulation, see Richard Falk, *The Making of Global Citizenship, in* GLOBAL VISIONS: BEYOND THE NEW WORLD ORDER 39–50 (J. Brecher, J.B. Childs and Jill Cutler eds., 1993); *see also* PAUL WAPNER, ENVIRONMENTAL ACTIVISM AND WORLD CIVIC POLITICS; THE STATE AND SOCIAL POWER IN GLOBAL ENVIRONMENTAL POLITICS (Ronnie D. Lipschutz and Ken Conca eds., 1993).

8. *See* COSMOPOLITAN DEMOCRACY: AN AGENDA FOR A NEW WORLD ORDER (Daniele Archibugi and David Held eds., 1995); *see also* Richard Falk, The Quest for Normative Democracy in an Era of Neo-Liberal Globalization, unpublished Hesburgh Lectures, University of Notre Dame (Feb. 19–20, 1997); Richard Falk, *Global Civil Society: Perspectives, Initiatives, Movements,* 26 OXFORD DEV. STUD. (1998) 99–110.

at the level of the state to deal with internal social demands. In this respect, regionalism becomes a response to globalization-from-above. Similar considerations seem to apply to non-European regionalism, including the slogan "the Asianization of Asia," as well as developments in Africa and Latin America. Whether regionalism should be understood as a means to carry forward the project of humane governance is a complicated and unresolved matter. It is necessary to ask the following question: Is regionalism serving primarily as an instrument for globalization-from-above or does it represent a potentially and actually liberating compromise that is able to preserve the gains from globalization while reducing or overcoming some of its highest costs?

This effort to identify the positive and negative world order effects of globalization is intended only to set the stage for an inquiry about humane governance within the historical setting of an emergent future. It is a setting that disclosed a recent capacity to generate surprises, both those that build hope and those that dash expectations. The great liberating experience of the end of the Cold War and the collapse of Soviet imperialism came about as a welcome surprise, startling "the experts" who had built their scenarios of the future without even contemplating the sequence of events that occurred as one of several possibilities. Similarly, the modern march of secularism was utterly unprepared for the religious resurgence that erupted initially in the Iranian revolution, and then spread in a variety of cultural spaces to the far corners of the globe. Also, few would have thought that the end of the Cold War would result in the weakening of the United Nations, especially as its weakness earlier had been so largely explained as a result of the gridlock produced by East/West tensions.

This lack of insight into the unfolding dynamics of history carries both a message of humility to those who would instruct us about the future and an invitation to all those who dream of a better world to extend the political imagination with boldness far beyond the horizons of possibility depicted by mainstream realism. It is this latter invitation, especially as we approach the threshold of the twenty-first century and embark upon a new millennium, that suggests the importance of reviving the project of humane governance despite the formidable obstacles that particularly seem at the end of this century to preclude success for such an undertaking: disillusionment with big visions; an economistic sense of the role of institutions; a passion for privatization; an autonomy for financial markets that is accentuated by secrecy and remoteness from regulatory authority; and a hegemonic reading of recent history that discredits any but the most inconsequential approach to social change.

## B. REFORMULATING HUMANE GOVERNANCE TO MEET THE CHALLENGES OF GLOBALIZATION

On the basis of the contrasting assessments in the prior section, it becomes possible to contextualize the quest for humane governance in this era of globalization. Instead of the emphasis on the attainment of discrete world order values as seemed appropriate in the Cold War era, there are now three more generic tasks that appear to link academic inquiry and world order activism: 1) theorizing the various issue-oriented struggles against globalization-from-above in a coherent manner that is sensitive to the unevenness of circumstances existing in various parts of the world; 2) giving ideological unity to the quest for humane governance by stressing its commitment to democracy as process and as outcome, but democracy reconceived and extended in light of the decline of electoral politics; and 3) stressing the importance of democratically accountable innovations in governance, both at micro levels to take account of pressures for self-determination *within* the state and at macro levels to address the problems of the global commons, and to offer the peoples of the world procedures and arenas that are capable of regulating global market forces.

### 1. Globalization-From-Below

The activation of civil society on a transnational basis has challenged both states and market forces in substantive areas in which global market forces and states were perceived to be endangering human well-being. These civic pressures were often focused on reshaping the outlook of governments to be more protective of a range of public goods, including economic and social rights, public health and the environment. In this regard, the ideological outlook of those closely linked to market forces tended to restrict most expenditures on public goods, leaving unattended societal suffering to the largesse of the private sector.

In this regard, it is notable to take account of the large, financial contributions to the satisfaction of global public goods made by such capitalist superheroes as Ted Turner and George Soros. These initiatives have as their objective the facilitating of the humanitarian activities of the United Nations with a gift of $1 billion spread across a ten-year period in the former instance, and the encouragement of the democratization of Russia with a gift of $500 million over a shorter period in the latter. What is striking and problematic here is that the scale of private resources possessed by the winners in the globalization sweepstakes seem often more readily available for these purposes than are the resources of rich states. Also relevant is the degree to which the posthumous portrayal of a saintly Princess Diana was associated with her acts of compassion directed at those outside her own country, especially the victims of anti-personnel land mines. These developments reflect innovative aspects of the response by elements of global civil society to the extent to which the state is losing its capacity and will to address the social and humanitarian agenda of the world.

Another type of response is connected with resistance activity, as when consumer power is brought to bear on behalf of the global commons. When Shell Oil proposed the sinking of its oil rig in the North Sea a few years ago, an oppositional effort was effectively orchestrated by Greenpeace that mobilized users of gas to boycott Shell service stations in Europe. The entire story is complicated, and the environmental argument not entirely resolved, but the political message was clear: if corporate action in the global commons is not regulated by the Westphalian institutions of government and intergovernmental character, then the civil sector can make trouble transnationally by mobilizing resistance efforts through the dissemination of information that harm will result unless the challenged activity is halted.

There are several related conclusions to be drawn. First of all, individuals are now commanding resources on a scale that permits them to provide support to global public goods that is comparable to what might be provided by enlightened state actors. This process weakens the position of the state in relation to the promotion of public goods, and it also means that society as a whole is not represented in the priorities chosen from among the various possible undertakings within the domain of public goods. It also creates a very real danger that affluent individuals will contribute significant assets to "negative global public goods," ranging from giving support to terrorist activity and regressive political causes across a wide range, including the financing of anti-democratic political movements in various parts of the world. Even the provision of "peacekeeping" capabilities, a task that was previously seen as an essentially falling within the domain of global public goods, particularly as it was regarded as the core assignment of the United Nations, seems to be in the process of being monetized and marketized. Former security officials associated with South Africa's apartheid regime have formed an organization called Executive Outcomes that sells its services to African governments confronted with internal unrest or external threats and often receives large shares of corporate and mining investments.

Whether the cumulative impact of this activation of civil society, and its transnational projections of influence by way of information, ideas, money, and organizational initiatives, can be considered as lending credibility and support to the project for humane governance is problematic at this point. There is no doubt that the rise of transnational social forces involves, to a significant degree, a reaction to globalization, but the multifaceted nature of this reaction makes it difficult to assess its overall normative impact. There was some earlier tendency to romanticize these transnational activities, but there is now a more nuanced realization that their roles are diverse and contradictory. Nevertheless, globalization-from-below is mounting an array of challenges to globalization-from-above, and confronting political elites in control of states with some hard political choices.

## 2. Normative Democracy

The collapse of progressive politics in the 1990s is closely connected with the discrediting of traditional left perspectives in the last stages of the Cold War and the impact of globalization as ideologized by neo-liberalism. The two serious consequences of these developments are to weaken support for vulnerable peoples and segments of society, and to make it more difficult to mobilize resources on behalf of global public goods. It seems evident, as well, that a progressive politics capable of meeting these two minimal challenges cannot expect to be successful if it relies on Marxist categories of analysis and socialist political language. There is an irony present here, as one consequence of globalization is to make economistic approaches to political explanation much more prevalent than ever before.

Globalization-from-below has been responsible for a variety of local and transnational initiatives based on democratic ideas of participation and direct action, and often animated by such world order values as human rights, environmental protection, and social justice. These initiatives have generated voluntary associations of citizens, as well as potent transnational networks focused on particular issues, and have made use of a range of arenas for promoting goals. The U.N. conferences on global issues, held during the first half of the 1990s, illustrated this new political energy as focused on environment, women, human rights, and development. But what was lacking was a cross-issue orientation that would be necessary to sustain a coherent politics from below that could in some ways balance the coherence of neo-liberalism in its differing, yet mutually reinforcing, forms. It remains the case that the politics arising from transnational social forces has so far been of an ad hoc and issue-oriented character, and thus neither effectively institutionalized nor ideologized. Without such steps, the capacity to challenge the excesses of globalization-from-above are likely to be transitory and, in the end, unsuccessful.

The possibilities of a new coherent progressive politics seems dependent upon the creative energies of globalization-from-below, as mainstream parties and perspectives seem generally subject to the discipline of global capital, or to be generating various reactionary forms of backlash politics, which embody narrowly protectionist ideas that are often combined with a chauvinistic ethos inducing the most dangerous of nationalist sentiments. In the 1980s, the green movement, especially in Europe, came forth with a new progressive politics that was both compassionate and committed to the realization of public goals, especially environmental protection. The greens had an impact, especially in relation to environmental policy, influencing the entire political spectrum, but their capacity to provide a progressive alternative seems limited. Their agenda was perceived as being too narrowly green, and although their actual concerns were far broader, generally extending to human rights and security policy, it has proved impossible for greens to mobilize sufficient support to take command of government. In most countries their bases of support included a coalition of former leftists and conservative libertarians, which limited their capacity to develop a comprehensive, coherent program. Further, especially in the crucial setting of West Germany, green ranks were badly split between reformist and radical orientations toward industrial civilization. But the green parties, acting mainly within traditional state/society frameworks, although active on a European level, suggested the possibility of a post-Marxist progressivism that was responsive to the particular challenges and opportunities associated with globalization, including tactical moves to reengage civil society in active, meaningful politics that relied on imaginative ways of gaining support.

At present, various political gropings toward a new outlook and language are becoming evident in various settings, especially relying on the widely endorsed normative frameworks associated with human rights and democracy. The striking feature here is a realization that democratic politics needs to be introduced into all political arenas, and can no longer be understood primarily as a type of politics at the level of the sovereign state. Various terminologies have been used to express this double movement in the direction of both the globalization and localization of democratic forms of participation, accountability, and legality, including references to "cosmopolitan democracy" and "substantive democracy."[9] A comparable deepening and expanding of human rights is also occurring, especially extending the reach of human rights to the social and economic agenda, as well as a variety of efforts to take account of cultural differences. These still embryonic efforts to shape a progressive outlook are also, by their very transnational nature, building political support for a coherent program of reform at all levels of social organization, which would in effect amount to a movement for humane governance. That is, the prospects of the project of humane governance, aside from its intellectual expression, depend on the potential political agency provided by the consensus and conception of democracy that is being evolved in different circumstances around the world. It is this orientation toward values and action that I am identifying with the term "normative democracy."

## 3. Governance

Globalization alters the substantive approach to humane governance, particularly with reference to the role of the state. In most earlier work, the sovereign territorial state was perceived as the obstacle, resisting efforts to achieve a disarmed world and opposing efforts to establish degrees of supranational authority to protect the global commons and to provide an effective alternative to geopolitics as the foundation of security.[10] The onset of globalization has disclosed

9. For elaboration, see sources cited *supra* note 8.
10. *See* sources cited *supra* note 2.

political elites far more disposed than their citizens to transfer sovereignty over economic activities to international institutions, as in relation to the establishment of the World Trade Organization or such regional initiatives as North American Free Trade Association. This pattern is evident, as well, in the European moves toward monetary union, as prescribed in the Maastricht treaty process.

With the rise of market forces and the acceptance of neo-liberal ideas, the state has lost a portion of its autonomy, and is no longer oriented, as fully, to the well-being of people, including its own citizens. Given this reality, from the perspective of humane governance it would be beneficial to reorient the state so as to enhance its willingness to be more people-oriented, including a renewed disposition to invest in global public goods such as an effective United Nations, an ambitious approach to climate change, and a willingness to create institutions for environmental governance that are comparable to those that have been established for the sake of economic governance.[11] In these regards, given the continuing capacity of the state to act and to mobilize resources, the only plausible means to respond to the harmful aspects of globalization is by reliance on the state to recover its role as guardian of people. Such a result can only be brought about by an active, organized civil society that is motivated by a reconceived, less territorial understanding of democracy, and is focused on challenging the neo-liberal ideas that shape economic policy, substituting a stronger sense of responsibility at the level of the state.

## C. A CONCLUDING NOTE

Globalization is not inherently opposed to the struggle to achieve equitable and effective governance structures for the planet, ranging from local to global settings, but there are tensions associated with the ideological and historical climate that prevails at the present time. Also, the structures of globalization are embedded so deeply in the dynamics of technological innovation and the efficient use of resources as to amount to an unchallengeable presence for the foreseeable future. In this respect, then, the political agenda for global reform involves two central undertakings: offering the perspectives of normative democracy as an alternative to the outlook of neo-liberalism;

11. I have put forward this argument elsewhere. *See* Richard Falk, *Will the State Lose Out?*, INT'L AFF. (1996).

and creating the local, national, and transnational pressures, by way of the further activation of social forces associated with globalization-from-below, to resituate the state so as to make it more responsive to people-oriented priorities, including the financing of global public goods. Against this background, it will be possible to revive the project of humane governance as a coherent conception of world order for the twenty-first century.

# INDEX